A Year of
Reformation

The Path of the righteous

is like the morning sun

Shining ever brighter

Until the full light of day

Proverbs 4:18 NIV

A Year of Reformation

By Cheryl Kvalvik

First published in the United states of America by
DimeSquare Publishing, 2025.

ISBN: 979-8-9913976-5-0

First edition.

DimeSquare Publishing

A Year of Reformation
© 2025 by Cheryl
Published by DimeSquare
541 S. Willow Ave. Ste 101 PMB 201
Cookeville, TN 38501

Forward

Reformation is the process of restoring something to its intended God-ordained purpose through repentance and a return to biblical principles. This is especially vital at this time in history for shifting wrong thinking, unlearning lies we believe about God, ourselves, our world, and for rescuing the next generation. Those who are ready and patiently waiting for Jesus' return will be a re-formed, overcoming people who will receive the promises revealed to the churches in the book of Revelation. *A Year of Reformation* is how to move into this never-before-seen dawning of a new day, one bringing in an amazing harvest of transformed souls. The mountain of the Lord's kingdom is rising with God's will being seen on earth "as it is in Heaven."

In 2014 I had a dream that a cold, eerie darkness came from the east. My family was in a car, but I could not close the door to protect them. I said three times, "The Sun will rise with healing in his wings." A jet-powered triangle rose over us, and through it I could see Heaven. The Lord is coming to heal us and to give us hope for the future. "To him who overcomes and does My will to the end, I will give authority over the nations...I will also give him the morning star" (Revelation 2:27-28).

These entries from my journals cover many topics, plus poems, quotes, a few dreams, and prophesies. I hope you read the verses and look at the websites I have included. I have given credit to everyone who has steered my understanding in the right direction. God bless them: Chuck Pierce, Robert Heidler, Dick Mills, Dutch Sheets, Tim Sheets, Cindy Jacobs, John Loren Sandford, Andrew Pudewa, Mark Virkler, Ira Mulligan, Jack Frost, Jamie and Donna Winship, and many more. A few have passed on and are now a part of the "great cloud of witnesses." Many thanks for their faithfulness in sharing their wisdom and life experiences. All thanks, praise, and honor to the Lord Jesus, and for Holy Spirit's wisdom, understanding, knowledge, and guidance.

The Sun of righteousness will rise with healing in his wings. Malachi 4:2

The Sun Will Rise

For those who revere my name
The sun will rise
With healing in His wings
But it also rises with
Scorching heat that withers
The plant, its buds, its blossoms
They fall; their beauty destroyed
The wicked will fade away
Even while going about their business
Revere the Name above all names
Escape the withering heat
And be healed

January 1

Some cultures begin their New Year's Day celebration on different dates than we do. The Chinese begin theirs on the Lunar New Year, and the Jews observe theirs in the autumn on Rosh Hashanah. Some dates have significant meanings and mark a new beginning, like a graduation day, a wedding, or a career change. Major change dates mark the start of a new season. What about the day you gave your life to Jesus? Not the day you decided to go back to church or read your Bible, but the day you laid down your life on the altar of God's will and picked up your cross to follow him, deciding to be led by the Spirit, wanting to hear his voice more than anything else, choosing to lay down earthly desires, and joining the battle for his kingdom to come. This is the starting line of a long but fulfilling race. Holy Spirit will guide your every step. If you have not yet experienced this new beginning, make the first move toward him, and he will run toward you. Are you ready for something new?

Genesis 1:1, *'In the beginning God...' Put the Lord at the beginning of your new year and of any new endeavor. He answers by saying, 'When my Spirit is invited to hover over something, what rises is good. I will make your years and your days good. What I bless is good; all you have to do is put me first. Is that too difficult? I ask so little of my creation. Other gods require so much more than I do. They require pain, sacrifice, and many useless obligations. Those who serve them receive nothing in return. I require only love. I created you for love; to receive it, then to give it. I desire to give you a good life of peace and blessing. Does that mean you will get everything you desire, escape every hard trial, or never experience sorrow? No, but it does mean that I will be there for every moment, and I will see you through. You will thank me one day, even as Job thanks me now in my kingdom, surrounded by the children of his suffering. You will have a good year!'*

January 2

After Job's trials, he had three beautiful daughters who received an inheritance with their seven brothers. They represent the bride of Christ, those who will receive an inheritance along with the believers who have finished their race. Job's daughter, Jemimah, meaning dove, is a representation of Holy Spirit. A dove is highlighted in the story of Noah's ark. After being sent out from the ark, it brought back an olive leaf symbolizing hope and peace. The Spirit, like a dove, came upon Jesus after his baptism in water. Solomon also refers to the dove when speaking of his beloved, a type of Jesus and his Holy Spirit-filled bride. Keziah, Job's second daughter, means sweet-scented spice. Nicodemus brought seventy-five pounds of spices and, with Joseph of Arimathea, anointed Jesus body before his burial. After the Sabbath, three women came with more spices, but the tomb was empty. Jesus has risen, and now we are his body. The spices represent how the Holy Spirit anoints us to present Father's love to a dying world that needs its own spiritual resurrection: "We are the aroma of Christ to God." Keren-Happuch, the third daughter, means child of beauty or beautifier. It has a particular meaning of the eyes being painted. The Holy Spirit makes us beautiful on the inside, giving us spiritual insight. We beautify the world by being the light and by sharing Jesus with others. (Revelation 3:18, Job 42:14-15, Genesis 8:10-12; 2 Corinthians 2:15).

The chief priests and elders met and devised a plan to trick the public. They gave the soldiers a large amount of money and told them to say, "Jesus' disciples came during the night and stole his body while we were sleeping." Matthew 28:12-13

January 3

Satan is called the devourer, which in Hebrew is *Akal*, meaning to burn up, eat, or consume. The writers of the Bible used this word to describe the results of fires, famines, wars, and plagues. "I will restrain the devourer for your sake..." (Malachi 3:11). The enemy's kingdom tries to steal our time, energy, and finances by distractions and evil temptations. Satan had no right or claim over Jesus, neither should he have a right or claim over us (John 14:30). The Lord made our protection so complete that the enemy cannot get his hands on us. The helmet of salvation, the breastplate of righteousness, and the shield of faith protect our thoughts, imaginations, and actions. The sword of God's word we speak drives the evil one away; he cannot touch us when we are wearing our armor! (1 John 5:18, Ephesians 6:10-20).

The enemy comes to kill, steal, and destroy, but I came that you might have an abundant life. -Jesus

Matthew 25
The kingdom of Heaven, a long time coming
All fall asleep, a watchman sounding the alarm
Some have no oil, "Hurry, go to those who sell it!"

"I do not know you," the Bridegroom declares
And closes the door on the half who arrive late
"Let us in! Did we not say, 'Lord, Lord?'"

"No money? Come, buy and eat
Buy refined gold of faith, white clothes of purity
Eye salve to see truth, buy with time spent with me."
Matthew 7:21-23, 25:1-13; Proverbs 23:23; Isaiah 55:1

January 4

The Charge of the Light Brigade, a poem by Alfred, Lord Tennyson, tells of the British cavalry's brave fight against Russian forces during the Battle of Balaclava in the Crimean War. The battle turned into a disaster for the British when their orders were misunderstood, and they stormed into a valley heavily guarded by the enemy. Lines from the poem read: *Someone had blundered.*
> *Theirs not to make reply,*
> *Theirs not to reason why,*
> *Theirs but to do and die.*
> *Into the valley of Death rode the six hundred.*

Sometimes we face troubles and sorrows and think that our commander and chief has deserted us, or we wonder if we have misunderstood his directives. Job felt that God had deserted him; his friends believed his suffering was punishment by God because of hidden sin; they named the sins he must have committed. The Lord did show up and ask Job seventy-seven questions that he could not answer. Seeing God's majesty and hearing his voice humbled him. He saw his own smallness in comparison to God's greatness. His three friends, however, were in danger of being judged for their folly of speaking ill of God by accusing him of punishing Job (Job 42:7-8). Never assume that a person's trial is related to their sin. Accusing is what Satan does. We can trust God; he is not distant or inept, he is aware of our troubles, and unlike the misunderstood order in the Battle of Balaclava, God has our back. If we misunderstand our orders, he will intervene.

In the gospels, Jesus asks 307 questions. Of the 183 he is asked, he answered few directly, they are: the greatest commandment is to love God and your neighbor, forgive 70 times 7, you could not cast out a demon because of your little faith, divorce is allowed if there is unfaithfulness, and "I Am," to the question of whether he was the Christ, the Son of God.

https://www.poetryfoundation.org. *The Charge of the Light Brigade*. Stanza II. Alfred Lord Tennyson.1854. Poetry Foundation. 2017.

Psalm 32:8

I will instruct you, and you will hear my voice clearly
A tutor to make you intelligent, skillful, and wise
I will teach you in the way you should go
Pointing the way so you will not miss the mark
I will guide you with my eye, watching your every move
Aiming you in the right direction, giving you a lighted path
As long as you will listen, I will speak. I have so much to say

January 5

There are times when shadows seem to loom over our lives, and nothing seems clear. We crave the voice of God and insist he isn't talking to us. Faith in these times is like when Rahab draped the crimson cord out of her window, and because of that one act, her whole household was saved. But she had to wait to be rescued; her family crowded around her while the walls of Jericho were collapsing. All her hope was in that red cord, that it would be seen and heeded by the troops of Israel. It was. She was not only saved, but she became one of the women listed in the lineage of Jesus. We must trust the red cord of the blood of Jesus over us to save us during times of darkness, chaos, and turmoil. Rahab's story speaks of faith and of cleansing. Her past was washed away; she became part of God's people and was given eternal honor in God's book. When life seems dark, watch and be sensitive to the little signs that he is sending: a dream, a song coming to mind, a friend's encouraging word, or a Scripture seeming to leap off the page. There are no coincidences; he will speak. Faith has the strength to wait, accepts the concealment of hidden things, puts God first—believing that he is and that he rewards those who seek him. Faith trusts, obeys, and has hope for the future.

Trust in the Lord with all your heart and lean not on your own understanding; in all your ways submit to him, and he will make your paths straight. Proverbs 3:6

January 6

The fruit of the forbidden tree of the knowledge of good and evil is still being eaten. Jesus is the Tree of Life who paid for the garden sin by hanging on a tree. He says, "Now eat of me, take my fruit and be healed." Which tree do you sit under? The one you choose will be the one you resemble, the one you serve. Will you be free and live in God's green pastures under the Tree of Life, or will you sit under the rebellious, disobedient tree of independence from God and his standard of good versus evil? It is a confining space of fleshly bondage where need and desire are the driving forces. The yin-yang symbol is the symbol of this tree. This Taoist philosophy teaches that these are complementary forces. The yin is associated with everything bad, negative, and sad; the yang with everything good, positive, and happy. This is not the truth; it is a destructive religious idea to be renounced. "I have created the spoiler to destroy" (Isaiah 54:16). God created this spoiler so that we would have a choice of whom we would serve. He gave Adam the choice between two trees: life or the spoiler of life. We are given the same choice. "Take, eat, this is my body, if you do not eat my flesh and drink my blood, you have no part in me." This statement by Jesus drove people away, but we must partake of Him; He is the Tree of Life! (Hebrews 12:2; Matthew 26:26; John 6:53-58).

'Don't eat from that tree!' What evil tree is he telling you not to eat from?

https://www.gotquestions.org. What is the meaning of the yin and the yang?

January 7

Could it be that the book of Job is a shadow of the redemption of Christ? We have always seen Job's trials as a picture of how the devil attacks us, no matter how godly we might be, and of how God may speak through a storm to make things right. But perhaps this trial is all about Job's friends. They were going down the wrong path. They thought of themselves as righteous, far more than Job, and accused him of hidden sin in long discourses. Is it possible that they had lost their right standing with God? They had not spoken truth about God, misrepresenting both his mercy and his judgment (Job 38, 42:7). Did they have hidden sin, hidden even from themselves? Romans 2:1-3 says, "You have no excuse, you who pass judgment on someone else, for at whatever point you judge another, you are condemning yourself, because you who judge do the same things. So, when you pass judgment yet do the same things, do you think you will escape God's judgment?" Were Job's friends doing what they were accusing Job of? The last chapter seems to prove it; the Lord was going to treat them according to their folly. They had to make sacrifices, and Job had to pray for his friends to rescue them. It is also a warning for us to avoid judging others, and we must ask the Lord to reveal any sin we aren't aware of.

I know my redeemer lives. Job 19:25

January 8

"If I, the Lord, announce that a nation or kingdom is to be unrooted, torn down, and destroyed, and if that nation I warned repents of its evil, then I will relent and not inflict on it the disaster I had planned. If at another time I announce that a nation or kingdom is to be built up and planted, and if it does evil in my sight and does not obey me, then I will reconsider that good I had intended to do for it" (Jeremiah 18:7-10). "I, the Lord, am the same yesterday, today, and forever" (Malachi 3:6; Hebrews 13:7). The Lord chooses to speak through his prophets, and we see by these verses that he sometimes changes his mind. It depends on how we respond to the word. If we brush off words of judgment, declaring them to be false, God probably won't change his mind. But if we repent like Nineveh, he just might!

Church History

You began with a revelation that became a list of rules
In came religion and division, greed knocking at the door
You focused on good works, burdened by iniquity,
Obligation, duty, and duplicity, you forgot "saved by grace."
THEN
Awaking, nine gifts, circuit riders, Holy Spirit
Dancing free, joyful praise, prophets, and apostles
Full armor and the sword, shield of faith, unity of love
God's glory coming down, life full of abundant grace
SOON
Back to Adam and Eve's religion, walking with Father
In the garden of delights, jumping in the river
Eating the fruit of life, healing in the leaves
Old things passing away, joy and peace to stay
Revelation 22:2

January 9

The king honors the prophet Mordecai. The wicked Haman, his family, and his friends hate this prophet. Haman's wife knows what is about to happen; she says to Haman, "You cannot stand against God's people–you will surely come to ruin." Esther, the bride, must intervene, for her people are marked for destruction. "Esther, the king holds his scepter out to you." She enters, not to beg, complain, or cry, but to invite him to a banquet. The king and the bride feast together for two days. The enemy is present; his plan to destroy Mordecai's people is in motion. After the second feast, the bride beseeches the king to stop the slaughter of her people. The king rises, leaves his wine, and walks out; the enemy falls on the bride, but in walks the king in anger. The enemy and his sons are destroyed in the same manner they had planned for the prophet Mordecai. The bride's people are allowed to fight back for two days. They rest on the third day, a day of joy and feasting. Queen Vashti missed out; she was sent away after her rebellion. Esther is the one who receives Haman's estate, and Mordecai, the prophet, looks after it. Can you see prophecy in this story? (Esther 6:13).

Jesus invites us to a banquet, joined by those brought in by fishers of men to a land flowing with milk and honey, where the food is the fruit of the Spirit, the bread of life, new wine, and the milk and meat of the word.

January 10

On August 31, 2024, I dreamed I was in a big church with my daughter. We sat in the front row, stage right, with a few others. The large and high stage was the focal point. The organist frowned at us—she didn't think we should sit there. We all moved to the center, and a huge motorized stage with unfinished wood boards in odd positions electronically moved out from under the stage in front of us. I knew it had cost $10,000. I guessed it was part of a presentation or play. Meaning: Big church boards make no sense. Wasting money to draw crowds isn't working and moves us away from the finished work of the cross. The organist is controlling, and the congregation sitting in the middle represents man-pleasing lukewarmness. The high stage represents a lack of connection between people and leaders. "These people come near to me with words only, their hearts are far from me. Their worship of me is made up of man-made rules" (Isaiah 29:13). Worship is not a slow song; it is a life of devotion, obedience because of adoration, acts of service, and righteous living. Ignoring God until you want or need something is not worship—it is lip service, holding to a form of outward godliness but denying its transformational power. Just because we have a God-given gift does not mean we have God's blanket stamp of approval on our lives. (2 Timothy 3:5)

'The church reformed but always reforming,' was the motto of the Protestant Reformation under Martin Luther and John Calvin. The church must never stop reforming into the image of Christ. When we stop changing, religion moves in, and we become stiff, cold, lifeless, and somewhat ineffective. God is preparing us by making us tired of the old wineskins so we will be attracted to the new ones. Matthew 9:17

Absurdity:

The quality or state of being ridiculous or wildly
unreasonable
Like the Capitol and the people of Panem in the *Hunger
Games,* who enjoyed watching the gladiator-like slaughter of
children while looking like clowns in their elaborate, bizarre
costumes
Gaudy, garish, and surreal, they are detached from reality
A dystopian city where everyone wants to be individually
unique
Covering up who they really are inside, empty, carnal, and
fake like mannequins
Detached and happy to be the predators instead of the prey
Do we have the absurd in our culture? People hiding behind
masks trying to be distinctive, a one-of-a-kind novelty, yet
becoming odd
Trying to highlight bangles, tattoos, and skin, drawing
attention away from the parts one despises, not wanting to
be ordinary or common
Beauty does not come from outward adornments, fancy
hairstyles, expensive jewelry, fine clothes, but from an inner,
unfading beauty
A gentle heart, doing what is right and not giving way to fear
Compassionate, rational, reasonable, and above all, loving.

"...Engraved with a flint point, on the tablets of their heart..."
What is engraved on your heart? (Jeremiah 17:1-2)

January 11

Imagine a dresser with three drawers. The top drawer is called "The Present," and it contains what is going on in your life now. Is this drawer chaotic, unorganized, and full of unnecessary time-wasters? The middle drawer is the past. Some do not want it open, others have it open all the time, and it interferes with the top drawer of "now." What is in your past that needs to be tossed? Is it unforgiveness, shame, anger, or regret? Or are the successes of the past consuming your time and attention? These may cause the "now" things to pass you by. We do not need mundane distractions, nor do we want lingering feelings of regret. It is important to respect and honor the Lord's forgiveness. He gave his life so that by his grace we are forgiven. If we hold on to our past sins and failures, then we are disregarding his sacrifice. If we hold on to someone else's offense toward us, then we are no better than the accuser of the brethren. If we comb deep enough into the middle drawer, we may find things we need to be forgiven for. When Jesus looks at our life, he sees the beautifully carved dresser he crafted with images of joy, love, and peace. He can turn our worst failures into our greatest successes. It is time to clean out the drawer of the past. Paul put it this way, "But one thing I do, forgetting those things from the past and reaching forward to those things which are in the future" (Philippians 3:13). "Do not remember the former things, the things of old. I will do a new thing, now it shall spring forth" (Isaiah 43:18-19).

To be a Christian means to forgive the inexcusable, because God has forgiven the inexcusable in you. -C. S. Lewis

QUESTIONS

When I look back, I back down
The past becomes my backdrop
Do impulse and desire rule me?
Do I love God for who he is
Or for what he can do for me?
Am I able to wait for God to answer,
Or do I impatiently take what I want?
Do I love God even when I suffer?
What is the darkness inside of me
Producing strong and violent responses?
A wounded emotion, a past trauma
To suppress or express?
Do I react to justify myself
Or respond without defensiveness?
Do I live by feelings or by principles?
No peace-no freedom
Know peace-know freedom
Is the Divine life inside of me?

January 12

The bottom drawer of the dresser represents our future; it contains our thoughts about death. Death can be ignored, but it is inevitable. Many fear death, will it come quickly or slowly? Will I suffer? Will I be able to complete everything I want to accomplish? The Bible tells us that death is the last enemy to be defeated, which is a nice thought, but it doesn't ease the foreboding feeling as we reach the golden years or encounter an incurable disease. We are commanded to trust the Lord, and he promises to take care of us. "Even to your old age and gray hairs I will sustain and rescue you. I have made you and I will carry you" (Isaiah 46:4-5). Open the bottom drawer, let the bats fly out, and fill it with the promises of God. Don't allow death to be on your lips; let your mouth be filled with truth, testimony, and gratefulness for each new day. Testimony means "Do it again." God wants us to see the challenging, exciting times ahead as we did when we were new believers. He doesn't want us spending our retirement years in a boring routine. Be curious to keep life interesting. Ask questions, embrace life, keep learning and exploring. Our eternal life begins the day we give our lives to Jesus; we will not perish but will quickly and easily be ushered by angels into glory when our assignments here below are completed!

We are called living epistles; we are God's book, recorded in his heavenly library. 2 Corinthians 3:2-3 NKJ; Malachi 3:16

Fears
Spiders, heights, water, fights, darkness, caves, sickness, graves
Fear like a sword, I want to run, I want to hide, cover me, Lord
"I am at your side, be fearless."

January 13

Bears or bugs, what are you afraid of? There are huge things we encounter in life, much like facing a bear: disease, disaster, death, loss. Then there are things that look small but for some reason cause terror: bugs, the dark, the future, failure, or any of the over 400 named phobias. The television show *Monk*, starring Tony Shalhoub, is about a brilliant man with many gifts and successes, yet he has unfounded fears: milk, elevators, germs, and more. It is a difficult show to watch; we want him to be normal and enjoy life, but he cannot. People watching this show have recognized their own compulsions and tendency to view life as an enemy. Phobias are connected to an underlying fear of death. Travel, adventure, and taking risks become a dread instead of a joy. God did not create us to be fearful. The Bible tells us to fear not 365 times. Gideon ground his meal in a wine press, fearing the enemy's notice; Moses didn't want to be God's mouthpiece because of fear and insecurity. They overcame their fear. There are times to run away, as when Paul climbed down a wall to escape persecution, but he did so knowing what he would face. He took risks, and yes, he suffered, but Paul never regretted his life of serving Jesus. Self-preservation can become idolatry; it is bowing to fear. We must give the future bottom drawer and its fears to Him.

When I felt great anxiety, your peace brought joy to my soul.
(Psalm 94:19)

Cowardice

The coward in us must die
The quitting when rejected
Running when threatened
Backing down when accused
Valuing status, fearing death
We must advance, take possession
Spies had a bad report-they died
Be a Caleb! Be a Joshua!
Stop wavering
It isn't for the faint of heart
The violent take it by force
Deception-FALL! Villainy-FALL!
Corruption-FALL!
Time to cross over
And face those giants!

January 14

This is the history of the box, not a cardboard one, but the one God was put into when the world entered the "Dark Ages" from 500-1500 A.D. Because the box was small, the light of God's truth flickered rarely and dimly. Father God was viewed as one who was angrily waiting to punish people for their slip-ups and who gladly sent rule breakers to hell. Martin Luther's 14th-century Reformation led to the rise of Protestantism, and the box grew a bit. He nailed his 95 Theses on the church door in 1517, revealing the truth: salvation is by faith, the Bible is the final authority, sin and its guilt can only be forgiven by God, and the church includes all the priesthood of believers. The box began to grow, and the Light grew brighter as sprouts of truth awakened the church, leading to Presbyterianism, Congregationalism, Puritanism, and Anabaptism. From the 1730s to the mid-1800s, leaders like Jonathan Edwards and George Whitefield brought about the First Great Awakening, and the church was reborn. Holiness was emphasized. John Wesley founded Methodism, leading to Evangelicalism. Then the Second Great Awakening began in the 1800s, and as more truth was restored, the box grew. Revivalist camp meetings led to a national revival in 1831. Charles Finney preached in Rochester, New York, and revival spread among the Southern Civil War troops. Then, on April 9, 1906, a revival led by William J. Seymour began on Azusa Street, California, and within 100 years, there were 400 million Pentecostals/Charismatics worldwide. Billy Graham began his evangelistic meetings, resulting in an explosion of salvations. Then came the truth of the gifts of the Holy Spirit and miracles, the presence and glory of God, worship, meeting in homes, intercessory prayer, and world evangelism. God is now seen as a loving Father ready to forgive. In 2016, Bill Hamon prophesied that this is the time of the Third Great Awakening, of preparing the way of the Lord's return, when God will bring everything under the headship of Christ. Looking at the history of God's plan for the church should be seen as an opening up of Truth. He does not belong in anyone's box; he will never fit! (Ephesians 1:10).

Are we hot or cold, warriors, deserters, or AWOL? Being lukewarm is dangerous. No more delay, be an on-fire warrior!

The Flood

For forty days it flooded, and all those mockers drowned
Forty days on Sinai, Moses heard from God
In the valley, a golden calf was worshiped
Another forty days, Moses on Sinai carving new tablets of stone
For forty years in desert sands, Israel wandered for doubting
"In forty days, Nineveh destroyed" in sackcloth they repented
Goliath taunted for forty days, David's stone ended those jeers
For forty days Jesus fasted, the forked tongue liar defeated
Jesus was forty days on earth after he rose from the grave
Forty is the time for testing, for going through the fire
Pass your test, do not cave, Jesus, your desire!

January 15

Are you the one? "For the secret power of lawlessness is already at work; but the <u>one</u> who now holds it back will continue to do so till he is taken out of the way. And then the lawless one will be revealed" (2 Thessalonians 2:7). This "one" has been assumed to be Holy Spirit being taken out of the world at the time of the wrath of God, but that contradicts Psalm 139: "Where can I flee from your presence? If I go up to the heavens, you are there; if I make my bed in hell, you are there." Holy Spirit does not completely leave the earth, only those with the Spirit in them. "Christ in us the hope of glory" (Colossians 1:27). Do we have the authority to hold back the secret power of lawlessness? Yes, we have access to the courts of heaven and must enforce what Jesus did in defeating the enemy at the cross. "Whatever you bind [or forbid] on earth will have been bound in heaven, and whatever you loose [or permit] on earth will have been loosed in heaven" (Matthew 18:19). "I have given you authority to tread on serpents and scorpions, and over all the power of the enemy, and nothing will injure you" (Luke 10:19). We are the ones who need to exercise our authority by speaking God's word and declaring his promises. The Holy Spirit, through us, is holding back the power of lawlessness.

The wages of death are earned. The gift of life is freely received. We were on Satan's payroll; now we are on God's gift list! -Dick Mills

January 16

"All the promises of God in Christ are 'Yes' and 'Amen'" (2 Corinthians 1:20). Believing and standing on his promises does not mean wishful thinking. "God does not lie...what he says, he will do; what he has promised, he will fulfill." (Numbers 23:19). Between promise and fulfillment is patience, a time of testing our faith and trust. It is the time to obey by waiting. Some promises are troubling. The Lord said that his followers would be sheep sent out among the wolves, some would be arrested, and persecution would even come from family members. "Do not fear those who are able to kill the body but are not able to kill the soul; but rather fear the one who is able to destroy both soul and body in hell" (Matthew 10:28). There are two hurdles we must overcome, our will and our way, because his ways and thoughts are beyond ours. As we wait for the fulfillment of his delightful promises, we trust him during the ones that are troubling. He is always with us. "In all these things we overwhelmingly, exceedingly conquer" (Romans 8:37, 12:21).

They will fight against you, but they shall not prevail against you, for I am with you to deliver you. Jeremiah 1:19

Psalm 149:6-9
High praises in their mouth, double-edged swords in their hands
Vengeance upon the heathen, punishments upon the people
Binding kings with chains, Nobles with iron shackles
Carrying out written sentences, this honor has all His saints.
To Him be all the Praise!

Unfaithful

Do you say you are on God's side, but your actions prove
otherwise?

Have you broken your vows, derelict in duty, untrustworthy?

A treacherous traitor betrays a country or a marriage

Disloyal, abusive, breaking covenant–a partnership
dissolved

God will forgive, confess, ask for help, seek Him
wholeheartedly

Put away apathy, a wavering opinion, dispassionate feelings

Become faithful, loyal, devoted, reliable, and steadfast

A solid follower of Christ, a dutiful citizen of your country

A spouse who is worthy of the vows that were made at the
altar

Be tried and true, enthusiastic, passionate, unwavering

A fervent on-fire follower of Christ, a pillar of society

Waiting for the Lord's affirmation in His glorious kingdom

January 17

False prophets are known by their conduct. Scripture reveals what to watch for in determining if they are false. Some teach a different gospel, speak in the name of other gods, and they deceive, lie, trick, and have worldly speech. The world likes them and speaks well of them, but they will not listen to the truth; they deny the Lord, are covetous, ungodly, and lewd. They turn from truth to fables and myths, and lead people away from Christ by flattery and smooth talk. Their prophesies and visions will have an element of divination. They exhibit questionable character qualities, serve their appetites, and some declare themselves to be "The Christ," magically performing false signs and wonders, then say, "Let us go serve other gods." They are rebellious against the Lord and will teach philosophies and human traditions based on "elemental spirits of the world," not on Christ. They do not expose iniquity or prophesy repentance. They are seductive and encourage idolatry; they demand payment, and they are fierce. Test the spirits to see if they are from God; do they say that Jesus Christ is Lord? Prophecies may take years to be fulfilled. Elijah's prophecies about Jezebel, Ahab, and Jehu came true after he died. "We see through a glass darkly...We know in part" (1 Corinthians 13:12). Prophets do not know everything; that is why there were communities of prophets in the Old Testament, and there still are. "Let two or three prophets speak, and the other [prophets] weigh what is being said" (1 Corinthians 14:29). Jonah's words of prophecy did not come true: "In three days Nineveh will be destroyed." Prophets give words of warning so we can pray and intercede so judgment may be lessened, and people will be saved. Old Testament prophets were killed along with John the Baptist and Jesus; they were hated for their message. We should be careful before accusing someone of being a false teacher or prophet. As for the "wolves in sheep's clothing," let the leaders in the church expose them, but let us be wary of wolves from the media, Hollywood, and education.

Matthew 7:15; Deuteronomy 13:1-5; 18:20-22; 1 John 4:1-6; 2 Corinthians 11:13-15; 2 Peter 2; Jeremiah 23:16; Jude 1:3-5; 2 Timothey 4; Romans 16:18; Luke 6:26; Jeremiah 14:14, 23:14-22; Matthew 24:15-16; Colossians 2:8; Acts 13:6; Lamentation 2:14; Revelation 2:20; Micah 3:11, Acts 20:29; Luke 10:3; 1 Corinthians 12:3

Surely the Sovereign Lord does nothing without revealing his plan to his servants, the prophets. Amos 3:7

Cut the Cord!

Sever the input of darkness, that box on a pedestal
Evil brainwashing conduit of hell itself, cut the cord
The umbilical hook-up to a Babylonian lifestyle
Full of debauchery, a vile, godless sacrilege, cut the cord
Remove the offensive high place, wash away duplicity
Cut it! That God-insulting venue, do not hesitate, amputate!
Be rid of hollow replacements, trade them for life, for Him

January 18

Jesus prayed in John 17 that his people would be brought into complete unity. Does that seem like an impossibility? Some believe that unity means we all think alike and share the same ideas and opinions about everything. If that were so, then why did Paul say, "If you disagree on some point, God will reveal that to you also" (Philippians 3:15)? Paul states, "We are God's household...being fitted together, growing into a holy temple in the Lord" (Ephesians 2:19-21). "And in him you too are being built together to become a dwelling in which God lives by his Spirit" (verse 22). Paul is speaking to a Spirit-filled church. Why would he say that we were "being built to become a dwelling" in which God dwells, or that we needed to "grow to be a holy temple?" We must be built and grow into the unity of Christ. Chapter 4 is how to achieve this miraculous goal. "Be completely humble, gentle and patient, bearing with one another in love. Make every effort to keep the unity of the Spirit through the bond of peace. There is one body, one Spirit, one hope, one Lord, one faith, one baptism, one God and Father of all, who is over all and through all and in all. Each one is given grace until we are mature and measure up to the standard of Christ." This process of unity comes through loving one another, maturing to the standard of Christ, and attaining to the whole measure of his fullness. Holy Spirit and God's people have work to do.

Live holy and godly lives as you look forward to and hasten the day of God. (2 Peter 3:12)

January 19

Paul tells the Ephesian church not to live like the unredeemed Gentiles. They are darkened in their understanding and ignorant from having a hardened heart. They have lost all sensitivity and indulge in every kind of impurity, with a continual lust for more. He encouraged them to stop lying, stealing, and displaying sinful anger, which gives the enemy a foothold. Paul condemns unwholesome talk and warns against grieving the Holy Spirit. He points out character flaws needing to be corrected: bitterness, rage, brawling, slander, and malice. "Have nothing to do with the fruitless deeds of darkness but rather expose them. For it is shameful even to mention what the disobedient do in secret" (Ephesians 5:11-12). He lists what the church needs to repent of: immorality, impurity, debauchery, idolatry, witchcraft, hatred, discord, jealousy, selfish ambition, dissensions, factions, envy, drunkenness, and pride (Galatians 5:20-21). The answer is to be crucified with Christ; we are not our own, we were bought with a price (1 Corinthians 6:20).

Be aware of godless teachers who say that after we become Christ-followers, we can do what we want without fear of God's punishment. These false teachers live immoral lives and mock those with authority, and in doing whatever they feel like, they ruin their souls. They are like Cain, who killed his brother; like Balaam, they will do anything for money; like Korah, they disobey God and die. They have no thought of others, and at potluck meals, they take more than their share. They are like trees without fruit, promising much but producing little. They complain and are loud-mouthed show-offs, only showing respect when they want something in return. They stir up arguments and love the evil things of this world. They do not have God's Holy Spirit. -Jude

Who hasn't been angry with Adam and Eve for ruining everything for a piece of fruit? But aren't we all tempted by a tree of the knowledge of good and evil, curious about what is on the other side of obedience, creating our own boundaries by self-determining good and evil? What about the temptations you have succumbed to? Do you remember the first time you sinned, and your conscience was pricked? Picture your tree; it doesn't have apples on it; it has other things. Call them idols, things we chose against our conscience, starting with our mom telling us not to take a cookie, and we did. Succumbing to the temptation was eating the fruit. God gave the command to Adam, who then repeated it to Eve after she was created. Satan's emissary, the serpent, twisted the command, which caused her to question what Adam had told her. She was deceived into taking the apple of an evil philosophy–that we can be a god. "Do not love the world or anything in it. If you love the world, the love of the Father is not in you. For everything in the world–sinful cravings, lusting eyes, and the boasting of what one has and does–comes not from the Father but from the world" (1 John 2:15-16). Eve's eyes lingered on the pleasantness of the fruit; she desired it, then considered the wonderful consequences of being like God. She was caught in the net, and so can we be. Instead of blaming Eve for our sinfulness, realize that we could have been blamed for being the first sinner to eat what God had banned.

Keep the serpent out! We wouldn't allow an uncaged snake to slither around our home, nor should we unlock the door to demons who prey upon our family.

UNITY

I'm a Charismatic Lutheran, the Just shall live by faith
I'm in the Church of Christ, God's Last Day Assembly Saint
I witness for Jehovah with those Pentecostal Methods
I'm baptized into Christ, and I've joined Salvation's Army
I work the Four-Square Vineyard and speak the Word of
Faith
Communion, confession, filled with Holy Spirit too
Cleansed daily by repentance, keeping Jesus' blood in view
I'm just a humble servant, passionate for Yeshua the Jew
A Non-Denominationalist, reading His Word each day
Evangelism, deliverance, and healing I pursue
I believe in the miracle to come, the unified Gentile and Jew
I've returned to Adam's religion, walking with Father each
day
Caring for orphans and widows and staying clean in God's
way
By grace through faith, I stand, and not by the works that I do

Believe it or not, there are people who actually think that Helen Keller faked her deafness and blindness. It must be because it is hard to believe that someone with so many disabilities can rise above to become a pillar of society. She made a difference. She met with presidents and wounded soldiers, attended a school for the deaf that taught them to speak, and then gave lectures in 35 countries. She wrote a dozen books and 400 essays, fought for women's rights, and garnered support for programs for the blind. In 1964, at the age of 84, Helen was awarded the Medal of Freedom for her service to her country. It may be that those who doubt have been put to shame by her accomplishments because they have eyes and ears and have not made a difference. Her tutor, Anne Sullivan, deserves recognition for her patience, determination, and dedication in giving her life to save one little deaf and dumb girl. Some of us will travel the world and be a beacon of light to millions, while others will serve one person. Those who serve the one are no less important than those who serve millions. God created us and knew the life that we would desire; He gives us those desires. He also cares about the one lost soul, and the good shepherd sends us out to rescue them.

He doesn't compel us to go against our will; He just makes us willing to go. From an old Kentucky song.

https://afb.org/about-afb/history/helen-keller *Helen Keller: Our Champion*. American Foundation for the Blind. 2024.

January 22

A scribe takes notes and writes what he sees and hears. He writes essays, books, songs, and poems. God is a mystery to be discovered. He speaks in the wind, the clouds, the thunder, and through his word. Scribe, write on; reveal more of God. Write down your dreams and thoughts; the revelations that you have never heard anyone else say. Document your journey, the surprises and miracles, the unexpected encounters, and the blessings. "Sing to the Lord a new song for he has done wonderful things!" (Psalms 98:1). You are God's epistle; he is not finished writing your story. His will is like golden threads hanging from Heaven, not in a symmetrical gradient, but a weaving in and out of reflected light and glory. We are in that tapestry of light with no dead ends because all things work together for good for those who love God and are called to his purpose. Be a scribe, see the eternal plan, and see your place in it. Do you hear him in the watches of the night? "Rise, my dove, and write."

Arise, shine, for your light has come, and the glory of the Lord rises upon you. Darkness covers the earth; thick darkness over the people, but the Lord rises upon you, and his glory appears over you. Nations will come to your light and kings to the brightness of your dawn. Isaiah 60:1-3

Ephesians is the book of our identity and warfare. In chapter 1, we are sealed by the Holy Spirit after we believe, then we are filled with wisdom, revelation, and power. In chapter 2, we are seated in heavenly places and are reminded that "we are God's workmanship, created in Christ Jesus to do good works which God prepared in advance for us to do." In unity, we are being built into a holy temple to the Lord, in which the Holy Spirit will dwell. In chapter 3, we see the mystery of God's many-faceted wisdom revealed through the church. This is accomplished because we are rooted and established in his incomprehensible and immeasurable love. Chapter 4 tells us what to be: loving, humble, gentle, patient, unified, and peaceable, no longer infants but mature as each one does the will of God. Then we are told to put off the old self and its corruption. Chapter 5 lists the things we are not to do and be. We are to live as wise children of light, having nothing to do with darkness except to expose it for what it is. Then lastly, chapter 6 begins with commands: children, obey your parents; fathers, don't frustrate, embitter, or discourage your children; slaves [and employees], respect your masters, serving them wholeheartedly. Masters (bosses), treat your slaves (employees) as you want God to treat you. Be strong and put on his full armor so you can stand firm against the devil's evil schemes. Take up the sword, which is the word of God, and pray in the Spirit often, with all kinds of prayers and requests. Be fearless and be alert (Colossians 3:21).

God loves everyman as though there were no one else to love, God also prepares every man as though there were no one else. - St. Augustine

January 24

Have you read the war poem by Alfred Lord Tennyson, *Charge of the Light Brigade*? That is what we are, a Light Brigade! We are children of light. Jesus told us to let our light shine before men so they may see our good works, then praise and acknowledge God. We are the light of the world, a city on a hill. The eye is the lamp of our body; if we allow darkness to enter through the eyes, then our soul will become darkened. Why are we a brigade? We are part of a military unit led by Jesus Christ, assisted by the host of Heaven, with headquarters both in Heaven and on earth. We aren't all in the same squadron, as each group has its own assignment, and each person has his or her own mission. Some fight for the education of our children, some for government, some for family, and others for media, entertainment, health, or business. We fight with our prayers and petitions, we fight through legislation, contacting the heads of these mountains of society, writing letters, and getting involved. Sometimes we charge by gathering to protest or pray, attending strategy meetings, and making our voices heard. (Matthew 5 and 6)

The importance of seeing ourselves as God's army is paramount!

Believing
Dreams, visions, signs, and wonders
Shadows becoming clear
Words like apples of gold in settings of silver
Mysteries revealed, miracles appear
The beauty of brokenness, dying to self
God's plan for a new year
Dying to gain, never bowing to fear

Church leaders are told to judge those inside the church; we are not to take fellow believers to court. "Is it possible that there is nobody among you wise enough to settle a dispute between believers? Instead, one brother takes another to court in front of unbelievers! Don't you know that you will judge the world? Why not rather be wronged?" A judge assesses and inquires through questioning, distinguishes good from evil, examines whether something is true, or decides whether something is appropriate by experience or insight. Discernment is the ability to determine the source of a thought or action and correctly respond to it. The Bible says that man looks on the outside, but God looks at the heart. Courts try to get to the heart of a matter, to the part that only God can see. They sometimes accidentally or on purpose convict the innocent or set the guilty free.

We are constantly tempted to judge each other. "Anyone who speaks against a brother or sister or judges them speaks against the law and judges it. There is only one Lawgiver and Judge. But you—who are you to judge your neighbor?" A trial consists of a judge, a jury, a defense lawyer, and a prosecutor. The burden of proof rests on the prosecutor, who must prove the accused's guilt beyond a reasonable doubt, using evidence of method, means, and motive. Motive is what is in the defendant's heart—that is the most difficult to determine. We must pray that justice will come from the 9 Supreme Court justices, the 1,770 federal judges, and the 30,000 state judges, and that the church will grow in love and discernment.

(1 Corinthians 6:7; Acts 17:11; Hebrews 5:14; 1 John 1:4; Philippians 1:9; James 4:11-12)

Taylor A Welch. *The types of Discernment* #short YouTube

The Holy Spirit always exalts Jesus; the evil spirit discredits Jesus; the human spirit attempts to exalt man and his cleverness, knowledge, ability and achievements. -Dick Mills

Agenda of Evil

The system has been prepared for those willing to sacrifice themselves
Procedures and experimentations, constructing a new world order
Pictures painted with enticing words, luring the ignorant to their doom
Those who won't comply are shamed, arrested, locked up, shut down

Seeing, feeling, and believing their own made-up media truth
Seeing may be trickery; feelings may tell lies
Believing in the false creates slaves to the counterfeit
Fraudulent, deceptive, and distorted, an illusion that isn't real

Decisions based on lies, virtual, CGI, fake
Fear controlling the masses is deadly. Wake Up!
You will live and not die! Find faith in God before the quake, now, not in the sweet by and by, do it for Jesus' sake!

January 26

Do the impossible, the assignments outside your ability and comfort zone. Why? Because when we are weak, then the Spirit can be strong through us. If you have a desire that seems impossible, don't let go of it. Pray, and God will lead you to see the impossible become possible. "If you have faith like the tiny grain of mustard seed, you will say to this mountain, 'Move from here to there' and it will move, and nothing will be impossible for you" (Matthew 17:20). "With men this is impossible, but with God all things are possible" (Matthew 19:26). "Lord God, you made the heavens and the earth, nothing is too difficult for you" (Jeremiah 32:17). "I am the God of all mankind, is anything too hard for me?" (Jeremiah 32:27). "What appears humanly impossible is more than possible with God, for God can do what man cannot" (Luke 18:27). Stretch your confidence, teach a Sunday class, volunteer to clean the church, feed the poor, talk to your neighbors. Start with the simple things, then let God move you into whatever mission field he knows you will love. He will equip you, and you will be blessed! "The days are coming when things are going to happen so fast you will be shocked, one thing coming quickly on the heels of the other" (Amos 9:13).

Faith sees the invisible, believes the unbelievable and receives the impossible. -Corrie ten Boom

Warfare words to say, "No, you are not going to do that!" That is how we speak to the enemy who is trying to kill, steal, and destroy. "That is not true!" That is how we speak to the enemy who is trying to lie to us about who we are, who others are, and who God is. "That is not coming in here." That is how we deal with the unclean things that try to sneak into our home through our eyes and ears. And lastly, "I am not doing that!" That is how we deal with temptations. We have to decide how clean we want our hands to be. When we decide to lay something down on God's altar, our hands are now empty for more of what God has for us. We wrestle by faith through our words. It is not hard to do, try it, say, "I submit to God and resist the devil, he will now flee. Fear, be gone. Rejection, be gone. Anger, be gone. Unforgiveness, be gone." But it must come out of the mouth; warfare isn't fought with thoughts. You will soon find that you have won that battle, and that particular wrestling match is over. Prepare for the next; the enemy does not give up easily. Before Christ came to earth, the devil was like a dog running around biting people. Now that Jesus has disarmed the enemy by giving his life for us, the dog is on a chain. He can only bite when we get too close. If we haven't resisted the world and the flesh, how can we resist the devil? (Genesis 3:15; Colossians 2:15; Hebrews 2:14-15)

The devil gives us a thought then condemns us for having it. -Ben Diaz

A BATTLE

One day, Satan crept into Heaven's library
He stole a book with each human's dying date
He cackled as he flew to earth; his intent was very clear
He would show each one that death was near
The day, the hour, the year
They would cower and tremble as he thrust the book to their face
He would gleefully torment the whole human race
A certain man did not recoil, but instead picked up a stick
And with it, pushed the book away
He was quite incensed with Satan's trick
"My God is sovereign," He shouted, "Hezekiah, a man,
Pled with God and received fifteen more years to his life span
So go away, you liar, I will not take your bait!"
The evil one flew back to Heaven, grumbling as he went
Seething with hatred for the wasted time he spent
He stealthily returned the book, angry from defeat
A sword of the Lord's angel suddenly blocked him from leaving
"I saw what you did there, how you were deceiving
And now I throw you out! Be gone in Jesus name!"
Like lighting the dark one fell to earth, back to his filthy lair
As he sat nursing his wounded ego, a book suddenly appeared
A name stood out, "Lucifer" it read, then a date and words–all caps
"CHAINED FOR A THOUSAND YEARS," it said
The vision ended, he fell back, he knew his time on earth would lapse
He would be chained and cast into a fiery pit, at last!

January 28

If one claims to be Christian because of earned righteous feelings from worthy good deeds, then he is no better than one belonging to a false religion. Jesus didn't die so we could feel good about ourselves, our successes, or our righteous deeds. Jesus himself will confront those who have their identity wrapped up in what they do, "casting out demons and doing many wonderful works," and will tell them to depart from him because he never knew them. He is interested in who we really are, not in what we do to try to impress, a works-based, fake identity (Matthew 7:21-23). The church in Ephesians had six great works to its credit, but because it had left Jesus as their first love, the future of their church was in danger. Christianity is not a world religion; it is a practice by a portion of the world's population based on a relationship with God the Father through Jesus Christ, his Son. Religion cannot forgive you or take away your guilt and remorse. But through Jesus Christ, Heavenly Father can. James put it this way, "True religion is caring for widows and orphans and keeping oneself unpolluted from the world." Being a disciple of Jesus, being a part of the family of God, the army of God, the building of God, is all about a relationship with God and with other believers. Our connection with God comes from praying, praising, worshiping, and listening to him, reading his word, and making time for contemplation. We don't go to church; we are the Church going. We take joy in pleasing him and in receiving the grace, mercy, and peace he freely gives. It excludes boasting about ourselves; it is all about Him!

If we cannot forgive ourselves, then the forgiveness from God is meaningless. -Dr. Kendall

"Then those who feared the Lord talked with one another, the Lord listened; a book of remembrance was written to record the names of those who feared him and meditated on his name. 'They will be rescued on the day when I act in judgment, they will be my own special treasure. I will spare them as a father spares an obedient child. You will again see the difference between the righteous and the wicked, those who serve me and those who do not" (Malachi 3:16-18). There are three throne room judgment times. One occurs after the tribulation and is when the sheep and goat nations are judged according to how they treated "Jesus' brethren" (Matthew 12:50; 25:31-36). Goat nations will be excluded during the thousand-year period of the reign of Jesus. Another judgment is for believers in Christ, "For we must all stand before Christ to be judged. We will each receive whatever we deserve for the good or evil we have done in this earthly body" (2 Corinthians 5:10). The Great White Throne Judgment occurs after the millennial reign of Christ when the books are opened, including the Book of Life, and all, living and dead, will be judged according to what they had done as recorded in the books (Revelation 20:12-15).

Many of His disciples turned back and no longer followed Him.
John 6:66

THREE IN ONE

We welcome you, Holy Spirit, you who hovered over the
deep
And over Mary, the mother, who raised Jesus from the dead
We accept your gifts, your peace, comfort, and joy
All that you bring to us, we reject nothing, thank you

In humility, we accept you, Jesus, the greatest gift of all
Praise you for coming, a baby, leaving your home behind
Bound for suffering that we may live and be a family
We leave the pigsties and the fields to worship and feast

We worship you, Father, you suffered the most
Offering your Son, who carried our sin and shame
You adopted us into your family, and run to us when we
come home
We leave the pigpens of the world, you care for us
We worship you

January 30

Dream 2/24

It was the first day of a college art class, and the teacher asked us to make a drawing. We then graded each other's work. I gave everyone high grades; 80% and above. The teacher then went around and graded the students' work; everyone did poorly; 30%. Then we did another project. I painted a nighttime scene of the ocean. The waves were small, the moon shone behind scattered clouds, and a woman was on the beach, her back to the water. I repainted her mouth from closed to open, and she was looking up; her face was in profile. Her arms were straight down; I wanted them up as a sign of worship. At the bottom, I wrote. "The Opera" and signed it CK.

Opera means work. The meaning of the dream is that we are in God's college, and we aren't supposed to grade each other's work or to take pride in our own. Our life and our works are worship to God. We worship with our backs to the darkness of the world, our arms raised in surrender, focused on the light. We need to see ourselves as always learning from our teacher, Holy Spirit, who corrects us when we take the glory for what we do instead of giving credit to the Lord.

Don't let the darkness rob you of your hope. God is in the darkness; he will be your light.

January 31

What is a right? It is something God gives to all humanity; a legal, inherent entitlement. It is claimed and recognized by nearly all people: life, liberty, speech, religion, family, the pursuit of property, and the right to become children of God (John 1:12). If someone takes your life, they are taking away your right to live, and they, in turn, forfeit their right to freedom and life. What is a privilege? It is a special advantage or opportunity given to certain individuals, or something granted to another as a favor that imposes an obligation on the one providing it. It can be taken away. In other words, we pursue what we have as rights, and others pay for the special privileges we receive. The free gift of salvation is a privilege that was paid for by Jesus' sacrifice on the cross. Reasons people reject the free gift of salvation are: ignorance, a hard heart, a dark soul, no regret or remorse, not mixing the truth of the word with faith, no conviction of sin, ingrained religious beliefs, wounds by church people or parents. These can be resolved by a near-death experience, a dream, a tragedy, a miraculous sign or wonder, a deep conviction or desire, or a prayer that says, "I don't know if you are real, but if you are, I want to serve you. Please reveal yourself to me." The Lord does not want any to perish!

Don't fight for rights, go to the front lines and fight the battle.

https://www.merriam-webster.com Privilege Definition & Meaning

February 1

Those of us who grew up in church might be like the people in Nazareth who rejected Christ because they thought they knew him too well and reasoned incorrectly about who he was and what he was capable of. Have we been raised in Nazareth and become disappointed by religion, losing our faith in Christ, and cynically equating him with the church? The people of Nazareth did not receive many miracles. Is that why we in America seem to get fewer supernatural interventions than other countries? Are we too sophisticated or self-conscious to believe we can fight through the crowd in desperation to touch the hem of his garment and be healed? Are we so indoctrinated by the world that we turn to doctors before going to the Great Physician? The poor of this world are rich in faith; they have no choice but to trust Jesus. We need more childlike, humble faith in his wonders. "Renew us, Lord, and wash away the cynicism, doubt, and unbelief of Nazareth." Don't let unbelief speak. There will be notable miracles, ones outside the four walls of the church (Acts 4:16), an unending stream of great miracles (Acts 6:8; 8:13), special miracles freeing people from evil entrapments (Acts 19:11), and diverse miracles for diverse needs (Hebrews 2:4). It is time to leave Nazareth and believe!

Being embarrassed is the opposite of being humble. Humble people are not focused on themselves and are never ashamed of themselves or of Jesus Christ. They are willingly joyful 'fools for Christ.' 1 Corinthians 4:10

February 2

"My burden is light. I do not expect you to carry the burdens of the world around like a heavy backpack; they are burdens you are to lift up to me. We partner together for the lost and hurting. I present to you what is on my heart, and you pray in faith and hand it back to me. I give you these burdens when we spend time together. I share my heart, and you share yours. As you focus on me and give the burdens for others back to me, you will notice that your burdens will become lighter. You will have peace and hope knowing I am working on your behalf. I carry your weights, but you must bring everything to me. You cannot live life on your own. I care about the little matters, and I care about the large ones. When you partner with me, your reward will be great." "Be joyful in hope, patient in affliction, faithful in prayer" (Romans 12:12; Revelation 3:20).

'Who then is the faithful and wise manager, whom the master puts in charge of his servants, to serve them food when it is time? It will be good for this servant to be doing so when the master returns.' The managers of God's kingdom are called servants. Luke 12:42-43

Isaiah 8:9-10
Raise the war cry
But be shattered
Devise your strategy
All of it thwarted
Propose your plan
It will not stand
God is with us

IN AWE

I stand in awe of you, Lord
I am hearing your quiet whispering voice
Seeing in the realm of your Spirit
Discerning your angelic forces
Smelling the aroma of your presence
You come, a tangible electric atmosphere
To change my mind, heal my heart
Washing away the old and stale
A new day, breaking out of the shell
Worshipping, the incense rising
Hearing and feeling God
His love is better than life

MY SHEEP

My sheep listen to my voice
I know them; they follow me
I give them eternal life, they shall not perish
No one can snatch them from my hand
Other sheep are not yet in the sheep pen
But they, too, will listen to my voice
One flock, one Shepherd
Follow me, and I will make you become

February 3

"The steps of the godly are ordered by the Lord" (Psalm 37:23). The Hebrew meaning for ordered is appointed. He doesn't just direct our steps; he has an appointment for them. He created us with a specific purpose, one that will fulfill the desires of our hearts. He provides us with the next step even when we mess up, and his work in us will be fulfilled no matter what obstacles seem to delay the plan. Obstacles are God's way of challenging us to grow our faith. We will either discipline ourselves to move forward, or we will slip backward into old patterns. He prepares good works for us to do and puts people in our path for his reasons. He knows the plans he has for us, and we can take confidence in that alone. Self-confidence, self-reliance, self-made, self-righteousness, self-serving, and selfishness will cause us to stumble. Less self and greater dependence on God are part of our process. It can be painful to be humble, but God gives grace to the humble and resists the prideful. To stay on track with God, keep him front and center, include him in your decision-making, and receive a green light before moving forward. "I know the plans I have for you, to prosper you and not to harm you, to give you a future and a hope" (Jeremiah 29:11). "May he give you your heart's desire and make your plans succeed" (Psalm 20:4).

I will instruct and teach you in the way you should go; I will counsel you and keep my eye on you. Do not lack understanding like the horse or the mule, which won't come near you unless controlled by bit and bridle. Psalm 32:8-9

February 4

The greatest sin is disbelieving God's words, the Bible ones, and the ones he speaks to us personally. The tests that we encounter are testing his words to us. Will we trust him? "Trust in the Lord with all your heart" (Proverbs 3:5). We see how the people in the Bible were tested. Noah heard from God about building the ark, and for 120 years, he worked, and God's words tested him. God tested Abraham by seeing if he would offer his promised son on the altar. He may also test us by having us lay things down on the altar of obedience. Gideon was given an angelic directive and finally had the faith to tear down the town's idols and lead 300 soldiers into victory over the enemy. Testing will come, and we hope to score a 100%. But seeing the patience of God through the examples of the Old Testament saints, we can forgive ourselves and move on when we fail. Abraham made mistakes, but he believed in God and is our example of the kind of faith we are to have. We cannot believe in God and at the same time *not* obey when he speaks. (Hebrews 11:8-12; Genesis 22:1-18)

Life is a test of our love. Do you pass the test?

Green Light
I will show you when to move
When to buy, when to sell
When to stand, where to dwell
Finally seeing your worth
Moving Heaven into earth
Ushering in the new
At My word, on cue

Jesus Washes Feet

Jesus wrapped a towel around his waist and knelt before the twelve

One after the other, he served them by washing away dirt from their feet

This was the task of the lowliest of servants, surely not the Son of God!

Peter protested and insisted with pride, "You shall never wash my feet!"

"Unless I wash you, you have not part with me," was Jesus' reply

"Wash my hands and head as well, then," Peter tried to hide his shame

Jesus replied, "You are already clean, you only need to wash your feet

Jesus finished, put on his robe, and returned to his seat

"I am your teacher and Lord, I have washed your feet, wash one another's feet."

Jesus is our example; you will be blessed if you let him serve you, then go serve another.

(John 13:1-17)

February 5

Cement an opinion, and you have a belief. Beliefs have consequences; bad beliefs have victims. Bad beliefs bring judgment. "Evil slays the wicked" (Psalm 34:21). Evil philosophies are beliefs with no positive conclusion and have driven a few philosophers mad. Searching for value and significance and questioning why we think what we think and act the way we do without a foundation of God and His Truth leads to philosophies like nihilism, the belief that life has no meaning, purpose, or value. How can we make sense of the world without the knowledge of the Creator's purpose and design? Many have been killed by evil drugs, evil friendships, evil underhanded deals, ignoring laws, ignoring common sense, ignoring advice from wise mentors, foolish and dangerous endeavors, and rebellious decisions. "The foolishness of man sabotages his life; his heart becomes resentful, and he rages against the Lord, blaming God instead of himself" (Proverbs 19:3). Beliefs have consequences; bad beliefs have victims.

Now it is required that those who have been given a trust to be found faithful. I care very little if I am judged by you or by any human court; in fact, I do not even judge myself. My conscience is clear, but that does not make me innocent. It is the Lord who judges me. 1 Corinthians 4:2-4

https://telegrafi.com/en/ten/-great-philosophers-who-have-suffered-from-mental-illness/ *Ten Great Philosophers Who Suffered From Mental Illness.* Agron Shala. 2016.

February 6

It is difficult to understand Judas's treason of betraying
Jesus. He saw many miracles and healings, but unlike the
Pharisees and Sadducees, Judas was part of the inner
circle, one of Jesus' elite twelve. Even though Jesus knew
what Judas was about to do, he invited him to the last
supper, washed his feet, and served him the bread and
wine. Nothing would change Judas' mind, and with a kiss, he
betrayed our Lord. The thirty pieces of silver immediately
became like a shackle of iron to his soul. Why couldn't he
predict his regret? Judas had given so much of himself to the
enemy by greed, stealing from the corporate purse, and
condemning Mary's offering of perfume, that he became a
tool in the hand of the enemy. He took communion in an
unworthy manner, and he drank judgment onto himself. He
did not discern the importance of Jesus' body and blood and
sinned against it. As soon as Judas took the bread from
Jesus' hand, Satan entered him. Just because we sit at
Jesus' table with his elite group, just because he washes our
feet with his forgiveness, and gives us his bread of life, does
not mean we are immune from falling into a ditch of sin,
allowing Satan's influence to enter us. "Beware, let him that
thinks he stands, take care lest he fall" (1 Corinthians 10:12).
Luke 22:3, John13:27, 1 Corinthians 11:27-32

*He sits on the throne of our heart, and someday we will sit with
him on his.* Revelation 3:21

February 7

God uses times of isolation for his purpose; they are not wasted. We see this with the apostle Paul, who wrote letters from prison. In our culture of busyness and impatience, God may intervene to get our attention. We are not to despise the day of small beginnings or uncomfortable situations (Zechariah 4:10). These hardships present us with a cloak of humility, then comes the time when the Spirit says, "Tuck your cloak into your belt and run" (1 Kings 18:46). The Lord told Elijah to do this, and he ran with God's power. Our belt of truth stays hidden under our cloak of humility until the Lord releases us into public ministry. Pride pushes us forward before we are ready, but after our "prison" experience, we will tuck humility in and run with the truth in the power of God. Voices will rise up and accuse us of pride and arrogance; they will not understand our boldness. Obedience is what matters, not the opinions of others. During the days of confinement, God will not leave you; he has a plan, have faith. Immerse yourself in his words. Bible saints were humbled from their fiery trials and times of isolation but went on to fulfill their purpose. God is the encourager of our faith, making us able to be "as bold as a lion."

An evil manager of God's kingdom thinks the master won't come for a long time. He becomes a drunkard, beating the fellow servants he is in charge of. The master will arrive unexpectedly, and he will be cut to pieces and assigned to a place with unbelievers. Everyone who has been given much, much will be required. A manager is any believer who leads others. Luke 12:41-48

February 8

JUDGE NOT

By Adelaide Anne Proctor (Revised)

Judge not, the working of his brain
And of his heart you cannot see.
What looks to your dim eyes a stain,
In God's pure light may only be
A scar, brought from some well-won field,
Where you would only faint and yield.

The look, the air, that frets your sight
May be a token that below
The soul has closed in deadly fight
With some infernal fiery foe,
Whose glance would scorch your smiling grace
And cast you shuddering on your face!

The fall you dare to despise,
May be the angel's slackened hand
Has suffered it, that he may rise
And take a firmer, surer stand,
Or, trusting less to earthly things,
May henceforth learn to use his wings.

And judge none lost; but wait and see,
With hopeful pity, not disdain.
The depth of the abyss may be
The measure of the height of pain
And love and glory that may raise
The soul to God in after days!
https://www.poetrynook.com/poem/judge-not

February 9

These are the days of Daniel, a time of unholy rulers, cruel, demanding, and ruthless. A time of protecting the holy, through the fire, through the water, up from the lion's den unharmed. A time to refuse the rich fare of Babylon. A time to pray three times a day.

These are the days of Elijah, a time of worshiping demons, of sacrificing to idols, a time of Jezebel's rebellion and Ahab's weak cowardice. A time of miracles and wonders, Elijah being fed near the brook by ravens, oil never running dry, bitter water turning sweet, the enemy halted at the gate. The cloud is small, but rain is on the way. The chariot will descend.

These are the days of David; worship is our battle weapon of choice. The ark of the presence is with us. Victory is finally ours. The kingdoms of this earth will soon become the kingdom of our Lord and Savior. He will rule with justice. He will rule with righteousness. His rule will never end.

FIRE
Through the fire, through the flood
You will not burn, you will not drown
A great rebellion released
The final trumpet sound
For one thousand years, the enemy bound
If my people will, I will heal their land
You too, Russia, you too, America
All people are invited

February 10

"In the beginning" is a phrase found in three places in the Bible: Genesis 1:1, John 1:1, and Hebrews 1:10. The first one states that God created the heavens and the earth by the Spirit hovering over the deep and by the words, "Let there be." The second says that Jesus, the Word of God, was with God from the beginning and through him all things were created. And the third confirms that God laid the foundations of the earth and created the heavens. It is a truth that God has emphasized in all three parts of the Bible, the Old Testament, the New Testament, and the time in between–the time when Jesus was on Earth, making the transition from the Old Covenant Law to the New Covenant Grace. It is also a reminder that God in three persons has always been and will always be.

God is not in the wind, the storm, or the fire. But with a still small voice, a gentle blowing, a whisper, "Be still, no fear." In the middle of chaos–hear the Word speak to you.

THE CORE
Love His Word
Love His people
Be faithful in small things
Spend time with Him
Have mercy and compassion
Desire to please God
` Desire to help others

JOKE

It would have been a joke in 1925
Saying our ancestors looked like apes
That a one-celled ameba evolved
Giving us brains and eyes
Primordial sludge with a mighty power?
Forty years later, God is removed
We are now considered animals
All without fossils, no missing link
"In the beginning God, He, with the power
Breathed into man, a crown of His desire
A soul made in His image
More valuable than an animal

Matthew 12:12

Realignment

The track is shifting to give you power
Power to take you over the mountain
"I think I can"–"You will!"
Watch out for a crash.
The crash will realign your future
The debris is removed from the track
Now cross over and receive
Accelerate into the new season
Designed for you from birth

After Jesus was baptized, he was sent into the wilderness to face Satan's three temptations. "Turn these stones into bread." Satan also tempted Eve through fleshly desire, telling her to eat the attractive fruit. "You will not surely die." The snake was calling God a liar by slightly changing the meaning of God's words, "In the day [within the thousand years since you were created] you eat it, you will die." Eve's body didn't die for 900 years (which to God "a thousand years is as a day"), but she immediately died spiritually. How could telling Jesus to throw himself off a cliff be a temptation? Satan was wrong to think that Jesus would test his Father's love by being pridefully reckless and self-motivated. This shows us that the devil is behind all suicides; he lies and says that it is a reasonable way to escape. Satan offered Jesus the kingdoms of the world if he would bow to him, the temptation of riches and fame. Jesus knew his death would be a hard trial, but he chased the enemy away and, for the third time, quoted from the book of Deuteronomy, "Only worship and serve the Lord your God." God created Lucifer, who fell because of his desire to receive worship instead of giving it. He was allowed into our world to give us a choice, whether to serve the Creator God or the fallen angel. We are tempted and lured by desires coming from what we see, from the desire to escape hardship, and from the desire to be wealthy and famous.

Do not be afraid. God has come to test you, so that the fear of God will be with you to keep you from sinning (Exodus 20:20). *Jesus is our model to follow. Anguish and pressure propel us to a new level of faith through death to self, so consider it pure joy when facing various trials.'* James 1:2

February 12

James 4:6 tells us that God resists the proud but gives grace to the humble. It was the pride of Lucifer that brought him down. "Your heart became proud on account of your beauty, and you corrupted your wisdom because of your splendor" (Ezekiel 28). In Isaiah 14, Lucifer says the words "I will" five times. Pride in his beauty, influence, position, and riches was his downfall. It is hard to be humble when you are at the top with the world at your feet. "He who exalts his gate seeks destruction" (Proverbs 17:19). The Hebrew word here for "gate" means a door or an opening. Some think that in ancient times, poor people would have doors no more than three feet high. This kept robbers from riding horses into their homes. Increasing the height of the door, or "exalting the gate," was for the rich who would welcome in their wealthy, carriage-riding friends. Nebuchadnezzar allowed the "low-gate" people to choose whether to go to Babylon or to remain in the land, but the "high-gate" folks were arrested, and their homes were burned to the ground (2 Kings 25:8-12). "Pride comes before destruction and a haughty spirit before a fall" (Proverbs 16:18).

The wide gate says there are many ways to reach God. The narrow gate is one person wide, and he is Jesus.

https://www.jewishvirtuallibrary.org/door-and-doorpost#: Door and Doorpost

BATTLES
Some battles are lost to reset our focus
Sometimes we stumble to keep us humble
If I am empty, He can fill me
If I am full of pride, I fill myself

PRIDE

Arrogance, conceit, snobbery
Evil behavior, perverse speech
Haughty eyes, conflict, strife
Blind to its own faults, only seeing others
Swearing falsely, boasting loudly
Practices and teachings of the Pharisees
Resisted by God, resulting in a fall
With the lowly is wisdom, grace, and blessing
Humble yourself before the Lord, let him exalt
you

THORNS

Pride of life, life's pride
Competition, serving self, a great faith braggart
Of impressive accomplishments
God will not allow it
Thorns of the flesh, flesh's thorns
Messengers to buffet me, keeping me humble
God will not share his glory with another
No one may take the credit
Have I, by my own hand, moved a mountain?
No one may claim greatness of faith or of works
We serve at the master's table
When he says go, we go
When he says act, we act
We are only a catalyst for His wondrous works
We must stay humble

February 13

"I created the destroyer to work havoc..." (Isaiah 54:16). Why does God want havoc? God left the enemy in the Promised Land so Israel would learn to fight. The opposite would have been complacency, idleness, lethargy, and apathy, which would have led to sin. This happened when King David stayed home during the time of war; it was his downfall. If we care, we fight. If we want a good life for our children, we fight. The word is powerful and mighty and active and near you, even in your mouth-use it! The spiritual battle we are in forces us to focus on God. We are being trained to be courageous, tough, strong, and trustworthy soldiers. Have you ever met a person who has gone through life without a single hardship? But what about Adam and Eve? Weren't they in this category of spoiled humans? Yes, but they had not yet eaten from the fruit of the tree of the knowledge of good and evil. They had no evil intentions, thoughts, or actions. They were full of kindness and love. Evil at that time was unknown and unknowable. Right now, though, we must fight. We fight our own fleshly and evil desires. Temptations will pass through our minds, but we cannot allow them to take root. We fight the unseen enemy who tries tirelessly to lead our loved ones and us astray. We also fight to be in the right relationship with God and others, and that takes humility.
(Hebrews 4:12; Revelation 20:7-10; 2 Samuel 11:1; Psalm 149:6-9)

Demons are diligent in their work to destroy, deceive, and divide; how much more should we be diligent in our trampling down of them?

February 14

There is one God who has three distinct yet united parts: Father, Son, and Holy Spirit. He created us in his image, so we too have three distinct parts: body, soul, and spirit. "May your whole spirit, soul, and body be kept blameless at the coming of our Lord Jesus Christ" (1 Thessalonians 5:23). Is the body less important than the soul or spirit? No, because we read in 1 Corinthians 6:19-20 that "our bodies are the temple of the Holy Spirit, who is in you, whom you have received from God. You are not your own; honor God with your body." 1 Corinthians 3:16-17 admonishes us that if anyone destroys God's temple, the body, then God will destroy him; for God's temple is sacred, "and you are that temple." Our soul includes our mind, will, and emotions (Psalm 42:1-5). When God creates us, he places in us a hole that can only be filled by him. When we accept him into that place, our spirit comes alive, and we are born again; all things become new. We grow strong in spirit by asking God to fill us, by reading his word, and by listening for his voice. We can command our body and our soul to submit to our own spirit and to the Spirit of God. It takes discernment to know which voice we are hearing: is it our own, God's, or the enemy's? Empty yourself of anger, unforgiveness, fear, and all lower-self feelings, ask him to speak, listen, and then you will be able to hear him clearly!
(Proverbs 17:22; Hebrew 4:12; John 4:24; Ephesians 4:24)

God uses all 5 of the love languages, and that is how we are to minister to him. They are: time spent, words of encouragement, acts of service, giving gifts, and physical touch. Yes, we can feel his presence.

"Behold, I stand at the door and knock, if anyone hears my voice and opens the door, I will come in to him, and we will share a meal together" (Revelation 3:20). Jesus doesn't knock with his fist, but with his voice. In the Song of Solomon, the bridegroom lingers outside the door of his bride and knocks, saying, "Open for me," but she does not want to get up, put on her robe, and get her feet dirty, so he leaves. The bride goes out and searches but cannot find him; the watchmen in the city beat her. This symbolizes a Christian who accepts the Lord but doesn't want to spend time with him. This is similar to the passage about the five foolish virgins who leave their "first love." They wake up to the watchman declaring that the bridegroom is on his way. They have no oil in their lamps, are excluded from the wedding feast, and are told, "Go, I never knew you." They were not filled with the Holy Spirit's oil; darkness had robbed them of hope (Matthew 25; 1 John 3:3). Not everyone who calls themselves "Christian" is a Christ-following disciple. "Many will say to Me in that day, 'Lord, Lord, have we not prophesied in your name, cast out demons in your name, and done many wonders in your name?' I will declare to them, 'I never knew you; leave me, you who practice lawlessness!'" (Matthew 7:22-23). Those without oil miss out on the wedding feast. They will need to repent and overcome perilous times by the blood of the Lamb and by the word of their testimony. "You can't be on the fence because the devil owns the fence" -Todd Coronato (Revelation 12:11; Jeremiah 30:7; Luke 12:35-48)

Except the Lord keep the city, the watchman watches in vain.
Psalm 127:1

February 16

Jesus told a parable of a man who built his house on a rock (Luke 6:47-49). When the floods and torrents struck the well-built house, it could not be shaken. The first thing the man did was to dig deep into the rock to secure his foundation. A newly born-again Christian must dig into God's word, taking time to develop his newfound faith. The Rock is Jesus; he is the Word, the Cornerstone of Truth. Reading in four parts of the Bible each day is a great suggestion, putting markers in Genesis 1, Psalm 1, Isaiah 1, and Matthew 1. Ask the Holy Spirit to help with understanding, and within a short period of time, the beauty of his history and character will become clear. "When you fix your eyes on Jesus and ask a question, the free flow of intimate and beautiful thoughts that comes to your mind is your answer. Don't ask 'Why?', ask 'What do you want me to know,' 'What do you want me to do?'" (Jamie Winship). Journal the verses that seem to stand out, your dreams, wise words, and revelations, which will be signposts to look back on. The parable also tells of a foolish man who built on sand, and the storm destroyed his house. Storms will come; we must have a solid foundation. "The Berean Jews were of more noble character and open-minded than those in Thessalonica, for they received the message with great enthusiasm and examined the Scriptures every day to see if what Paul said was true" (Acts 17:11). (The Bible App is also an audio Bible for those who prefer to listen).

Building on sand is the easy way, based on our own theories and ideas, a short-sighted view. Building on the Rock of Truth, with Jesus as the cornerstone, and digging deep into the foundation of His Word secures our future.

When Jesus gave his famous Sermon on the Mount, he said he knew when a bird fell out of a nest. God loves his creation, and he knows the number of hairs on our heads. God is motivated by love; everything he does comes from love. He wants us to be rooted and established in love, knowing how wide, long, high, and deep it is (Ephesians 3:17-18). John 13:35 gives us a standard to determine whether or not someone is a disciple of the Lord, "All men will know we are his disciples if we love one another." 1 Corinthians 13 describes love and God: they are patient, kind, not envious or boastful, not proud or dishonoring, not self-seeking or easily angered, nor do they keep a record of wrongs, nor do they delight in evil but rejoice with the truth. God and love always protect, trust, hope, and persevere. God and love never fail. "Lord, increase our love for each other so the world will know we are your disciples. We want to be more like you. Forgive us, Lord, for the times we have not been loving. Holy Spirit, fill us with your love." "Owe nothing to anyone except to love one another, he who loves his neighbor has fulfilled the law. Love does no wrong to a neighbor, therefore love is the fulfillment of the law." Therefore, every sin is a sin against love; we have a debt that needs to be paid; it is a love debt! (Romans 13:8-9).

If God forgives us, we must forgive ourselves otherwise it's like setting up ourselves as a higher tribunal than Him. -C. S. Lewis

February 18

For eighty days on Mount Sinai, Moses received the Ten Commandments and the history of mankind, the first five books of the Bible, or the Torah. The Israelis were coming out of a pagan, hedonistic society, one that lived in opposition to God's intent for mankind. The evil that had permeated the surrounding people groups would eventually tempt and draw God's chosen ones away from him. God wanted the Israelis to be separate from these other nations to preserve the lineage that would eventually give birth to the Savior. God had to give laws to rein in and discipline them so they could learn to be self-disciplined. This is the goal of parents when raising children. "The secret things belong to the Lord our God, but the things revealed belong to our children and to us forever, that we may follow all the words of this law" (Deuteronomy 29:29). Jesus quoted many times from the book of Deuteronomy. He said in Matthew 5:17, "I did not come to abolish the law or the prophets, but to fulfill them." "Through the law we become conscious of sin. Where there is no law, there is no transgression, but the law does not produce heirs-only faith does" (Romans 3:20; 4:14-15). Is the evil surrounding us drawing us away from God? God wants our lineage preserved for the Second Coming of Jesus, the Lion of the tribe of Judah, King of kings and Lord of lords!

The foolish Galatians were bewitched because they started out by faith, then tried to earn their salvation by living under the law. Have we been bewitched? Holding onto a sliver of our good works to feel good enough, just in case God's grace isn't enough to cover our sin, is an offense to the finished work of Jesus' sacrifice. We must trust in His grace and our receipt that says, "Paid in full!" That is what faith is for! Galatians 3:1; Ephesians 2:8-9

Daniel's Vision

I watched until the thrones were in place
The Ancient of Days was seated
His garment was white as snow
His hair like wool, his throne a fiery flame
Its wheels are a burning blaze, a stream of fire
Coming out from before him
Thousands upon thousands ministering to him
Ten thousand times ten thousand
Standing before him
The Court was seated, and books were opened
Daniel 7

God Hates

Robbery and iniquity
He who loves violence
Haughty eyes
Lying tongues
Hands that shed innocent blood
A heart devising wicked schemes
Feet rushing into evil
A false witness pouring out lies
A man stirring up dissension among
brothers
Esau
Proverbs 6:16-19; Malachi 1:2

February 19

Revelation 2:24 says that we are not to learn Satan's so-called deep secrets. There are many: pagan idolatry, rituals, sacrifices, hexes, vexes, voodoo, witchcraft, spells, crystals, incantations, fortune telling, seances, astrology, horoscopes, palm reading, philosophies, and false worship. "The sacrifices of pagans are offered to demons, not to God, and I do not want you to be participants with demons. You cannot drink the cup of the Lord and the cup of demons too; you cannot have a part in both the Lord's table and the table of demons. Are we trying to arouse the Lord's jealousy?" (1 Corinthians 10:20). Replacing God with an idol altar opens demonic portals. Eating the fruit of disobedience cursed the land at the time of Adam, and it still does. Cruelty and dominance are a result of the sin of witchcraft. "When someone tells you to consult mediums, spiritists, and wizards, those muttering their enchantments and incantations, should not a people inquire of their God? Why consult the dead on behalf of the living? Consult God's instruction. If anyone does not speak according to this word, they have no light of dawn" (Isaiah 8:19-20). "Let no one be found among you who practices divination or sorcery, engages in witchcraft, casts spells, or is a medium, spiritist, or who consults the dead. Anyone doing these things is detestable to the Lord. You must be blameless (Deuteronomy 18:10-14).

Human history is the long terrible story of man trying to find something other than God which will make him happy. -C. S. Lewis

February 20

Does God hate? The word "hate" in Hebrew is *sane*; it is not an emotional word, but a choice to reject, ignore, turn away from, push aside, or leave behind. Yes, and some things he calls detestable, a word stronger than hate. He hates haughty eyes, which look down on others, hands that shed innocent blood, a wicked scheme, feet rushing into evil, false witnesses in the courtroom, and judges who twist the meaning of the law. A man who stirs up dissension among brothers, who spreads gossip and rumors with malice and bitterness, then rejoices when divisions are created–God hates. He hates pride, evil behavior, perverse speech, burning incense to and worshiping other gods, plotting against a neighbor, swearing falsely, evil practices and teachings, and Esau. Why would God hate Esau? Because he could see into the future, and he could see the depravity, violence, murder, discord, strife, and desire for vengeance in Esau's heart and in the hearts of the Edomites, "For their country is named 'The Land of Wickedness'" (Malachi 1:4). God hates because God hates pain. Obadiah 1 says that Edom gloated over Jacob's misfortune, handed them over to the enemy, and seized their wealth on the day of their disaster. They took vengeance against the house of Judah and had no mercy (Ezekiel 25:12-13).

(Psalm 11:5, 137:7; Hosea 9:15; Deuteronomy 12:31,16:22; Leviticus 20:1-23; Malachi 1:2-4; Romans 9:13; Revelation 2:6; Proverbs 16:5, 8:13; Isaiah 1:13).

A few years ago, signs were going up in yards that read, 'Haters Not Welcome.' Seems like a hateful thing to say. Everyone hates something, even if it's just liver and asparagus.

https://eitan.bar/articles/hebrew-word-study-hate-sane/

February 21

Jesus predicted that family members would become divided. We must fight for unity and live in peace with one another as much as possible. Jesus prayed in John 17, "I pray also for those who will believe in me through their message, that all of them may be one, Father, just as you are in me, and I am in you. May they also be in us so that the world may believe that you have sent me. I have given them the glory that you gave me, that they may be one as we are one." David wrote in Psalm 133, "How good and pleasant it is when brothers live together in unity! It is like precious oil poured on the head...for there the Lord bestows his blessing, even life forevermore."

The tactics of the devil are division and deception, always through lying.

Build
Build a good foundation
A large and sturdy one
Jesus the cornerstone
His word, the solid rock
Storms won't sway you
Move or destroy you
He's the one on whom to stand

END TIMES

Wars, famines, earthquakes, diseases, fearful events, great signs from heaven

Signs in the sun, moon, and stars, anguish at the sea's roaring and tossing

Men fainting from terror, confusion, and distress, grief, and suffering increasing

Every country persecuting believers and Jews, murder, prison, and poverty

Many are turning away from the faith, betrayal children rebelling against parents

Brother betraying brother to death, a father killing his child, families dividing

Wickedness increasing, love growing cold, a never-before-seen wretchedness

False prophets and Christs, deceiving the elect with great signs and miracles

Lightning flashing from the east to the west, like a thief, one taken, one left

The sun darkened, the moon gave no light, and the stars fell from the sky

Heavens being shaken, the sky-sign appearing, Jesus coming on clouds

With great power and glory gathering his elect from the winds, earth, and heavens

When you see these things begin, know the time is near, right at the door

It may be evening, at dawn, or at midnight, be ready. Watch!

(Matthew 24-25, Mark 13, Luke 21)

February 22

The inspired word of God has sixty-six books, thirty-nine in the Old Testament and twenty-seven in the New Testament. Matthew, Mark, Luke, and John are books of transition from the Old Covenant given through the Law to the New Covenant of Grace sealed by Christ's death and resurrection. Forty inspired authors wrote the Bible in three languages across 13 countries and three continents over a period of 1,500 years. The writers were kings, peasants, herdsmen, philosophers, tax collectors, fishermen, poets, and scholars. We know God inspired the Bible through its continuity and the 2,000 incredibly accurate prophecies, at least 300 of which concern Jesus' birth and death. Over 60 prophecies predicted the destruction of Babylon, which had a wall 200 feet high and 87 feet thick with 300 towers on top. Over 25,000 archaeological sites have confirmed the stories of the Bible. Because the Old Testament was written on papyrus, it disintegrated. Before 1947, the oldest of these dated to around 900 A.D. Then the Dead Sea Scrolls were found at Qumran, and many of them dated to about 150 B.C. These read identically to ones from 900 A.D. and are the same as the Hebrew texts of today. More than 24,000 partial and complete copies of the New Testament exist today, dating from 200 years after Christ. Only 11 verses of the New Testament are not in this collection. All the books of the New Testament were written within 30 years of Christ's death, and our earliest copies date from 125 A.D. (Frank Harber, PhD)

To reject Scripture is to reject Jesus since he used the Old Testament to validate who he was. 'And beginning with Moses and all the Prophets, he explained to them what was said in all the Scriptures concerning himself' (Luke 24:27). *He said to them, 'This is what I told you while I was still with you; everything must be fulfilled that is written about me in the Law of Moses, the Prophets and the Psalms'* (Verse 44). *Jesus quoted Scriptures to put Satan in his place and to end debates* (Matthew 4:4-10; John 8:17). *'All Scripture is given by the inspiration of God, and is profitable for doctrine, for reproof, for correction, for instruction in righteousness'* (2 Timothy 3:16).

Psalms 82:1-4

God presides over Heaven's court
He pronounces judgment on the judges
How long will you judges refuse to listen to the evidence?
How long will you shower special favors on the wicked?
Give fair judgment to the poor man, the afflicted, the fatherless, the destitute
Rescue the poor and helpless from the grasp of evil men

February 23

Jesus, God's Son, the Lamb of God, was the replacement for the Old Covenant animal sacrifices for sin. The blood of a lamb on the doorposts at Passover saved the Jewish tribes when the death angel came over each house in Egypt and killed the firstborn. We put our trust in the blood of God's Lamb for our eternal salvation. It isn't just knowing God exists; it is a deep personal commitment and trust in the saving power of Jesus, God's Son. There is a hell. Jesus used the word "Gehenna" to describe it. Gehenna was a refuse dump outside of Jerusalem that was perpetually on fire. He also said it was a dark place of worms, fire, and trouble (Mark 9:43-48). He also called it the outer darkness, where there would be weeping and gnashing of teeth (Matthew 8:12; 22:13). Matthew 25:41 speaks of a lake of fire reserved for the devil and his angels. It was never destined for humans, but some choose darkness rather than light. God is very forgiving and said that though our sins be as scarlet they will be white as snow (Isaiah 1:18). "I will forgive their wickedness and remember their sins no more" (Jeremiah 31:34). A key element to salvation is humility, falling to our knees in repentance, forgiving others, and being forgiven. "Come let us bow down in worship, let us kneel before the Lord our Maker; for he is our God, and we are the people of his pasture, the flock under his care" (Psalm 95:6-7).

If you want the pearl, you must buy the whole field.
Matthew 13:45-46

James says that we are perfect if we can control our tongue, because the greatest temptation to sin is with our words. "Out of the abundance of the heart the mouth speaks." We say many things we wish we hadn't. Those words come from a heart of fear, insecurity, unforgiveness, bitterness, jealousy, or anger. Another great sin of the tongue is complaining. The Israelis couldn't get past their victim identity and grumbled all along their trip to their Promised Land. God refused to allow them entry. A negative attitude not only blocks our ability to learn, but it also cuts off our communication with the Lord. An unforgiving heart blocks God from forgiving us. "If you forgive men when they sin against you, your heavenly Father will forgive you. But if you do not forgive, your Father will not forgive you" (Matthew 6:14). We must go to those we have hurt and with humility say, "I was wrong, I am sorry, would you please forgive me." "Therefore, if you are offering your gift at the altar and remember that your brother has something against you, leave your gift there in front of the altar. First go and be reconciled to your brother; then come and offer your gift" (Matthew 5:23). God does not accept when we blame others for how we are, nor does he forgive excuses. "All have sinned and fall short of the glory of God" (Romans 3:23).

I have sinned, by my fault, by my own fault, by my own most grievous fault. -From the Confiteor

Abraham was called the friend of God; Solomon, the wisest; Moses, the most humble; and King David, a man after God's own heart. Noah was the most righteous in his lawless generation when everyone did what was right in their own eyes. These men are known as the greatest of the Bible, and yet they had serious flaws. Abram lied twice, putting his wife in peril, then took Hagar as a substitute for God's promise. At age 99, Abram and Sarai, at 89, received new names and new identities: "The father of many nations" and "the mother of nations; kings will come from her." After this identity change, the promised son, Isaac, was born. Solomon married 1,000 wives, who eventually turned his heart toward idolatry. Moses was a murderer, and so was King David. What made these men so special? David humbly repented and is known for his worship of God. He built the tabernacle that had continuous praise. Moses was humble and obedient and led the Israelis out of Egypt. Solomon prayed to God for wisdom after the Lord said he could ask for anything. Enoch, at age 365, the seventh from Adam, walked with God and then was not, for God took him. That is the best example to aspire to! (James 2:23; Numbers 12:3; Genesis 6:9, 12:10-20, 17, 20:1-18; 1Kings 11:3; Exodus 2:11-15; 2 Samuel 11-12; Psalm 51).

Then the Lord came down in the pillar of cloud and stood in the door of the tabernacle and called Aaron and Miriam and said, "Hear now My words: if there is a prophet among you, I, the Lord, make Myself known to him in a vision; I speak to him in a dream. Not so with My servant Moses, He is faithful in all My house. I talk with him face to face, even plainly, and not in dark sayings; he sees the form of the Lord. Why then were you not afraid to speak against My servant Moses? Numbers 12:8

February 26

There are two different ways to look at the world. Through God's word or through the secular, human viewpoint. The world says don't murder or commit adultery. Jesus said being angry with your brother or calling him a fool deserves the same judgment as murder, and lust is the same as adultery. Jesus' famous sermon in Matthew 5-7 did not cancel the law but made it less like a hammer and more like a scalpel. Jesus cuts at the heart of adultery and murder, revealing the heart issues as being the crime. The world will tell you that all paths lead to Heaven and that truth can't be known, but the Bible says that Jesus is the only way, truth, and life, and the only way to get to the Father is through him (John 14:6). Religion will tell you to follow rules and laws; the Bible is clear that we are to follow Jesus. People may say that Jesus was a good man, but he is God, born of a virgin, sent to save us from eternal punishment (Isaiah 7:14). Religion insists that we get to Heaven by being good, but no one is good enough; we are saved through God's grace by faith in Jesus' sacrifice alone (Ephesians 2:8-9). The world loves to show off its good works, but Jesus says to do your giving and good works in secret. The world sneers at women who have children, but God says that mothers are doing God's work (Proverbs 1:8; Deuteronomy 4:9, 6:6-7). The world will insist you save up lots of money, whereas Jesus says to store up treasures in Heaven. We are tempted to look good and be accepted instead of living to please our Heavenly Father, but that is a destructive path (Matthew 5-7).

Dream 1992: I was taken to heaven to a place of judgment after death. People were given a test to see if they would be allowed entrance. I saw a man's test before he arrived. It was a microscope with three lenses. The tall lens was what he spent his time doing. I saw a television. The second medium-sized lens was the good works he had done; it was blank. He had no good works to his credit. I looked into the small lens, and there was one drop of Jesus' blood. I knew he would get in.

Courts of Heaven
By faith, know it is true
Then proceed
We must confess and repent of the
Iniquity of our forefathers and
Covenants with the enemy
Wiped out and nailed to the cross
Every ordinance against us
Disarming principalities and powers,
Those sniveling public spectacles,
Triumphing over them through the cross

Do not taste, do not touch, do not handle
The regulations which perish
Let no one judge you
Concerning the Sabbath
A shadow of things to come
The substance is of Christ
He is the only one
(Colossians 2:14-17)

February 27

"Accept him whose faith is weak, without passing judgment on gray-area matters. We who are strong ought to bear with the failings of the weak and not to please ourselves. Each of us should please his neighbor, to build him up. For even Christ did not please himself. Why do you judge and look down on your brother? Therefore, let us stop passing judgment on one another. In the same way you judge others, you will be judged. First, take the two-by-four out of your own eye, and then you will see clearly to remove the speck out of your brother's eye. If your brother sins, rebuke him, and if he repents, forgive him. If he sins against you seven times in a day and seven times comes back to you and says, 'I repent,' forgive him." "Judge nothing before the time of the Lord's coming, he will bring to light the hidden things of darkness and reveal the motives of the heart. Then each one's praise will come from God." "The spirit of man is the candle of the Lord, shedding light on one's inmost being" (Proverbs 20:27).
(Romans 14:1,4,10,13,15:1-3; Matthew 7:1,5; Luke 17:3; 1 Corinthians 4:5)

As soon as you judge someone for their character flaws, you have just exposed your own.

BE CURIOUS

Ask yourself questions, be honest
Why do I do that? What makes me tick?
Why did I say that? Do I really believe it?
What is important to me and why?
Be interested in others, ask them questions
What do you love to do? What is your passion?
They will feel valued and remember that you care.

February 28

A fact is a concrete reality to acknowledge simply; it is arrived at by evidence, observation, measurement, and is proven to be true. It cannot be combated with reasoning, for it is logical in itself. Science, through experiments using the scientific method, with math and chemical equations, discovers facts. The Bible reveals its truth by interpreting itself, taking into account the whole canon of scripture. Jesus is the Truth with a capital 'T.' How do we see truth being exposed in the courtroom scene? Each attorney puts his own spin on the facts, adds his own opinions using emotional, ethical, and legislative appeals, and then adds flowery words to sway the jury to his side. If he is a prosecutor, he makes the defendant seem guilty; if he is the defense attorney, he makes the defendant look innocent. Lawyers want to win; their reputation is at stake. That is not how the courts of Heaven operate; the guilty ones, who have repented of their sins and have accepted Jesus' sacrifice, are declared innocent. That's a fact.

Christians do not know that they can come before the Courts of Heaven to request a divine restraining order to restrict, revoke, or cancel any activity of Satan. Daniel 7:10

February 29

This is for all of you who were born on this day and feel gypped. Your identity is not about when or where you were born, what job you have, or the good or bad things you have done. Your identity is who you are, what God calls you. It cannot be the lies you believe about yourself, feeling you aren't enough, falling into the trap of thinking you owe God something, needing his approval, needing to compete with others for his attention. When Jesus tells people that he doesn't know them, it is because they carry a false identity, and God cannot connect with what is false. We must be honest with God about what we believe about ourselves, others, and him; that is how he knows us. God came to Cain and addressed his attitude, "Why are you angry? If you do what is right, you will be accepted." Cain was angry in his heart before he offered the sacrifice. After he murdered his brother, God reached out to him, placing a mark of protection on him. His identity went from "murderer" to "one protected by God." God isn't disappointed with us, nor does he pour responsibilities and expectations upon us. "I have called you by your name so you will know you are mine" (Isaiah 43:1b).

What is your identity? What does Jesus call you? What are you afraid of and why? Take captive that thought.
https://www.identityexchange.com Jamie and Donna Winship

March 1

A successful life includes the character qualities of humility, gratitude, generosity, teachability, a positive attitude, mercy and kindness, and, most importantly, love. Actions for success are putting God first every day, reading and meditating on scripture, praying, asking Holy Spirit for wisdom, and building bridges instead of burning them. A bridge is a person appointed by the Lord to move you into your next step in life. God uses all kinds of people and sometimes animals to advance us. Balaam's donkey kept him from being killed! God may want you to stay in a job, a church, or a family longer because of a larger unseen plan. There are times when God will use an enemy or an uncomfortable situation to bring about a victory in your life. We can't see the future, but he can, so don't bail out too quickly or reject a possible God-bridge.

Jesus focuses on the good in each person, even if he has to use a magnifying glass, so should we. -Donna Rigney. *In essentials-unity, in nonessentials-liberty, in all things-love.* -Andrew Whalen

Offense
Some people say all that is on their mind
It may hurt and it may sting
But at least you know what they are thinking
Others hide their angry seething
Behind a smile of pursed lips
And unsmiling eyes. What is worse?
At least one who speaks his mind
Won't be insulted by my careful words
In response

March 2

Were there any positive biblical sibling relationships? Yes, Moses, Aaron, and Miriam seemed to get along. There was an instance in which Miriam and Aaron did not approve of Moses' choice of an Ethiopian wife and argued that God had also spoken through them, not just to Moses. God came down and told them that he had chosen to speak to Moses face-to-face. He rebuked them, and Miriam became leprous, white as snow. Moses cried out to God, who agreed to heal her. Usually, though, biblical siblings did not get along: Cain and Abel, Jacob and Esau, Joseph and his brothers, and Rachel and Leah. Even Jesus' brothers did not receive him until after his resurrection—jealousy, greed, unforgiveness, competition, bullying, or feeling second best cause these rifts. Philippians 2:3 tells us to do nothing from rivalry or conceit, but in humility count others more significant than yourselves. It is difficult to have a positive relationship with someone you are always in competition with. Impatience leads to frustration and anger and throws fuel on fiery conflicts. Division and disunity are what God hates the most and what Satan works the hardest to achieve. "If a kingdom is divided against itself, it cannot stand. If a house is divided against itself, that house cannot stand." Love heals conflicts. Ask the Lord how you can show those you have conflict with that they are valuable to you. (Mark 3:21-25; John 7:5; Acts 1:14; 1 Corinthians 15:7)

Eve lost her blessing and future over a piece of fruit, Samson over a woman, Saul over impatience, Israel over grumbling, David over covetousness, Absalom over rebellion, Eli over not disciplining his sons, Ananias and Sapphira over a lie, Jonah nearly lost it over disobedience, and Lucifer over pride.

March 3

Many are called, but few are chosen. This verse can be difficult to understand. Look at it this way: the phone rings for everyone, but not everyone picks up. God is working overtime to get our attention. If we answer, then we are chosen. If we ignore the call, he does not choose us. "I called, but you did not answer; I spoke, but you did not listen." (Isaiah 65:12). What is he calling us to do? The first thing is to confess and repent and accept him as Lord over our lives. He calls us to spend time and develop a relationship with him. He is our much-needed daily bread. He calls us to do good works, to a purpose we will find fulfilling, and gives us gifts to help us in that calling. When Jesus ascended, after first descending into the lower parts of the earth, he led out the captives and gave gifts to men. These gifts are not organized by hierarchy or title, like the world's systems are, but rather by function. Some are to be apostles (sent ones to start and encourage churches), prophets (God's spokespersons), evangelists (ones called to spread the good news of Jesus Christ, and to inspire others to do so), pastors (caring shepherds), and teachers (those able to explain God's word clearly, leading us toward maturity), to prepare us for works of service, so we are edified and unified in faith and in the knowledge of the Son of God; becoming perfect and attaining to the whole measure of the fullness of Christ. Pick up the phone and ask what Jesus is calling you to be! (Ephesians 4:8-11).

If we need pastors, teachers and evangelists, then we also need apostles and prophets.

Mach 3

Happening quickly
Miracles
Persecution
World revival
Healing
Demons manifesting
Apostolic authority
Betrayers and mockers
Coming from family and
Teachers of the law
Satan's kingdom divided
God's family revealed
(Mark 3)

Marriage

Like a lion roaring
The one I was wed to
Next to me is snoring
An irritation supreme
But my life has not been boring
He is kind, considerate, gentle
Patient, funny, and loving
We have had a great life
With strong and amazing children
I will drift off now, and start snoring

March 4

A hypothetical statement is an if/then statement. The Bible is full of them. "If you eat that fruit, then you will die." "If you do what is right, then you will be accepted. If you do not do what is right, then sin is crouching at your door ready to have you" (Genesis 4:6). "If you are willing and obedient, then you will eat the good of the land" (Isaiah 1:19). Parents often use hypotheticals giving positive or negative consequences. They can be presented as rules, promises, threats, or motivators. The Bible gives a hypothetical to children, "Children, obey and honor your parents in the Lord, so it may go well with you, and so you may enjoy a long life" (Ephesians 6:1-2). To know how to be a great dad, study the ministry of Jesus to his disciples because he said that he and his Father were one, "If you have seen me, you have seen the Father." Jesus rarely rebuked his disciples; he taught them everything they needed to know, he gave them responsibilities and trusted them. He washed their feet; there was no religiosity between them–they broke sabbath rules together; he gave them their identity and died to save them. He did the same for us.

God cannot give us happiness and peace apart from Himself because it is not there. There is no such thing. -C. S. Lewis

Once
Once I was in darkness, now I walk in light
Once I was weak, now Christ strengthens me
Once I was in want, now God supplies my needs
Once I was sick, now with His stripes I am healed
Once I was a victim, now I am more than a conqueror
Once I was lost, now I am found -Dick Mills

March 5

We call them the Be-attitudes from Jesus' *Sermon on the Mount*. "Blessed are the poor in spirit, those empty of themselves, for theirs is the kingdom of heaven." The poor in spirit are humble, willing to associate with people of low position. "For I say to every one of you: Do not think of yourself more highly than you ought" (Romans 12:3). "Blessed are those who mourn, for they will be comforted." Quickly go to the Lord when you are sad and troubled and be comforted. "Blessed are the meek, for they shall inherit the earth." Meek doesn't mean weak; it means humbly and patiently enduring without resentment. The opposite is impatient, bossy, or willful. "Blessed are those who hunger and thirst for righteousness, for they shall be filled." This is a deep curiosity about God, a desire to know his thoughts, plans, and desires. "He reveals his thoughts to man" (Amos 4:13). "Blessed are the peacemakers, for they will be called sons of God." Peacemakers aren't pacifiers but arbitrators, caring about unity and speaking up on behalf of others, willing to face the backlash from telling the truth. "Blessed are those who are persecuted, reviled, and are lied about for righteousness sake. Rejoice, for great is your reward in heaven, for in the same way they persecuted the prophets who were before you" (Matthew 5).

Judgment without mercy will be shown to anyone who has not been merciful. Mercy triumphs over judgment. Blessed are the merciful, for they will receive mercy. James 2:12; Matthew 5:7

March 6

There are immutable laws; we don't have to go back and re-prove them, and everyone (who isn't trying to be obnoxious) agrees that they are rock solid in their truth value. We have laws in mathematics: communicative, distributive, associative, and so on. There are laws of English grammar: every sentence begins with a capital letter, ends with a punctuation mark, and has a subject and a noun. The laws of thought studied in a logic class are: The Law of the Excluded Middle–any statement is either true or false, The Law of Identity– if a statement is true, then it is true, The Law of Noncontradiction–a statement cannot be both true and false. We can use these laws to defend our faith. Lastly, there are God's Laws, the 10 Commandments from the Old Testament, and the Law of Love, stating that love is the fulfillment of the law (Romans 13:8-10). Do you believe this hypothetical statement? *If I have love, then I can do as I please. Since all sin is a sin against love, then if I am loving, I will not sin while doing as I please.* There is no law against love (Galatians 5:22-23). "Whatever other commandment there may be, are summed up in this one command: 'Love your neighbor as yourself.' Love does no harm to a neighbor. Therefore love is the fulfillment of the law" (Romans 13:9-10).

The law of the mind is 'what you think about controls you.' Both God and the devil want your mind. What bad thoughts are cemented into your mind? Romans 7:23

March 7

"When I was a child, I talked, thought, and reasoned like a child. When I became a man, I put childish ways behind me" (1 Corinthians 13:11). Childish ways include expecting people to take care of you, viewing them as objects to meet your needs, and needing instant gratification. It is also childish to be happy only when you get what you want, and if you don't, to complain, withdraw, manipulate, or get even. It is childish to break down emotionally when stressed by trials and disappointments, to be unable to calmly talk about needs and wants, and to be easily hurt and offended. Immature people are defensive and threatened by criticism. They keep a mental record of wrongs, and in a conflict, they blame, gossip, pout, or ignore. They are self-centered and struggle to understand others' needs and pain. They are critical and judgmental. Mature adults are honest, take responsibility for their own emotions, and, under stress, can calmly relay their thoughts. They know people aren't perfect, so don't expect them to be. They are open about their own weaknesses and try to resolve conflicts by developing solutions that consider others' ideas. Spiritual maturity is loving well, not just loving God, but being dedicated to loving people. "Love your neighbor as yourself" (Matthew 22:37-40). If you want to see an example of a lack of love, read the words and actions of the religious leaders of Jesus' time. We are not the sun around which all others revolve; Jesus is!

Scazzero, Peter. *Emotionally Healthy Spirituality.* Zondervan. 2017

The problem is that you do not realize how important you are. Self-importance is rooted in pride. You are important because you are a creation of the Almighty, and you have a responsibility to others.

March 8

"Where there is no revelation of God and his word, people cast off restraint and lose control; but blessed is the one who heeds wisdom's instruction" (Proverbs 29:18). We are promised wisdom if we ask, but we waver when we doubt the instruction that Holy Spirit gives us. "Like a wave of the sea, that person should not expect to receive anything from the Lord. Such a one is double-minded and unstable," (James 1:6-8). Wisdom speaks, and we must obey without the instability that comes from doubting. Listening when we ask for wisdom gives the guidance and restraint we need. Restraint is like a leash; it holds back for safety, not to quell freedom. Freedom does not mean we can do whatever we feel like doing. Freedom of speech does not mean you can say whatever comes into your mind. If my freedom interferes with your freedom, it is not freedom. Loud music at 3 A.M. may interfere with a neighbor's freedom to sleep. If I say something threatening that sparks fear in someone, it is not freedom of speech. Restraint is the law and being unrestrained leads to places like prison. Freedom in a society is freedom for everyone.

Good people do not go to heaven, and bad people do not go to hell. Holy and righteous people go to heaven, and unholy and unrighteous people go to hell. We are righteous and holy only through God's saving mercy and grace. -Pastor Landon Mauricio, Called Church Honolulu

March 9

On a podcast, a man was criticizing a line in a Christian worship song. The line was, "When I open up my mouth, miracles start breaking out." This line is a hyperbole, not meaning that every time we open our mouths, a miracle pops out, but rather referring to believing in one by declaring God's will and word. Why pray if we aren't expecting a miracle? It also refers to the verse, "Death and life are in the power of the tongue," or perhaps it's about our authority to trample on snakes and scorpions. We do not do that with our feet, but with our mouths. Jesus knocks with his mouth, a sword comes out of his mouth, and with words, everything was created. Words have the power to curse and to bless. Worship songs have many lines that we make untrue. When singing about raising hands to God in worship, we should raise our hands. Worship is sacred ground, and it must come from our spirit and heart, the core of our being, not an emotional uplift from fondness of the song; it is not about us. We must worship in truth. We cannot truly worship if we are living in a false identity, pretending to have "holy hands," when we are living a sinful lifestyle. Worship in your "prayer closet," then you will be ready to worship corporately, in spirit and in truth. Read or sing the Psalms, "Come let us worship and bow down and kneel before the Lord our God, our Maker." "Sing to the Lord a new song, for He has done marvelous things." (Psalm 95:6, 98:1; John 4:24).

*...my tongue is the pen of a skillful writer. Psalm 45:1
Psalms (in Greek, songs) were written to be sung; some encourage and motivate others, some express grief and cry out to God, and others thank, praise, or deeply worship the Lord. They are humanity reaching out to God, desiring his divine presence. 'Hallelujah' appears only in the Psalms.*

March 10

"Anyone claiming to be in the light yet hates his brother is still in darkness. Whoever loves his brother lives in the light, and there is nothing in him to make him stumble. But whoever hates his brother is in darkness and walks around in darkness; he does not know where he is going, darkness has blinded him." (1 John 2:8-11). Darkness is hate, feelings of loathing and disgust, or a hardened, uncaring heart. "Brother" means a brother in Christ or a sibling. Jesus warned that calling a brother a fool puts one in danger of hellfire. "God is light; if we claim to have fellowship with him yet walk in darkness, we lie and do not live by the truth. But if we walk in the light, as he is in the light, we have fellowship with one another, and the blood of Jesus purifies us from every sin" (1 John 1:5-7). Walking in darkness blocks the blood of Jesus' ability to purify us. "If we claim to be without sin, we are deceived, and the truth is not in us. If we confess our sins, he is faithful and will forgive us our sins and purify us from all unrighteousness." This was written to believers. We go through life being washed by the blood of Jesus, confessing when we become aware of our sin and are cleansed. We are commanded to love our enemies and pray for them, and in doing so, we are closer to the perfection of our Father (Matthew 5:22-48). "Jesus is not ashamed to call them brothers those whom he is making holy" (Hebrews 2:11).

Repent therefore and be converted, that your sins may be blotted out, so that times of refreshing may come from the presence of the Lord (Acts 3:19).

The end time's not-attitudes are listed in 2 Timothy 3:1-5: self-loving, abusive, disobedient, boastful, proud, ungrateful, unholy, lovers of money but not of people, crude, rude, foul, unforgiving, slanderous, brutal, without self-control, not lovers of the good, treacherous, rash, conceited, lovers of pleasure rather than lovers of God– having a form of godliness but denying its power. In verse 2, "lovers of themselves," in Greek means kissing themselves. This word is not used anywhere else in Scripture. The last day's people will be a selfie generation. Having a form of godliness is attending church, giving money, serving the poor, praying, yet denying that God's power is available, not just for the works Jesus did on earth, but the power to make us holy. Rewards are for those who pray and give in secret. Putting your name on church offering envelopes in hopes that the pastor will honor and respect you is giving to be noticed. This "I am" last days generation forgets that God revealed Himself to Moses at the burning bush as "I Am." When we say, "I am" followed by other words, we must be careful what those other words are. They should be words about our true and unique identity, what He calls us. "My Heavenly Father loves me; I have worth and am valued!" Our faith is rooted in God's love for us. Have faith in what God says about you!

We regard God as an airman regards his parachute; it's there for emergencies, but he hopes he never has to use it. -C. S. Lewis

March 12

Where does wisdom come from? It is not a commodity that we are naturally born with. We know that the fear of the Lord–the reverential awe that we have for our all-powerful, all-seeing, all-knowing Creator is the first step. "To fear the Lord is to hate evil" (Proverbs 8:13). We receive wisdom from listening to God, his word, to parents, and wise people. It comes to those who want to change, who are open to rebuke and correction, who call out to God for it. "For the Lord gives wisdom and from his mouth come knowledge and understanding." "Wisdom builds a house, a life, a home, a family, and by understanding it is established on a solid foundation. By knowledge the rooms are filled with all kinds of riches" (Proverbs 2:2-6; 24:3-4). The benefits of wisdom are: protection, long life and riches, pleasant ways and peace, blessings and confidence with no fear. It can distinguish that which is evil. The opposite of wisdom is folly or foolishness. James 1:5 says, "If you lack wisdom, ask God, he will give it generously without finding fault. But when you ask, believe that what you hear are words from God and be ready to do what the Lord shows you; if you don't, you should not expect anything from the Lord; you are double-minded and unstable."
(Hebrew 5:14; 12:28-29; Proverbs 1, 2, 3; 8:23-36; 13; 9:13)

A man who has riches without understanding is like the beast that perishes. Psalm 49:20

March 13

Five things occurred the moment Jesus died. The temple curtain was torn in two from top to bottom; the earth shook, rocks split, tombs opened, and the bodies of many holy people were resurrected. (Matthew 27:51-52). The rending of the curtain was God's message that the Holy of Holies was no longer a place for the yearly visit by the high priest; God's people could freely enter and commune with God. That red-letter day was the beginning of a new era on God's calendar. Gentiles, no longer excluded by the law, could be saved; the law written on their hearts. It was the beginning of the New Testament, a New Covenant written in Jesus' blood for the forgiveness of sin. The earth quaked in response to this offering being poured out upon it, and many holy Old Testament saints came out of their graves and were seen walking around Jerusalem. Jesus, the warrior, entered paradise, released the captives, and then took them to heaven. Mary was not allowed to touch Jesus until he had received his new body; then he returned from heaven and told Thomas to touch his hand and side. He departed from the earth in Acts 1, then in Acts 2, Holy Spirit came with flames of fire. (John 16:7-8,13-14; Matthew 27:51-53; Ephesians 4:7-9; Luke 16:19-31; John 20:17).

Then Peter and John placed their hands on them, and they received the Holy Spirit. Acts 8:17

Building

The foundation has been laid
On Christ the solid rock
The house is being built
Using gold, silver, and costly stones
Or wood, hay, and straw
The works will be exposed by fire
On that Day, all brought to light
To test the quality of the work
Will it burn and turn to ash?
Suffering the loss of rewards?
Or will it survive with congratulations?
"Well done, good and faithful servant
Come and share your master's joy."
(1 Corinthians 3:11-15; Matthew 25:23)

The Table

I was seated at a table
Facing strangers, not a few
Each one bore a label
The tension grew
I rose to speak my heart
My knees began to quake
How to compose a start?
Here I go, for Jesus' sake.

March 14

Things are not always what they seem; that is why we should not jump to conclusions. We judge by what we see, based on our own assessments. Lady Justice is blindfolded for a good reason. "The first to state his case seems right until another comes and cross-examines him" (Proverbs 18:17). "I, the Lord, love justice" (Isaiah 61:8). "Let justice roll down like a river, and righteousness like a mighty stream" (Amos 5:24). Our justice system is based on giving the accused the benefit of the doubt, "innocent until proven guilty." Giving someone the benefit of the doubt comes from a merciful heart and takes into consideration other possible explanations. Making hasty decisions, taking rash actions, jumping to conclusions, making snap judgments, or being impulsive leads to mistakes. Slow down. Gather the facts first, and there will be no regrets, embarrassment, or apologies later. Assume the best, not the worst, in people. "Love believes all things" (1 Corinthians 13:7). We should assume the best possible scenario, not being gullible, but listening to both sides of a story, then, with prayer and our God-given ability to discern, we can decide. I saw an elderly man stagger and fall in front of a grocery store. People ignored him, thinking he was drunk. He wasn't; he had just fallen, and I was able to drive him home. Things are not always as they seem.

To answer before listening to the facts is foolish and shameful.
Proverbs 18:13

March 15

The Catholic religion instituted confessionals where people could confess their sins. Is there a scriptural basis for this? James 5:16 says, "Therefore, confess your sins to each other and pray for each other so that you may be healed. The prayer of a righteous man is powerful and effective." In some of the older Greek texts, "sin" here means "a deviation from what is true." When we confess, we are telling the truth about how we have moved away from what the Bible says about God, ourselves, and others. Moral failure carries regret and results from this deviation. After you confess, the trusted leader is to pray for your healing. Rats feed on garbage; if we hide things deep in our hearts, the guilt and shame of it eat away at us and invite evil to reign. We become isolated in our unworthiness, thinking that we are unlikable; it isn't true. Remove the garbage, and the rats will go. Counselors are ministers to help us deal with our past. We, as humans, are in the same boat as 8 billion earthly sinners and, "No temptation has seized you except what is common to man" (1 Corinthians 10:13). God not only removes our failings as far as the east is from the west, but he also removes our guilt. "I acknowledged my sin to you and did not cover up my iniquity. I said, 'I will confess my transgressions to the Lord,' and you forgave the guilt of my sin" (Psalm 32:5). God does not remember Moses' sin, or David's, Noah's, or ours once we confess and repent. If you bring it up to God, he says, "I don't remember that." Neither should we bring up others' sins.

God cannot forgive excuses, only sins. -Calvin Thielmen

March 16

The most beautiful things on Earth are unity and babies. God loves babies. His first commandment was to multiply and fill the earth. He also repeated this to Noah's family after the flood. "Children are a heritage from the Lord, offspring a reward from him. Blessed is the man whose quiver is full of them. Like arrows in the hands of a warrior are children born in one's youth" (Psalm 127:3-5). "Jesus took a child and put him in in the midst of them, and taking him in his arms, he said to them, 'Whoever receives and welcomes one such child in my name receives and welcomes me,'" (Mark 9:36-37; Matthew 19:14). "Jesus said, 'Let the little children come to me, do not hinder them, for the kingdom of heaven belongs to such as these'" "At that time the disciples came to Jesus saying, 'Who is the greatest in the kingdom of heaven?' And calling a child to himself, he put him in the midst of them and said, 'Truly, I say to you, unless you turn and become like children, you will never enter the kingdom of heaven'" (Matthew 18:1-5). God is the creator of the unborn, "For you created my inmost being; you knit me together in my mother's womb, all the days ordained for me were written in your book before one of them came to be" (Psalm 139:13-16). "Before I formed you, I knew you" (Jeremiah 1:5).

Fill the earth; everything is food for you; don't eat blood. These are the commandments after the flood. We are to fill the earth, eat what we want, except blood. Pretty easy directions; eat and have babies. (Jeremiah 29:6; Acts 15:20,29)

ARROWS

Arrows in the warrior's hand, shape them
Teach them what you know
Reproduce what you are
Sharpen the arrows–prepare them for life
An arrow without a point won't make an impact
Make them sharp
Gentle parenting does not prepare
The arrow for future success
A time and place for disciplining
With love and forgiveness, point them back to Jesus
Form the arrow to look like Jesus
But you must look like Him, too
Nock the arrow, a straight shot
Aiming toward the future
Draw the bow, the tension is tight
Testing their faith and character
Growth arising from healthy tension
Aim and shoot in the right direction
With a warrior's eye, help them see the target
Release the arrow, let go
Trust the builder of the house
The arrow will fly on its own

Pastor Landon Mauricio on training children
–Proverbs 27:17; Psalm 127

March 17

Every thousand years has marked important beginnings in God's timeline. A thousand years after creation, Noah was born, ushering in a new day. After another thousand years, our father Abraham brought a new example of faith in God. Moses came on the scene five hundred years later, bringing the Law and the Torah, securing the future of the Messiah's lineage. After another five hundred years, David became king, the one whose lineage would produce the Messiah. After another thousand years, the Messiah came; his death and resurrection brought us the Age of Grace. Around 1,000 A.D., the Vikings were brought into salvation, and the Norse explorer Leif Erikson landed in the Americas. Jerusalem was won and lost during the Crusades, and the Kingdom of Hungary was established as a Christian state, becoming the foremost cultural power in Central Europe. In 1948, prophecy began to be fulfilled when Israel became a country again, and Jews returned to their homeland. It has been 6,000 years since the creation of mankind. The next thousand will be the Sabbath day of rest when Jesus rules and reigns. Then Satan is released, and another short-lived rebellion against God will arise. At the end of the age, on the 8th day, God will give us a new heaven and earth. "And on the eighth day, a sabbath rest..." (Leviticus 23:39). It will be like the first garden without an evil tree. "Do not forget, dear friends, that with the Lord a day is like a thousand years, and a thousand years is like a day. The Lord is not slow in keeping his promise, he is patient, not wanting anyone to perish, but that everyone would come to repentance" (2 Peter 3:8-9).

(Jeremiah 24:6-7, 30:3; Isaiah 11:11; Joel 3:1-2; Joshua 13-21)

The Crusades were a response by western European Christians to the centuries of Muslim expansion into Christian lands. These early and later battles ended in the 16th century with the Protestant Reformation.

https://www.britannica.com/event/Crusades Gary Dickson, Marshall W Baldwin April 19, 2025

Will You?

Ask, then listen, then do
Spirit sending ideas
All new innovative ones
Don't say, "I can do that!"
It may take some time
But all things are possible
With endurance, climb

Jesus asks you questions
Will you listen, will you answer?
Answer the call, say you're a trier!
He waits till you ask to go up higher
He always waits for your will
Are you ready to leave the treadmill?

March 18

You must have thoughts before you can think critically; you cannot do this without knowledge. Students need help in the learning process; don't hold back with your assistance. The goal isn't to sink or swim; it is to swim. Eventually, they will catch on and won't need your help. Teachers must not overcorrect; give three positives before the negative; many students already feel stupid. Be clear in your expectations and do not compare children with each other. Each one will have a unique identity and will develop their own skills, gifts, and strengths at different ages. Classical and worship music should be a part of each day, with a wide range of rhythms and patterns. Listening to music is a good way to extend a student's attention span. Study the instruments, listen for the different ones you hear. Read aloud and have them narrate back what they have learned; this will develop an attention to detail. Encourage journaling. Model wonder. Respect their ideas and interests. Spelling should be a verbal practice with no paper. Twenty minutes is the optimal attention span. We want improvement, not perfection. Your style as a teacher/parent will match your personality; is it clinical, relational, or military? Do you control your children with anger, threats, manipulation, bribery, shame, guilt, or do you pursue a close relationship with them, and do they grieve when that relationship is broken?

This chapter is from a conference taught by Andrew Pudewa
Smalley, Gary. *Key to Your Child's Heart*. 2010

Schools should be welcoming, each one greeted and appreciated. This will surely decrease the number of bullies.

March 19

Classical education begins with knowledge, where the youngest students learn by repeating, memorizing, and expressing what they have learned, reinforced through storytelling. All lessons were memorized in the past, but in 1920, John Dewey was anti-memorization, so he introduced rote learning by drills; it killed motivation. Memorizing grows the brain, and it doesn't matter what it is –Scripture, drama, dance, poetry. Students will do well on their pre-college tests if they have spent time memorizing. In college, they will learn the material rather than cram for tests and then forget what they were taught. When students are nearing middle school age, they enter the understanding phase of learning, where the memorized knowledge begins to make sense, and they start creating their own ideas. Then comes the wisdom stage, where students can compare time periods and the people in them. They connect relationships, recognize cause and effect, view circumstances in a broad context, and appreciate experts in their fields of study. The students can arrange their thoughts on paper using an outline then present a memorized speech with style and confidence. Half-truths, hearsay, a mixture of true and false, and judging without evidence become discernible to the student. Finally, these well-educated students learn to form opinions and can debate these opinions, citing resources. The goal is to know God and make him known, engaging in learning through peer discussions, learning to speak, write, and debate persuasively, confidently, with grace, humility, and wisdom. Rhetoric is a good man speaking well, persuading men to believe and act. It loves seeking the truth and sharing it.

Sophistry uses false arguments or seemingly logical reasoning pointing to a false conclusion with the intent to deceive.

The Classical Conversation model of education
(Proverbs 2:2; 3:13,19; 4:7)

Ignorance comes from ignoring. We are not ignorant when we dig for truth and gain understanding, leading us to wisdom. Ignorance may be bliss, but it has consequences.

LIFE

It may shame me
But it won't break me
It's a roller coaster
Being stuck in a toaster
Some ups, climbing high
Plunging down, time to cry
An opera of not knowing the words
A drama, a dark comedy
A sci-fi with no "Beam me up, Scotty"
Trying not to lie
Trying not to be naughty
End of days, things are slowing down
Waiting on death row
Waiting for the burial
Feeling like fifteen more years
Would be good
Time to turn off the TV

March 20

The formal art of debate is a learned skill rarely seen today. Our opinions are affected by our biases, prejudices, and past experiences. Express opinions as opinions, not as facts. To persuade someone to your point of view, use ethos–the appeal to right versus wrong; pathos–an emotional appeal based on truth and justice; and logos–using logical reasoning or the law to make the appeal. We never make fun of a person's looks, mock, or ape people (mimic for the purpose of degrading), make fun of someone's health or disabilities while in a debate, or otherwise. Let your logic, ethics, and morals be the presenter of truth. Passion is fine, but be sure it is passion for principle, not a desire to win the argument. Always show respect for others' opinions. Do not show disdain for their views by your body language or facial expressions. Do not use terms such as 'idiot,' 'stupid,' 'ignorant,' or 'fool.' The goal isn't an ambitious, self-exalting desire to triumph and feel good about your debating skills; it's for truth, and the attitude is humility.

Classical Conversations formal debate and mock trial notes

Truth is for all time, all people, and all places. If it is true for me but not for you, it is not true. The Truth is God's truth, and it never changes.

March 21

On January 1, 1863, in his Emancipation Proclamation, President Lincoln changed his rhetoric from saving the union to abolishing slavery when he said, "...all persons held as slaves...shall be then thenceforward, and forever free." The media attacked Lincoln for his ancestry, lack of formal learning, appearance, and morality. No matter what he did, it was never good enough for one faction or another. He received both praise and abuse, even from those dedicated to his cause. The Richmond Enquirer ran editorials vilifying Lincoln, "He ought to be removed by any means necessary." The newspaper, Charleston Mercury, said that ridding the nation of Lincoln would be cause for celebration. Some Northern newspapers called for his assassination, and called him a deceiver, trickster, coward, an idiot, and the "original gorilla" by his own General McClellan as seen in his letter to his wife dated November 1861 (McClellan, Civil War Papers, 135), as did Edwin Stanton who became his secretary of state (Stanton, Thomas and Hyman,135). William Lloyd Garrison Jr. called his murder providential because he wanted Andrew Johnson to be the leader. Elizabeth Cady Stanton, a famous abolitionist, fought against his renomination and swore in a letter to Wendell Phillips in 1864 stating, "if he is reelected, I shall immediately leave the country for the Fijee [sic] Islands." "A monstrous usurper," said the Chicago Times, 1863. Of the states that had an article of secession, Georgia, Mississippi, and Texas cited the main reason was slavery (56%, 73%, 54% respectively). South Carolina cited slavery as a reason by 20%. Other reasons were states' rights, context, economy, military protection, and Lincoln himself.

Sounds like politics and the media haven't changed in a hundred fifty years. "Now he [Lincoln] belongs to the ages."-Edwin Stanton, 1865.

Even when our prayers seem all unanswered and our champions are defeated, the great cause is just assuredly marching to its radiant goal. FW Boreham

www.battlefields.org. "The Reason for Secession: A Documentary Study." Oct. 3, 2023.

www.archives.gov. "Transcript of the Proclamation," January 1, 1863, May 5, 2017.

www.thealtantic.com. "'Idiot,' 'Yahoo,' 'Original Gorilla': How Lincoln was Dissed in His Day." *The Atlantic*. June 2013.

Foner, Eric. *The Fiery Trial: Abraham Lincoln and American Slavery*: W. W. Norton, 2010.

Holzer, Harold. *Lincoln and the Power of the Press*: The War for Public Opinion, 2014.

McPherson, James M. *Battle Cry of Freedom*: The Civil War, 1988.

ROAR

Roar and let the enemy's house divide and fall
Your response now will affect the end of the year
Resist all that produces grief, emotions, and all that
wars against faith
Be dead to fleshly desires, operate in new faith levels
with no fear
Dispatch the Host of Heaven to do His glorious work
Link arms with believers, agreeing in prayer
"In the name of Jesus, we dislodge hell's
assignments
Over this city, over this country, over the world
We speak confusion into the evil camp of the enemy
We tear down all communication structures
Between you and those demons serving you."
Victory belongs to the Lord. It is His kingdom,
His glory, for His honor, King of kings, Lord of lords!
Glory of Zion–2015

March 22

Andrew Pudewa talks about the four types of stories. The whole story is about the good being good, the bad being bad, and the good winning. We crave this type of story; it is the Cinderella story in which justice is finally meted out to the evil stepmother. The healing story is where the good is good, the bad is bad, and the ending is not good but redemptive, like Hans Christian Andersen's fairy tales and Aesop's fables, which teach a moral, a character quality, or a consequence of actions. This is the true story of Jesus dying on the cross, a healing story with terrible evil and death, but having a glorious resurrection ending. A broken story is one where the good is good, the bad is bad, and evil wins; there is no redemption, as in *Strange Case of Dr. Jekyll and Mr. Hyde* and *The Lord of the Flies*, full of sadness and peril. Lastly, a twisted story where good is stupid, evil is good, and evil is glorified. Stories model an author's worldview and philosophy. For thousands of years, dragons have been the archetype of the devil to be hated and fought. Now we have *Puff the Magic Dragon, How to Train Your Dragon*, and *Pete's Dragon*, to name a few. It is a subtle twisting of bad into good. The symbolism is destroyed. Children are checking out books on becoming witches or wizards and casting spells. Boys need stories like Pinocchio, where they can cry out in their thoughts, "No, don't do it." Notice movies, some written by atheists, are impossible unless there is a powerful God who cares, like *Nim's Island, 2012, The Jungle Book, City of Ember,* and *Castaway*.

We tell truth through fiction. -Neil Gaiman

Grammar is not a perfect science—not like math, some rules are not clearly defined; it is also an art. We have language because God does. Latin was understood and used across the Greek and Roman cultures until after the Thirty Years' War, when society broke up and people no longer understood each other because Latin was no longer used. In 1544, Henry the 8th declared that schoolmasters must use *Lily's Grammar of Latin in English*, and within one generation, there came an explosion of literature, including Shakespeare. Many languages today are highly influenced by Latin. The first sentence of the Declaration of Independence has 42 words, and the subject comes last! Our government hires people to translate the difficult writings of our forefathers and legalese. For instance, "in flagrante delicto" is a legal term, meaning "in blazing offense," and is used when someone is caught in the act of a crime. Learning Latin is a great way to learn grammar because it is consistent, and we can focus on its writing as it is rarely spoken. Latin is the foundation of English, 60% of our words are rooted in Latin. Over 90% of the technical words used in law, science, medicine, and government are derived from Latin or Greek. Learning Latin early will help with higher education later on.

The Bible interprets itself, so we can make deductions from linking Scriptures, and then by using Greek and Hebrew translation tools, we increase our understanding of the deeper meaning of words.

https://oldshirburian.org.uk/lilys-grammar/ *Lily's Grammar*–Sherborne School's oldest textbook. The Old Shirburnian Society. Rachel Hassall

March 24

Read children's books above their grade level and talk about what you read. In 1853, students attended school for 6-12 weeks a year but were very literate. They spent time reading to each other by candlelight. In his book *Orthodoxy*, Mr. Chesterton wrote a chapter titled "The Ethics of Elfland," in which he argued that children learn about the real world from fairy tales. They need to know that dragons can be slain, and that kings, in their proper role, are good and loving. If there is an evil king in a fairy tale, he will be replaced by a true and kind one. Trolls, dragons, goblins, and witches aren't tolerated—they are evil. Princes can be frogs, and frogs can be princes. The supernatural exists, which is hard to believe until you can imagine it. Half of adults today don't read anything, and less than half read books in high school. They are choosing not to read, so they are illiterate. Even college students struggle to understand what they read. In 2025, a student was beginning her freshman year of college, having graduated from high school with honors. She sued her high school because she could not read or write!

Fairytales express what we all know but have forgotten—the world is a mysterious and wonderful place...fairytales bring us back to reality, as we recognize that our world doesn't have to be the way it is. There are glass slippers, glass mirrors, and glass castles—a reminder that happiness is shiny and beautiful—but also brittle. Strike [the] glass and it will not endure...do not strike it, and it will endure a thousand years. ..The joy of man...depend[s] on not doing something which you could at any moment do...G.K. Chesterton.

https://dckreider.com/blog-theological-musings/orthodoxy-4-the-elf/ 8/19/2016.
https://amp.cnn.com/cnn/2025/02/27/us/connecticut-aleyshe-ortiz-iliterate/

March 25

Andrew Pudewa recommends Belloc's *Poems for Boys*; he
says it will help them fall in love with words. There are 700
noticeable differences between boys and girls and
separating them in classrooms improves education.
Cochlear cells are larger in boys and smaller in girls, who
are more tightly compacted. Girls hear sounds 10 times
softer than boys, so speak louder to boys. Women use both
hemispheres when listening to audiobooks; boys use only
one. Female eye P-cone cells show greater intensity, and
male M-rod cells show clearer speed and direction. Boys
draw verbs, girls draw nouns. Women use adjectives and
nouns; men use verbs and adverbs. Stress and pain in
males increase their temperature and heart rate, helping
them think more clearly. Females experience decreased
blood flow during stress, but tend to forget their pain. It
takes a lot for females to fight or flee–they freeze. Boys move
around more and sometimes pace or stand to do
homework. When chairs became optional for boys, their
scores went up. Boys are competitive and need the
possibility of winning with a tangible reward. Intrinsic
relevancy is when one is interested in something for no
apparent reason–like when a child begs for a violin. Let them
do what they find interesting since they cannot do
everything, then learning will be lasting and internally
driven. Inspired relevance is an interest in something
because someone we love and respect is inspiring us.
Contrived relevance is doing something one is not
interested in. Enforced relevancy means "do it or else." This
produces a form of learning; it is not real, and learning
becomes a punishment. Children like to do what they can
do. Don't ever tell them, "I know you can do it if you just try."

They prefer punishment to failure, and if they feel like they are failing, they will hate what they are doing. Let them do what they can do 80% of the time, what they think they can do 20% of the time, and what they hate 0%. When they know they are loved, learning is a smooth ride. Give them 10 positives to 1 negative and smile; no nagging. -Andrew Pudewa, founder and director of the Institute for Excellence in Writing (also used in home education), lecturer, and father of seven.

A negative word is like a germ; a positive word is like a gem.

If

If you repent, I will restore you that you may serve me
If you utter worthy, not worthless words,
You will be my spokesman
You must influence people; do not let them influence you!
They will fight against you, but will not prevail,
I will protect you
You will be as secure as a fortified wall of bronze,
I will save you
I will rescue you from the grasp of the cruel and ruthless
You will be delivered for a good purpose,
Your enemies will beg for mercy
I, the Lord, search the heart and examine the mind,
to reward man for his deeds
If you obey me when I tell you where to go,
I will give you my message
Blessed is the man who trusts and has confidence in Me.
Jeremiah 15-18

March 26

Every religion precludes all others, starting with atheism, which says there is no god. Building a god or creating an imaginary one makes us the god. Having a god means being in submission to it. Casting off restraint to be one's own god leads down a dark path. There are unseen entities trying to lead victims of amorality into a life of immorality and wickedness. The God of the Bible has qualities that no other god claims to have. He has the divine attributes of being infinite and eternal, self-existing and self-sufficient, he is immutable, meaning unchangeable, omniscient–containing all knowledge, omnipresent– surpassing all space and time yet present in space and time. He is omnipotent with all power and is incapable of being defeated and is absolutely sovereign–the source of all rule and authority. God allows himself to be perceived by the youngest and simplest of creatures, knowable yet unknowable, close yet far above us. He is absolutely good and is the epitome of love. Who can be compared with God Almighty, Creator of the universe, who knows when each bird falls from its nest and how many hairs are on our head! In spite of all his power and magnificence, he respects each person's decision on whether or not they will love, serve, and honor their Creator. God doesn't control everything but has everything under control (Job 38-40).

March 27

When the Holy Spirit leads us, life is never dull. We can expect our daily bread to be fresh, not old and stale. But we like our safe, comfortable ruts; God is not a safe rut. We look for something to fill our longing while stuck in our routines, a television show, a vacation, or retirement. Serving God is a daily adventure of Him talking with us, leading us, and giving us purpose. Obligation also kills love and passion. If we give money to the church because it is a safety blanket against disaster, we are missing the joy of giving. Arrive at your fellowship with the flame of God already in your heart. Be excited about what God wants to do corporately. Each person is to be a partaker and a participant. We are told that when two or more are gathered in his name, he is there in their midst. Any time we are together for his purpose, we are the church. "Parachurch" is not a Biblical term. Organizations with a purpose in God's kingdom are no less important than any other gathering. They are vital. God hasn't called us to go to church on Sunday; He called us into all the world to preach the gospel to every creature, being disciplers of nations. We come together as a family then go out as an army. "Truly, the Lord's great power goes far beyond our borders!" (Malachi 1:5)

If the devil can't make us bad, he will make us busy. -Corrie ten Boom

March 28

Confusion occurs when deciphering the biblical differences between the catching up of the saints and the Second Coming of Christ. These are two different occasions separated by at least 7 years, depending on your ideas of eschatology (end-times study). The word "rapture" is taken from the Greek word *Harpazo*, from 1 Thessalonians 4:17, meaning "snatch, seize, or take away by force," or the Latin word *raptus,* meaning "carried away," the verb being *rapere*, "to catch up." The rapture is when the dead in Christ rise from their graves first, then those who are alive are caught up together with them to meet the Lord in the air. "But your dead will live, Lord; their bodies will rise—let those who dwell in the dust wake up and shout for joy" (Isaiah 26:19). This is a rescue of the bride of Christ, or the group of believers "who have made themselves ready." They are taken to heaven for a wedding feast and are shielded from the judgment wrath of God. This day has always been imminent, meaning that it can happen at any time; the only requirement is that the bride is holy "without spot or wrinkle." He will claim his own special treasure. Prophetic events will be triggered when this happens. People on earth during the ensuing intense time of trials will need to turn to Christ, refuse the mark of the beast's kingdom, and be brave; cowards will be judged. The courageous ones will receive rewards and a feast. They will overcome by the word of their testimony and by the blood of the Lamb. The Second Coming is when Jesus comes back with the saints to end the antichrist's rule. Satan will be bound, the false prophet and the beast will be cast into the lake of fire, and the millennium reign of Christ will begin.

"Gather to me my consecrated ones, who made a covenant with me by sacrifice" (Psalm 50:5).
(1 Thessalonians 4:16-17; Revelation 3:21, 19:7-9, 20, 20:4, 21:8-9; Matthew 8:11, 22:1-14, 25:1-13; Luke 12:36; John 3:29; Isaiah 25:6-7; Jude 1:14; Deuteronomy 7:6)

The seven raptures in the Bible: Enoch and Elijah went without dying, Jesus was caught up into the clouds, both Paul and John–whether in the flesh or in the spirit- they did not know, the bride, and the 144,000. Eight, if you count that Moses was taken up from 'Abraham's Bosom' at the same time as Elijah, causing Satan to be angry. This is similar to the prophecy in 1 Thessalonians 4:16-18, 'The dead in Christ will rise first, then we who are alive and remain will be caught up with them to meet the Lord in the air. And we will be with the Lord forever. Encourage one another with these words.'
(Jude 1:9; Acts 1:9; Luke 16:22; 2 Corinthians 12:2)

Sow and Reap
Time to till the readied earth
Planting, watering, then reaping
Fields turning white, ready for harvest
Ready for Jesus' return
John 4:35

March 29

Some believers are called to be watchers whose job it is to warn the church to wake up, like the parable in Matthew 25, "And at midnight a cry was heard: 'Behold, the bridegroom is coming; go out to meet him!'" These are prophets who know the Scripture, have their fingers on the pulse of the world, and are watching. God reveals to them the progression of the signs of the times, and they remind us to stay awake. "Believe in the Lord your God, and you shall be established; believe His prophets, and you shall prosper." It is like a surprise birthday party, with a scout at the door ready to alert the crowd to the honored guest's arrival. Sometimes there are false alarms, like a car driving by that looks like his. People make mistakes because the glass they are looking through isn't always clear. We cannot reject the watchers, telling them they are wasting time on things that we cannot know for sure. But the watchman in the parable knew. "If you do not wake up and be wise, you will not know at what time I will come to you; I will come as a thief" (Revelation 3:3). The inverse is true: the wise will know, will be prepared, and will not be surprised at all when the Lord comes back. It will be very exciting when the shout goes up, "He is here!" and it really is him. (2 Chronicles 20:20, Mark 13:34; John 3:29)

Noah was not caught by surprise by the floods; he had been preparing for them by building an ark. Lot, who lived in a wicked city, barely escaped the fire. Jesus gave these examples of how the time of his coming would be. One was taken above the earth in an ark while a flood judged the world; the other was preserved in a town, then in a cave, kept safe from the judgment of fire. One represents the church's catching up, the other a rescue for those remaining on earth. (Luke 17)

March 30

Our flesh and our spirit war against each other. The flesh, our lower, sinful nature, is what we inherited from Adam. "The flesh profits nothing; it is the spirit that makes us alive" (Galatians 5:7). We may have a willing spirit, but our flesh is weak and lazy. It is powerless and does not want to do what our spirit is ready for. Our spirit is alert and full of desire for more of God. It is energized by the Spirit of God to move ahead, but our flesh drags us down. What can we do? It seems like a hopeless dilemma! "Walk by the Spirit, and you will not gratify the desires of the flesh" (Galatians 5:16). We can ignore the apathetic voice of our flesh that is only interested in comfort, a full belly, and a smooth ride with no conflicts. The Spirit within us says, "Let's go, it's time for a win!" To walk means to move. When you start moving, the Spirit will start leading. Stay connected with other passionate believers, stay sensitive to the Holy Spirit's voice, and go outside to ask him to take you on an adventure of meeting needs and bringing Jesus to hungry hearts. Fight the flesh with passion and zeal and command it to submit to Holy Spirit.

That you might be filled with all the fullness of God. Ephesians 3:19. The Greek word for fullness is *pleroma,* meaning 'completely full'!

First Love–First Deeds
He is the source of all I own; it is his. I use what He gives me and multiply what I have. I seek His kingdom first. My first-fruits giving stirs up my first love. Reflecting Jesus, hearing his announcements every day, and being a disciple. Revelation 2:5

March 31

"Then the man and his wife hid from the Lord God" (Genesis 3:8). We hide from God because of fear, guilt, and shame. We feel we deserve the separation from God because we have been bad, so we wait in fear of his punishment. We avoid reading the Bible, praying, and being among believers, because we feel sick inside. This is the kind of sickness that a crimson splash of sin brings. Confession is delayed as we drown out the voice calling from the quiet garden of his presence by being loud and busy, until we are weary to the bone, never quite able to smother the guilty soul. We keep the closet of prayer closed and padlocked. How simple it would be to open it up, confess, repent, and be free! Why live life chained to the ball of heaviness that comes from hiding? God sees it all anyway. He came out at the same time in the cool of the evening, even after Adam and Eve sinned. They had to have that discussion, and God wanted it immediately. He quickly made coverings for them before he sent them out of the garden. He was still with them. In his eyes, their identity had not changed; it had only changed in their own eyes. Jesus died carrying the sin of the world from the beginning of time to the end of it because he values everyone. Run to the garden, don't hide any longer. He is waiting. He will wash the stain away and remove the guilt. The garden is such a nice, peaceful place.

Repent immediately, obey quickly, listen quietly, read the word often, and pray without ceasing.

April 1

We must master that thing wanting to chew us up and spit us out. We blame God for our misery when it is sin causing the pain. Do we want to do well? A stubborn character won't admit the need to confess and repent. If we live like the devil, instead of forsaking self-gratification, our end will be like his. God gives us a choice. He knows that we will fail; those are the moments to apologize and be accepted. Slam that door in sin's face and give it a bloody nose. Master the tyrant. God will help. What we have encountered in life from relatives, teachers, friends, enemies, and strangers does not give us permission to become an abuser. Offended people think that everyone is out to get them. This striving to be justified and vindicated, and the desire for the recompense we deserve, drives loved ones and friends away. Self-vindication is alien to love. If you are feeling hurt and hated by someone, that person probably needs a good friend who will love them to freedom. Love ends conflicts. Peace and an absence of self-protection are the signs of forgiveness. A broken heart breaks hearts. Hurt people hurt people. The good news is that when we unload that burden of sin and regret onto God, at the foot of the cross, the forgiveness will feel like Heaven itself. He will wash and cleanse us. The one who holds on to resentment, unforgiveness, bitterness, malice, or hate will not feel that release. (Genesis 4:6).

The Israelis said, 'If only we had died in Egypt or in this desert.' God said, 'I will do to you the very thing I heard you say.' Numbers 14:28

April 2

"His heart was filled with pain" (Genesis 6:6). God knows pain; the sad truth is that we often cause it. He allows himself to be affected by our actions, thoughts, and words. The flood came after God felt the pain of what had become of his creation, an unholy mixture of humanity with evil. But he had a plan to redeem mankind even before he created the world (1 Peter 1:20). He created us in his image and after his likeness; of course, he has feelings. We want all the joy and happiness he gives, yet we never bother to ask what he desires. Do we cause him pain by harboring resentment? Is our thinking full of imagined hurts or fantasy revenge? David prayed for the Lord to "see if there be any wicked way in me" (Psalm 139:24). King David had many things for which he was guilty, but he was finally willing to be humble and repent. The joy of forgiveness caused him to love the Lord even more. Being honest and taking the hidden things of the heart to the Lord will lead us to goodness and will make God happy.

Christianity without a relationship with God is a free get-out-of-jail card. It is a life of going round and round the Monopoly board, living for mammon, buying and selling, and staying in a box called 'going nowhere.'

Shingles
A pain of a thousand needles
But worse are migraines, earaches, childbirth
Stepping on a safety pin
You get the point
Worst of all is the pain of
Broken relationships
And the regret of mistakes that were made

April 3

We must teach our children the ways of God and to love what is good. Share the story of Elijah and how he told the Israelis to quit wavering between two opinions, how we have a choice, and we must decide. Instruct them to reject the religion of secularism to avoid a lifetime of materialism that leads to an empty life of moronism. Show them that life submitted to Jesus is an exciting adventure of seeing beauty in his creation and in people. It is about losing to gain, giving to receive, dying to live, and how serving leads to greatness. It is about leaving the 99 and the comforts of home, wherever and to whomever God leads, and doing so while leading children so they will know how to answer God's call. The laws given to Moses emphasized the importance of teaching children, but notice how most of the godly men of the Old Testament had children who failed terribly: Eli's, Abraham's, David's, Samuel's, Noah's, to name a few. Our children will be drawn to our light and will want a relationship with God and with us because they like what they see. We must protect, teach, and guide them, giving them our undivided attention. The heart of Father is to bring cheer in the home and to the world by adding truth, beauty, and laughter. It is all about the children. "I am convinced that you are full of goodness, complete in knowledge, and competent to instruct one another" (Romans 15:14).

The Christian must be consumed with the infinite beauty of holiness and the infinite damnibility of sin. -Thomas Carlyle 1795-1881

April 4

God sends us and moves us. Those we love may turn against us and drive us away, but never forget that God is sending us. If life were always lovely, then we would never move. He has to light fires under us to get us going, and often those fires are lit by friends and family members. Learn from Joseph and be a blessing, even to those who hurt you. A disappointment can be God's appointment. "Eye has not seen, nor ear heard, neither has it entered into the heart of man, the things God has prepared for them that love him" (1 Corinthians 2:9; Genesis 39:5). "From one man he made every nation of men, that they should inhabit the whole earth; and he determined the times set for them and the exact places where they should live. God did this so that men would seek him and perhaps reach out for him and find him, though he is not far from any one of us" (Acts 17:26-27).

Shall what is formed say to him who formed it, 'Why did you make me like this?' Does not the potter have the right to make out of the same lump of clay some pottery for noble purposes, and some for common use? I will call them 'my people' who are not my people, and I will call her 'my loved one' who is not my loved one.
Romans 9:19, 25

Dark the sin that soiled man's nature
Long is the distance that he fell
Far removed from home and heaven
Near deep despair and hell
But there was a fountain open
The blood of God's own Son
Purifies the soul and reaches deeper
Than the stain has gone
(An old hymn)

April 5

No matter what your problem, sin, or disaster, Heavenly Father wants you to go to him. You will probably lose the need for vices or pity parties. He is the best stress reliever, problem solver, comfort-giver, peacemaker, soul quieter, body healer, crisis averter, relationship mender, and life-saver. This isn't abracadabra, this is trust. Trusting God is knowing that no matter what happens, God is in control. He always has our best interests in mind; he knows our beginning and our end. When we gather in heaven, and God reveals to us the mysteries of life, we will nod in agreement with every one of his decisions (Exodus 20:4-5).

What is in us that is resistant to worshipping God? Worship is an act of submission, a surrendering of our will, and a realization that God is in control. Every time you worship, you are humbling yourself, putting God on the throne, and removing self. It is in direct opposition to pride. Exodus 23:25

Juggling
Are you juggling your troubles, fears, and tears
A constant activity like running in place
Going nowhere?
Juggle them high, let another grab ahold
Keep going till all that remains is peace
Then go, have an adventure with Him

April 6

Moses, Aaron, Nadab, and Abihu, and the 70 elders of Israel went up the mountain and saw God; they ate and drank in fellowship and in a relaxed manner; this was not a religious meeting. Then Moses climbed the mountain to hear from God, and the others went and built a golden calf to worship. Afterward, God was still with them, but as a consuming fire. They lost their fellowship with the God who speaks when they bowed to an idol that can never speak (Exodus 24:10-11, 17; 32:1).

The beautiful, priestly garments of Aaron and his sons gave them dignity and honor, but after putting them on for the first time, they were splattered with blood from an animal sacrifice. God wants us to be respectable, but only through his blood, or we become puffed up with pride (Exodus 28:2; 29:21).

Prayers Of:

Awe:

You are Worthy; You are Great; You are Awesome

Confession and Cleansing:

I am afraid and angry; Have mercy; Remove my stain

Seeking:

I want to know you; Enlightened my heart; What is my identity?

Silence:

What to pray? Wordless groans; Contemplation

Hearing:

Creativity; Innovations; Strategy

Psalm 145:1-3, 51:1-4; Ephesians 1:17-19; Romans 8:26

April 7

The priestly breastplate was for making decisions. This shows us that our mind isn't the decision-making method the Holy Spirit uses; it is the heart. We must completely quiet our mind to our own will, submit to his will, expectantly wait on him, and trust him to speak. He has purified our hearts, written the law on our hearts, and even entered our hearts–that is where he will talk to us. Pray, then listen to God in the closet of seclusion, away from noise and distractions, and listen, don't talk, listen. Write what he says because his words are precious and life-changing. When you leave your closet, keep listening, he is never finished speaking (Exodus 28:15, 30). "Priests' lips should flow with the knowledge of God so the people will learn God's laws. Priests are messengers of the Lord of Hosts, and men should come to them for guidance" (Malachi 2:7). We are a kingdom of priests and God's messengers with lips flowing with the knowledge of God!

He has clothed me with garments of salvation and arrayed me in a robe of His righteousness...Isaiah 61:10

If we live, we live for Christ. If we die, we go to Christ. -Spurgeon

April 8

Giving out of a grateful heart pleases God, but what he really enjoys is cheerfulness, not wads of cash or bars of gold. But without riches, the Gospel doesn't travel far. Saving money is encouraged, investing is smiled upon, being wise with money is good, but burying the bundle out of fear is a serious crime. In the parable of the talents, the servant said that he buried the money out of fear because the Master was a "hard man." He did not want to work to earn more for the master; he was selfish and lazy. Some believers fear that God may demand they sell all and give to the poor. Fearing that the future will be as bad as the past stunts growth, fear of lack leads to hoarding, and fear of losing keeps one from running the race. These are heart issues to be confessed and renounced (Matthew 25:24-26). "...Whose heart prompts him to give" (Exodus 25:2) is a willing offering. When leaders get involved and meddle with the heart by coercion, by making tithing a law, or by presenting God as a punisher of those who don't tithe, it may be challenging to have the right motivation. The Holy Spirit's job is to speak to the heart about when and where to give, and those in ministry need to trust God with their finances as well. "Find out what pleases the Lord" (Ephesians 5:10).

When those who are called to fish don't fish, they fight. When energy intended for use outside is used inside, the result is explosive. Instead of casting nets we cast stones. Instead of extending helping hands, we point accusing fingers. Instead of being fishers of the lost, we become critics of the saved. Rather than helping the hurting, we hurt the helpers. When those who are called to fish, fish, they flourish. (In the Eye of the Storm, by Max Lucado)

April 9

Leviticus 14 is so odd that it must have a deeper meaning. This is the ritual of cleansing when someone was declared healed from leprosy (representing sin). This law was important because a person with leprosy was not allowed to serve in the temple. A male lamb was slaughtered (Jesus), the priest would put the blood on the right earlobe of the healed person, the right thumb, and the right big toe. Then, in the priest's left hand, olive oil would be poured, and with his right forefinger, he would sprinkle it seven times "before the Lord." Then the oil would be placed on top of the blood on the earlobe, the right thumb, and the right toe. We are healed from sin by the anointing of the blood of Jesus sacrifice and anointed for service by the oil of Holy Spirit. This was put on the ear for hearing the Lord's voice, on the thumb for doing the Lord's work, and on the toe for walking in righteousness with the Heavenly Father. Leviticus 8 has a similar process for the ordination of Aaron and his sons. When serving God or leading people, we can do nothing without the saving blood of Jesus Christ and the anointing of the Holy Spirit on every part of our lives from top to bottom. We, full of faith, take communion to remember what we have gained from his sacrifice, and we are anointed by Holy Spirit to accomplish his purposes.

Every sin and blasphemy will be forgiven men, but the blasphemy against the Spirit will not be forgiven. Anyone who speaks a word against the Son of Man will be forgiven, but anyone who speaks against the Holy Spirit will not be forgiven, either in this age or in the age to come. Matthew 12:31-32

"Leaders try to put shoes on my church other than the Gospel of peace. These shoes pinch and restrict my body. They become stunted and deformed and are not free to carry out my will. These leaders put their own will above mine and force my people to fit into this rebellion. It is rebellion to wear on your feet other than what I give you, trying to achieve goodness on your own, choosing your own ways, and allowing others to control you, restricting the movement of my Spirit. This is offensive to me and moves you away from the place of blessing. The new babes of my kingdom drown in rules, and their beginning zeal wanes; what is left is a religious experience and a feeling of self-righteousness. Only those with my shoes will have peace and will do great exploits for God." The Greek word *apostasia* is where we get the word "apostasy," a falling away from the original faith, defecting to the other side, abandoning a previous loyalty, and departing from God's holy word. Daniel was told, "And some of those of understanding shall fall, to refine them, purify them, and make them white, until the time of the end; because it is still for the appointed time." "We know that when Christ appears, we shall be like him, for we shall see him as he is. All who have this hope in him purify themselves, just as he is pure" (1 John 3:2-3). Many who fall away will return. "Continue in him, so that when he appears we may be confident and unashamed before him at his coming" (1 John 2:28). (Hosea 4:8; 1 Timothy 4:1; Daniel 11:35)

Deception likes to draw a crowd and get a following. Deep down, he knows he isn't right, but he likes the attention, the money, and the accolades.

April 11

David sings Psalm 18 after he was delivered from the attack of his enemies. "The earth trembled and quaked, the foundations of the mountains shook; they trembled because He was angry. Smoke rose from his nostrils; consuming fire and burning coals blazed out from his mouth. He parted the heavens and came down; He mounted the cherubim and flew; He soared on the wings of the wind. He made darkness his covering, his canopy around him—the dark rain clouds of the sky. Out of the brightness of his presence, clouds advanced with hailstones and bolts of lightning. The Lord thundered from heaven, the voice of the Most High resounded. He shot his arrows and scattered the enemies, and great bolts of lightning, and routed them. The valleys of the sea were exposed, and the foundations of the earth laid bare at your rebuke, O Lord, at the blast of breath from your nostrils." This may have been precisely what David saw; it is similar to what Elihu described in Job chapter 37. In Psalm 18:21-26, David declared himself blameless. He said that God had rewarded him for his own righteousness and cleanness of hands. No doubt that David was in right standing with the Lord at that point. Then he said, "To the faithful you show yourself faithful; to the blameless you show yourself blameless, to the pure you show yourself pure, but to the crooked you show yourself shrewd. You save the humble but bring low those whose eyes are haughty." After David became king, these words would ring true. His eyes did become haughty; he did become crooked, and the prophet had to come in shrewdness to expose his sin (2 Samuel 12:1-7).

Then we read Psalm 51 of David's repentance, sorrow, and humility for what he had done. There were consequences to his actions, but he was again in right standing with the Lord.

I will set before my eyes no vile thing. Psalm101:3

Suffering

In captivity, trapped
Oppressed and tyrannized
The devil's so-called secret plan
Like the woman with a crooked back
Whom Satan had bound for years
Like all who are in shackles
Yet God anointed Jesus
Who went and healed all
Those oppressed by the devil
No more negative grumbling
About afflictions and troubles
Talk about deliverance instead!

Have you suddenly felt guilt for something you have done or said? It is the Holy Spirit calling you to repentance. Have you suddenly felt a burden for a family member, a friend, a nation, or an issue? It is a call from the Lord to intercede. Have you had a surprising thought that seemed to have come out of nowhere? It was the Lord giving you a revelation, either for you or to share. Have you felt red flags of warning, feeling not quite right about where you were going, or, while driving, felt uneasy about a particular route? Take these warnings seriously; they may be coming from the Lord's angels to protect you from impending danger. Don't shake these feelings off as ludicrous; take them seriously. You do not know what is around the corner, but your Heavenly Father does. "Surely he will save you from the fowler's snare and from the deadly pestilence. He will cover you with his feathers, and under his wings you will find refuge; His faithfulness will be your shield and rampart." He gives us a burden, then we stand in the gap, pray, and resist the enemy's plan. We strike and hit the mark, but we must have God's strategy. Intercessors hear and war against the enemy on behalf of others and do it with fervent prayer, praise, worship, and declarations (Psalm 91).

Our God is meant to be experienced through our five senses. 'Taste and see that the Lord is good.' 'We bear the fragrance of God's Presence.' 'Behold, a hand touched me.' 'My sheep hear my voice.' 'Now my eyes have seen you.'
Psalm 34:8: 2 Corinthians 2:14-16; Daniel 10:10; John 10:27; Job 42:5

April 13

A monk named Bede used the word "Easter" to refer to Christ's resurrection in the 7th century A.D. This word originated from the Anglo-Saxon "Eostre or Eastre," a fertility goddess celebrated around the spring equinox. We now celebrate it on the Sunday following the first full moon after the spring equinox. The symbol was eggs and rabbits to represent fertility. Passover is translated as Pesach in Hebrew, Pascha in Latin, Pascua in Spanish, Pasqua in Italian, Páscoa in Portuguese, Pâque in French, Påske in Danish, Pääsiäinen in Finnish, Påske in Norwegian, Påsk in Swedish, Pasg in Welsh, Pascha in Greek, Paskha in Russian. Bulgaria, Poland, Czechoslovakia, Slovakia, Serbia, and Japan call it Grand Day, Grand Night, or Resurrection. The United States and Germany are the only countries that name the resurrection of our Lord and Savior, Jesus Christ, after a pagan goddess. God instituted the Passover, the day when a lamb was slain in each Israeli home. Its blood was placed on the doorway in the shape of a cross, to keep the death angel from killing the firstborn, the tenth plague of Egypt, which secured their release from bondage. God said that this holiday was to be held throughout the generations on the 14th day of Nisan (Exodus 12:14). We remember Jesus as the Passover Lamb when we regularly take communion (1 Corinthians 5:7). Constantine changed the time and name of Passover to coincide with the spring equinox at the Council of Nicaea in 325 A.D. He and his biographer, Eusebius, hated the Jews and changed "Passover" to "Feast of Salvation" and would not use the Jewish calendar. Acts 12:4, King James Version, uses the name Easter, but in Greek it is Pascha. Let's go back to

God's name for His Holy Day–Passover, or Resurrection Day, or Jesus Day!

Get rid of the old yeast, so that you may be a new unleavened batch–as you really are. For Christ, our Passover lamb, has been sacrificed. 1 Corinthians 5:7-8

https://www.diggingdeep.info. What did Constantine say about Easter? Dr. Steven L. Smith. 2015- Digging Deep Inc.
https://lifehopeandtruth.com/life/plan-of-savation/holy-days-vs-holidays/
Origin of Easter. John Foster. 2025
 https://ukip.com/how-to-say-easter-in-europeans-languages/
https://www.infostarbase.com/holidays/easter/easter1.php The Word "Easter" in Other Languages
https://thecleartruth.com/christianity//passover-vs-easter/

Psalms One and Ninety-One

Comes the enemy creeping around at night
In the darkness, bringing a pestilence or a snare
Wicked sinners and mockers, chaff blown by the wind
Not invited with the righteous, the ones like a tree
Those planted by streams of water, dwelling in His shelter
Resting in His shadow, saved from the snare
A thousand may fall at your side, ten thousand at your right hand
None shall come near you; you will only observe and see
The punishment of the wicked

April 14

Do we have Hagars in our lives? The rushed and desperate moves we make instead of waiting for God to make good on his promises, like Sarai's promised child given to Hagar to fulfill. The Lord has given us more than 7,000 promises in his word. Do we replace his promise of being saved by grace through faith with our own religious acts of trying to earn our way into Heaven? Do we exchange the Lord's promised peace of mind with conscience-deadening substances instead of resting in him? Do we forget the promise of the Lord's provision and, in fear, focus on earning money instead of trusting the Lord? Have we exchanged belief in our Great Physician who heals, for the medical industry, a business to make money? Can we not believe him for the glorious promises of his word? Find a promise you can hold on to, quote it until you believe it, then wait for God to open the door. Make no decisions based on fear, tell Jesus what you are afraid of, and only move ahead when you have perfect peace. Satan may give us what we desire: riches, fame, and protection for a season, but he is a slave driver, and he pays with misery. God wants us to believe that he is good, that he wants us healed and successful, and that is why he gave us so many promises.

Don't exalt your trials by focusing on what you are going through, because the Word can change facts. By-pass your brain; turn it off and turn on faith.

April 15

Deception is a darkness that covers the soul; its demonic trickery hinders our knowledge of truth. Paul talks about foolish hearts becoming darkened by suppressing the truth by their wickedness. With Eve, it was a sudden, quick deception, but it can happen over time. "For although they knew God, they did not glorify him or give thanks to him." This is the first step to deception, removing God from his rightful position as the one to be praised and worshiped. "For since the creation of the world, God's invisible qualities–his eternal power and divine nature–have been clearly seen, being understood from what has been created, so that people are without excuse" (Romans 1:20). Knowledge about creation is increasing. The earth and the universe move together in perfection; the order and systems we see in nature must have an originator. If it is unbelievable to think that Stonehenge's circularly positioned monoliths were an accidental placement caused by meteors, then it cannot be reasonable to say that an accidental explosion causes all we see in nature. Our eyes, brains, and bodies are more complex and intricate than a computer chip. Yet no one would dare believe the chip came about by accident, even after billions of evolutionary years. "In your light we see light." We can see truth through the light of God's word; if we cannot see truth, we are in darkness.
(Psalm 36:9; Isaiah 60:1; Romans 1).

Do we know what it is to sin so grievously that a lesser sin seems right? That is Satan's deception.
-Dr. R.T. Kendall

April 16

For 1,500 years, beginning around 325 B.C., theological debates over the interpretation of scripture and the nature of God divided the church into sects. Then the Lord sent revival movements. Recent, wide-reaching spiritual reforms have prepared us to disciple nations as Jesus commanded. (Matthew 28:19). The church, without being awakened and empowered by Holy Spirit, is incapable of doing this work. Jesus told his disciples to wait for the Holy Spirit. He didn't begin his own ministry until he was anointed at his baptism. We cannot "go into all the world and preach the gospel" unless we are full of God's Spirit. How can we minister to the hurting, sick, demonized, and deceived on our own? Keep on being filled, continually immersed through and through with the power and life of God (Ephesians 5:18). He must have the preeminence in our life, or we will be powerless and have trouble hearing his voice. "My sheep hear my voice." Is that a statement, a command, or both? Our mission is to push back and punch holes in the darkness, fully revived, ready to go, dependent on Father. As we prepare for the influx of seekers who will soon join us, we must be united so they can experience the healing love of God. So many of these lost ones are alone, engulfed in sorrow, and hopeless; they have no peace. Help us be the light, Lord. "You will receive power when the Holy Spirit comes on you; and you will be my witnesses" (Acts 1:8).

Revivals movements are usually highly controversial. They are messy and often stretch the bounds of what is considered acceptable 'church behavior.' True revival also brings unity among believers. Cindy Jacobs, page 228, *Reformers Arise.*

God is the author and finisher of our faith. This doesn't mean he is the author and finisher of our life, but that he places in us a mustard-seed-sized faith that he tends, prunes, and watches over, all with the hope of us attaining "the measure of the stature of the fullness of Christ" (Ephesians 4:13). Spiritual growth is intentional; a forty-year-old who has been saved for many years may continue to be a one-year-old Christian. Here are a few markers to measure whether you have left the baby stage: screaming and out-of-control emotional outbursts have ceased, complaining is rare, no more blaming others and justifying self, being in love with God's word, and living in your true identity. The Lord will give a baby believer opportunities to grow as he allows the Lord to transform him into a full-grown faith adult. Mature people are patient because they have walked through the wilderness of grief and pain, have accepted the limits of who God has made them to be, and they know their purpose. These are men and women of great faith who have dedicated their lives to serving God and others. Knowing that you have freedom to do whatever you want, yet do what you ought, what God expects of you, and what he says is essential, is maturity. "Solid food is for the mature, who by constant use have trained themselves to distinguish good from evil" (Hebrews 5:14). Milk, or the basic teachings of God's word, is for baby believers. The deep things of God are like chewing the steak of seeking God and being curious about him and his mysteries.
(I Corinthians 3:1-2; Hebrews 5:12-13).

I have given you everything you need for righteousness on a silver platter, My Blood and My Body. -Jesus

April 18

We are commanded to be braver, bolder, and bigger. "Be men of courage, be strong!" "The righteous are as bold as a lion." "You make me bold and stout-hearted." "Enlarge the place of your tent, stretch your tent curtains wide, do not hold back, lengthen your cords, strengthen your stakes. For you will spread out to the right and to the left." Be who God made you to be. Let him take you further than you could ever dream of going. Don't be satisfied with ankle-deep or knee-deep; let go and float down the river he has planned for your life. "Everything lives where the river flows." "Let the weak say, 'I am strong!'" Boldness in Greek is defined as "freedom of speech, unreserved utterance with confidence." Some are locked up verbally, some because of childhood trauma. The Holy Spirit specializes in giving us the ability to speak. Ask Him to loosen your tongue and be brave, bold, and strong. (1 Corinthians 16:13; Proverbs 28:1; Isaiah 54:2; Psalm 138:3; Ezekiel 47:9; Joel 3:10).

You do not have because you do not ask. James 4:2

First Aid
Four things are needed
In our survival kit:
Silence, prayer, the Word
And listening
"Sheep, hear my voice!"
This is the model for
Christianity and for
Endurance

April 19

Some of the fallen angels polluted the genetics of mankind and were imprisoned by God. Other fallen ones in a hierarchy of evil have become emboldened by curious and ignorant people opening doors for them. Satan knows he has a short time to try to deceive and distract mankind by the tantalizing temptations of the dark arts of witchcraft. Mankind replaces the Glory of God with the devil's evil power. Even the elect ones are drawn into these exciting facades of mystery, intrigue, and imagination. These creatures will eventually be locked up. We must focus on serving the Lord and exposing darkness for what it is: manipulation toward fear. "Don't call everything a conspiracy that they call a conspiracy; don't fear what they fear. The Lord Almighty is the one you are to regard as holy; he is the one you are to fear" (Isaiah 8:12-13). The Lord has everything under control; in fact, he laughs at the enemies of God, the kings and rulers who plot against him (Psalm 2:4). Many are in the valley of decision, ready to take sides. There are only two sides (Joel 3:14). Jesus was falsely accused by hired liars and murdered as a result of fake news. His own people believed the lie. We must watch and pray because lies will seem like truth and truth will seem like lies because the enemy is the great deceiver and counterfeiter. (streaming.lamarzulli.net for teaching on the Nephilim)

People believe their own imaginations yet say the Bible is a fairytale.

April 20

The five governmental functions given by Holy Spirit to equip, build up, unite, and mature the body of Christ are apostles, prophets, pastors, teachers, and evangelists. Spiritual gifts given by the Holy Spirit are prophecy, messages in tongues and interpretation, faith, healing, miracles, discerning of spirits, words of knowledge, and words of wisdom (1 Peter 4:10-11). Inborn gifts are perceiver, servant, mercy, teacher, administrator, giver, leader, exhorter/encourager. Imagine this scenario. At a fancy dinner party, a child spills his milk. A perceiver has already recognized the possibility of this happening; the administrator will organize the clean-up process. The mercy gift will hug the child. A teacher shows him where to place the cup to avoid future spills. The servant will mop it up. The giver hands the child more milk, and the encourager says, "You will do better next time." The leader, after overseeing the process, congratulates everyone on a job well done. The fruit of the Spirit is love, joy, peace, patience, kindness, goodness, long-suffering, self-control, and gentleness. Faith, hope, and love are the greatest of spiritual qualities, with love being number one. Our life should be one of righteousness, peace, and joy in the Holy Spirit. And finally, the foundation of God's throne is righteousness and justice. What are your gifts? What fruit are you needing?
Ephesians 4:11-13; 1 Corinthians 12; Romans 12; 2 Timothy 1:6; Psalm 84:10; Ezekiel 3:17; Deuteronomy 17:14-18; Galatians 5:22-23; 1 Corinthians 13; Romans 14:17; Psalm 89:14

The three friends of the crippled man made a hole in the ceiling and lowered him down to Jesus, who forgave and healed him. Now that Jesus is in Heaven, we punch a hole in the heavenlies with our prayers, lifting people to Him for salvation and healing.

April 21

Perceivers love to solve problems, have boldness, and know the power of truth. They see what is going to happen by principle and see the damage sin does to the church. Walking into a room, this person can tell if something is not right. They are drawn to brokenness and to leadership and recognize rebels and hypocrisy immediately. Time is critical for the prophet; they understand the times and seasons in which they live. This gifted person needs to rely on the Holy Spirit and always have a heart of love for the people they minister to.

Issachar were men who understood the times and knew what Israel should do...1 Chronicles 12:32

The person with the gift of the exhorter is a world changer, is relational, and has never met a stranger. They share their faith with ease and understand people. They can have loud arguments without losing friends. They are skilled at creating and maintaining relationships. They do not like being alone and are most fulfilled when having many friends. They are master communicators, are flexible, and are not intimidated by new truths and ideas. They like approval, whereas the prophet doesn't care. They inspire, motivate, exhort, and give knowledge of God to others. Finding time with God can be a challenge; they need to say no to activities. "I saw an altar with this inscription: To an Unknown God. So you are ignorant of the very thing you worship! –Now I will tell you what you need to know -Paul (Acts 17)

Asking questions makes people feel valued. Be curious about them and be curious about God. Ask Him questions too!

April 22

The giver has a generational worldview and likes to focus on the future of their family. They are nurturers and peacemakers who want to donate to noble causes. They sense false people and hidden agendas. They find options and opportunities, read the fine print, and get the timing right. They receive supernatural resources and give wisely, not impulsively. They do not care to help start-up companies or invest in the poor. They are frugal and see money as a form of security. They are creative and have many interests and projects. God wants to bless them, but they need to recognize that all they own comes from God. *Give, and it shall be given to you in abundance.* Luke 6:38
The merciful person rarely has enemies and is a safe person who recognizes the wounded and those who feel rejected. People often bare their souls to them. They want to help everyone but must first get the green light from Holy Spirit. Feeling the pain of others can sidetrack them into getting involved when the Lord isn't guiding them to do so. They avoid judging and easily forgive when they are offended. They do not like warfare or choosing sides, but when they see the pain caused by the demonic realm, they will deal with it. They are happy with one or two friends and are drawn to the prophet gift. They are the most complex and sensitive. They need all the other gifts, and all the others need him. Their hearts and souls are to be, not to do. They enjoy and savor being with God and sanctify time with worship. They take sinlessness very seriously and often go to the Lord in repentance.

Mercy triumphs over judgment. James 2:13

April 23

The administrator is gifted at and necessary for organization, for seeing what needs to be done, and for making sure it is accomplished. The leader needs the administrator because he has the big picture but often overlooks the details. They both need to include input from other giftings to further God's kingdom. Most people have three prominent gifts. There is a test in the book *Discover Your God-Given Gifts* by Don Fortune to help determine your strengths and weaknesses.

Let all things be done decently and in order. 1 Corinthians 14:40

The teacher loves to dig for truth and then to share it but is slow to change his opinion. He is not quick to speak but ponders an issue before making a judgment. The teacher is the most untouched by the world. He can focus on what is essential and not care much about what he deems unimportant. The purity of the word is his passion. The teacher needs to develop a life of faith and belief in what God says in his word and what the Spirit is saying to his heart.

If anyone speaks, let him speak as the oracles of God...1 Peter 4:11. *The word oracle in the original Greek means a brief, terse, concise utterance. One word from God lasts a lifetime.*

April 24

Those with the gift of a servant want to empower others and are fulfilled in knowing they have been helpful. They notice external needs and move quickly to meet them. They see the best in people, work hard, and compete. They can go to any church; labels don't matter to them. They minister to fewer people but can take on the most complex cases. They have high authority in the spirit realm and can defeat death over a person or a nation. This is because they prefer not to have authority and can stay humble. The greatest pastors are the servant pastors–they model Jesus' ministry. The servant must deal with his identity. Ask, " Do you believe what God says about you?" You are not unseen, ignored, used, or taken for granted, so don't take yourself for granted. God has your back, choose dignity, and positivity. Obedience is easy for the servant; they are willing to do whatever God wants them to do.

Thoughts affect our beliefs about our identity, but we are not our thoughts. -Ben Diaz
Our own thoughts lead us astray; seek the Lord's opinion. If you know what you are called to be, then you will see what you are called to do.

April 25

This is part of a dream from 1992. My husband and I died in a fire (didn't feel a thing), then flew to Heaven in a gondola-type vehicle driven by an angel. I was given a wedding dress by another angel to put on so I could meet with Jesus. I walked down a curved hallway and began feeling his presence. Then I saw him and immediately faced him. He hugged me and told me he was sorry for the things I had suffered, and I responded by saying that my suffering was nothing, that I was sorry for what he had suffered. I stared at his face and could see, under his beard, a facial feature people deem uncomely. He then said, "Never make fun of what someone looks like, you don't know what I look like." The dream went on to teach me many things, but making fun of someone's looks is something the Lord takes very seriously. Was I prone to that? I hope not! Psalm 35:16 says, "Like the ungodly, they maliciously mocked." Webster defines mocking as treating someone or something with scorn or ridicule. We must be careful with our words. There are times when we are angry at injustice, but ridiculing and mocking are not acceptable. "Drive out the mocker and out goes strife; quarrels and insults are ended" Proverbs 22:10.

Those who make fun of others will be judged. Proverbs 19:29

April 26

The Old Testament points to Jesus, to future events, to God's end-time kingdom of Eden and its four rivers of Pishon, Gehon, Tigris, and Euphrates, meaning: increase, breakthrough, acceleration, and fruitfulness. Moses and Elijah being taken to Heaven is a picture of the dead in Christ rising and of "we who are alive" being caught up as well. The New Testament tells us that Lot symbolizes those going through tribulation, Noah, and those taken before God's wrath. Israel, suffering the first three plagues of Egypt but was protected from the last seven, is like Jesus saying we would have tribulation in this life, but will be rescued from the seven years of judgment. Nehemiah 3 maps our walk with the Lord through the gates of the city of Jerusalem: Sheep Gate, "All we like sheep have gone astray," the Fish Gate, we were fished out of the ocean of the world to serve the Lord, the Old Gate, the ancient scriptures our guide, the Valley Gate, he leads us through the valley of the "shadow of death," the Dung Gate refers to our ongoing deliverance and sanctification, The Fountain Gate, where he is the fountain of living water and all our fountains are in Him. There is a place making room for the Pool of Siloam, which speaks of our healing. The Water Gate is for baptism, the Horse Gate for warfare, the East Gate reminds us that he is coming again from the east, and the Inspection Gate speaks of the days when all will be judged according to what they have done on earth. The Jews worked hard to repair the walls and the gates. Now we must fix them also.

1 Thessalonians 4:16-17; Isaiah 53:6; Psalm 23:4; Matthew 6:13, 24:27; Luke 21:36; John 4:14; Psalm 87:7; Jeremiah 12:5; Revelation 3:10; 20:13

April 27

"Be dressed and ready for service, keep your lamps burning as if at any moment your master will return from the wedding feasts. Then you will be ready to open the door and let him in immediately upon his arrival. Those who are ready and waiting will be rewarded, and he will dress himself to serve and will wait on them. He may come at midnight, or just before dawn, but whenever it is, be ready all the time, for he will come when you least expect him." (Luke 12:35-40). This speaks to the last day's Laodicean church, who shut the door on Jesus; they do not need him, they feel wealthy, righteous, and wise. He is on the outside, desiring a relationship with them. Notice that in this Scripture, Jesus is returning from the wedding feasts to those who have endured the tribulation time, the five foolish ones, and the believers whom he did not know. "There will be great distress like has never been seen before. Unless those days be cut short, no one would survive, but for the sake of the elect those days will be shortened" (Matthew 24:21-22). God calls those going through tribulation his elect, and if we assume a particular period of time for this trouble, then we are wrong. Those days will be cut short. The Lord Jesus will come back to earth after the wedding feasts (plural in Greek and Hebrew), seat them, put on an apron, and serve them. "But if the servant thinks the master won't be back for a while (seven years) and begins beating other servants, partying, and getting drunk, then the master will banish him with the unfaithful. A servant who knows what the master wants and does not do it will be severely punished. But if someone does not know and does wrong, he will be punished lightly.

Those who are given much will be required much, and those entrusted with much even more will be required." (2 Timothy 3:5; Luke 12; 13:25-27; Revelation 3:20).

It was the best of times; it was the end of times.

Jesus came as a servant; he is still serving us. Do not deny his help, recognize it when it comes, and receive it with a glad heart.

Discipleship

Shut off the voice in your head; you are not a failure
Failing is for learning the lessons of life
You are not a disappointment or a loser full of fear
That is the wrong view of self, a false identity
You are not powerless and alone
When did you think you weren't enough?
Put that lie to death; what you are is important
Falling off the cliff? Don't worry, He will catch you
Backed into a corner with no way out? He has the answer
In a tunnel with no light? He is your light; you will get through
Through the fire, through the flood, what are you afraid of?
Being left behind? Being rejected? Of not belonging?
Ask Him. "What is my true identity?"
"What do you want me to know?"
"What do you want me to do?" He is speaking
Never ask "Why," you wouldn't understand anyway
Take every thought captive, listen, and respond
Stay in the present, ready for the rough road
No self-protection, no self-promotion, a true disciple

April 28

Self-pity keeps one helpless. It is like pathetic Smeagol from *The Lord of the Rings*, who listened to the inner Gollum's lies, keeping him controlled and powerless. A pity party is no party; it may feel good to be the victim needing empathy and recompense, but pity is never satisfied. Nursing grudges and licking wounds is unpleasant and leads to a prison of isolation, broken relationships, and a victim spirit that attracts more predators. Holding onto grudges is yielding to the sin nature. Out loud, yield to Holy Spirit, renounce self-pity and all the rejection that goes with it. Quit focusing on the failures and sins of others; focus on the Lord and his forgiveness toward you. Start thanking him by faith for deliverance and sanctification. In fact, thank him for the sin nature; it makes us see our need for the Lord; otherwise, pride would dominate. Failure does not define you; it is how you learn and grow. Ask the Lord to talk to you about your failures, and you will be surprised by what he says. Thank him for helping you die to sinful thoughts. Meditate on Scripture, ask him questions, "What do you want me to know? What do you want me to do? What is there not enough of in my life? Journal what the Lord reveals. Speak to self-pity and tell it to go. You are not a victim; you are the child of the Most High!
(John 8:32; Romans 8; 2 Corinthians 10; Galatians 3:3; Zechariah 4:6)

There is no condemnation for those who are in Christ Jesus, because through Him the law of the Spirit of life has set me free from the law of sin and death. Romans 8:1

April 29

There are three categories of stress: acute, which comes on suddenly; episodic, which recurs; and chronic, a serious, ongoing problem. God desires to heal you! Remember that the promises of God are, "'Yes,' and we say 'Amen'" (2 Corinthians 1:20). To have access to these promises, memorize and declare them until you believe them. "Do not be anxious about anything, but instead bring everything to God in prayer, with thanksgiving, present your requests to God, and the peace of God that surpasses all understanding will keep your heart and mind through Christ Jesus. Cast all your anxiety on him, for he cares for you." Time reading the Bible and praying is how we purchase what we need from God. "I counsel you to buy from me gold (wisdom) refined in the fire, that you may be rich; and white garments (righteousness), that you may be clothed; and anoint your eyes with eye salve (spiritual vision) that you may see." "Ho! Everyone who thirsts, come to the waters; you who have no money, come, buy wine (joy) and milk (purity) without money and without price." Ask, knock, seek, and wait, allowing faith to grow. Cast your anxiety, PTSD, fears, worries, and stresses on him. "Whatever you have learned, put into practice, and the God of peace will be with you" (Philippians 4:9)
(Revelation 3:18; Isaiah 55:1-3; Philippians 4:6-7; 1 Corinthians 1:19-20; Proverbs 16:16).

Faith is to believe what you do not yet see; the reward for this faith is to see what you believe. -St. Augustine

https://www.psychologytoday.com/us/blog/open-gently/201812/the-three-types-of-stress Psychology Today. Open Gently. Temma Ehrenfeld. December 7, 2018.

April 30

Life may seem like a roller coaster, and times of elation can turn into times of distress. The Israelis were miraculously rescued from their enemies when God opened a path through the Red Sea; they danced and celebrated. But soon they doubted his love and began to grumble about having no water, then about having no food; they grew tired of the manna God was sending them. They should have said, "Thank you for rescuing us, providing water and food, but we would really like some meat, please." It is tempting to look at them and wonder how they could have possibly complained instead of trusting in God the ten times they were tested. How many times have we done this? "Why is God letting me down. Why doesn't he speak to me?" Instead, we should have a grateful heart and pray. "Whatever you do in word or deed, do all in the name of the Lord Jesus, giving thanks to God the Father through Him" (Colossians 3:17). "Give thanks in all circumstances" (1 Thessalonians 5:18). Be thankful even in suffering, counting it all joy, and accepting it graciously. Pass the test now, or the future refining fire may be turned up. (James 1:2-4; Romans 5:3-5). Why would we thank the Lord for the bad things in our lives? Because "we know that all things work together for good to them that love God, to them who are called according to his purpose" (Romans 8:28). We know that faith works together with patience, and faith grows every time we patiently wait for God's answers.

I fill up in my flesh what is still lacking regarding Christ's suffering. The suffering of Christ flows over into our lives. Colossians 1:24; 2 Corinthians 1:5

Armor is strong and defends us in an attack. The sword is our offensive weapon; it is God's words coming out of our mouths. The enemy cannot approach as we wield it, but most do not pick it up, making them defeated and weak. The faith shield protects our hearts from attacks. Yes, the helmet, shoes, and belt are on, but the soldiers are bruised, discouraged, and ineffective. They despise war and run from it, then arrows are shot into their backs. They are defeated, and the kingdom does not advance. This is not a time of peace; that time is to come. This is a time of war. Those who cower and run will unknowingly become victims. They may not mind for their own sakes, and may not see their own bondage, but it will be the bondage of their children that will motivate them to fight. The enemy is after the children. That is his goal. Those who fight early on will be able to avoid the wounds of the future. Nations led by righteous leaders will arise; those under the unrighteous will fall. Peace at all costs means bondage without freedom. "Jesus" is the most powerful word to cry out when facing the enemy. "The people of Ephraim, though fully armed, disobeyed and turned their backs and fled when the day of battle came; they forgot about the wonderful miracles God had done for them" (Psalm 78:9-12).

Answers to prayer are available to us; the determined, persistent, fervent, and energetic take them by faith. James 5:16

May 2

Chuck Missler, a well-known Bible scholar, said that the more he studied the Bible, the more he realized he must take it literally. Jesus was specific and noted when his stories were parables. The story of Lazarus and the rich man was not a parable. This was a true story with real people (Luke 16:19-31). Scriptures like Revelation 12 are clearly symbolic. When we are told that Jesus will rule and reign for a thousand years, or a millennium, that is what he means. When we are told that hell is for eternity, that is not a play on words. Mary was a virgin; Jesus did turn water into wine; God did part the Red Sea; he did judge the world with a worldwide flood; and Jesus did die on the cross and rose to purchase our salvation. Scripture interprets itself. Reading the Old Testament is key to unraveling the symbols in Revelation. Few people like to study the last book of the Bible, but there is a literal blessing for hearing and reading it. "Write down the revelation...for it awaits an appointed time; it speaks of the end and will not prove false. Though it linger, wait for it; it will surely come and will not delay" (Habakkuk 2:3).

'Stephanus' is the Greek word for crown, used for the conquering athlete that the rider of the white horse in Revelation 6:2 is wearing. This is not Christ, but one who is bent on conquest. In Revelation 14:14, Jesus is wearing a crown, and the Greek word here is 'diadema,' the crown of royalty.

May 3

God gives us faith to believe for the impossible, for the future, for miracles, for provision, for overcoming obstacles, for obeying, and for dying. Faith sees the cloud as small as a man's hand and knows that God is coming with a breakthrough. Hope carries us through to faith, and patience takes us all the way home. Faith is knowing and trusting without seeing. Without faith, we cannot please God because faith makes us righteous. By faith, Enoch did not experience death. In holy fear and by faith, Noah built an ark to save his family. By faith, Abraham left his hometown at God's command to live in tents as a stranger in a foreign land. By faith, Isaac, Jacob, and Joseph prophesied into the future. They saw their reward and were willing to wait for it. The saints of the Old Testament saw the invisible, conquered kingdoms, administered justice, shut the mouths of lions, quenched the fiery flames, escaped the sword, turned weakness into strength, and raised the dead. Others, by faith, were tortured, flogged, made fun of, stoned, and killed. The world was not worthy of them. They are the cloud of witnesses cheering us on, so together with us they would be made perfect. Saints from the past are passing the baton to us. What did they have that we do not? We have more! The blood of Jesus washes away our sin, the Holy Spirit fills us, and now we should be living extraordinary lives full of faith and miracles! (Hebrews 11; 1 Kings 18:44; 2 Corinthians 3:18; Acts 2:17-18; Ezekiel 36:26-27; John 7:39, 20:22).

Desire, then hope, then hold on until it comes to pass and faith hits a critical mass. He is waiting on you.

A conditional statement is an if/then hypothetical statement from the study of logic. The Bible has many. The antecedent of the statement follows the "if", and the consequent follows the "then." Here is a consequent (or consequence), "The Lord delivers him in times of trouble, and will protect and preserve his life. He will bless him in the land and not surrender him to the desire of his enemies. The Lord will sustain him on his sickbed and restore him from his bed of illness." So, what do we need to do to receive these incredible blessings? What is the antecedent? "[If you] have regard for the weak." That is a tremendous promise. So, who are the weak? Children, the disabled, the broken-hearted, ill, depressed, and the elderly. We need to look out for, honor, respect, and help anyone weak in body, soul, or mind (Psalm 41:1-3). Making fun of the habits, looks, and quirkiness of others may be dangerous; you may end up with those very same qualities one day.

We tend to take Jesus' words and turn them into object lessons. 'Turn the other cheek. If you are forced to go a mile, go two. Do good to your enemies.' This is a clear message, but one we would deem unfair. We must take a long, hard look at his words, not just a glance.

May 5

A fallacy is a mistaken belief based on an unsound argument. It is a failure of reasoning used to mislead. A fallacy called "Appeal to Force" is used to control people by threatening them. When discussing a matter turns into name-calling, that is called "To the Man." This is when a person is attacked instead of the argument. Creating an argument other than what your opponent means is called "Straw Man." "I didn't like the outcome of that last protest." Then the opponent says, "You just don't like freedom of speech!" "An Appeal to the Masses" is the fallacy that asserts that if most people believe something, it must be true. "Post Hoc Ergo Propter Hoc" is a false assertion that one particular thing causes another. "The rooster makes the sun rise, because when he crowed, the sun came up." "Appeal to Authority" is using a person's credibility as evidence when the person is not an expert on the subject. "Darwin said there is no God, so there must not be." A "False Dilemma" occurs when only two options are given when there may be more. "Either he will fail his grade, or his teacher will pass him anyway." He could get a tutor, go to night school, do extra work; there are many other options besides failing. Studying the 231 fallacies opens our eyes to how the media tries to control us and helps us learn how to have great discussions and debates.

And some things which should not have been lost were forgotten.
-Galadriel in *The Lord of the Rings*.

https://iep.utm.edu/fallacy/ Fallacies | Internet Encyclopedia of Philosophy

May 6

For two thousand years, people have been reciting the prayer that Jesus gave his disciples. He began with "Our Father who lives in Heaven." He was teaching a group of people that we are part of a family who prays to our Heavenly Father, one we can have a close relationship with, an all-present Father, who cares about every detail of our lives. "Holy is your name." God presented himself with many names, all of which are holy. The word "holy" means sacred. Using the word "holy" to describe things that are not holy is a careless use of words. Smoke is not holy. Holy is a part of the name of God, as in Holy Spirit. The things that are holy according to the Bible are God and the call for his people to be holy, "Be holy in all manner of conversation; because it is written, be holy; for I am holy" (1 Peter 1:16). "Thy kingdom come; thy will be done on earth as it is in Heaven." God wants his will to be done here and now, just like it is done in Heaven, where there is joy, peace, and perfect love. It is time to believe that this is possible. Why else would Jesus have us pray this?

I tell you that men will have to give account on the day of judgment for every careless word they have spoken. For by your words you will be acquitted, and by your words you will be condemned. Matthew 12:36-37

"Give us this day our daily bread." Jesus said, "I am the bread of life; he who comes to me shall not hunger but will live forever." "Man shall not live by bread alone, but by every word that comes from the mouth of God" (Matthew 4:4). Jesus and the word are our daily bread. We need him at the beginning of every day. A hungry soul is weak and can easily give in to temptation and wrong thinking. "And forgive us our debts, our intentional and unintentional sins, as we forgive those who owe us and have sinned against us." "Forgive us in the same manner as we forgive others." Matthew 18 tells of a servant whose master forgave a large debt; he then turned around and threw his servant into prison for a small debt. The master, because of this, turned his servant over to torturers! Let us make sure that we forgive every sin and debt owed to us, even the one that says, "He owes me an apology." And never say, "I hope they get what they deserve." John 6:31-35, 51-59; Matthew 18:22-35

'Lord, how many times shall I forgive my brother or sister who sins against me? Up to seven times?' Jesus answered, 'I tell you, not seven times, but seventy times seven times.' Matthew 18:21-22

Harvest
The servants of the enemy
Are running to the altar
A billion souls or more
A kingdom in the making
Thank you for the shaking
Thank you for the quaking
Thank you for revival
Thank you for awakening

"Lead us not into temptation" is another part of the Lord's prayer. James 1:13 says, "When tempted, no one should say, 'God is tempting me.' For God cannot be tempted by evil, nor does he tempt anyone." This part of the prayer is asking the Lord to protect and guide us away from situations that could lead us into sin. We need to pray each day for spiritual protection because temptation is real. Satan knows how to get to us, as he has spent 6,000 years perfecting his methods. We also need to pray the other half of that sentence, "Deliver us from evil." This is the prayer for when we have given in to temptation and have given the enemy a foothold. A foothold is a place in our soul or body where we have given Satan a legal right. If we play with the devil's toys, there are consequences. We must stay far away from the things of darkness. The last part of Jesus' prayer example gives the Father all praise and honor, reminding us that it is His kingdom, His power, and His glory now and forever.

There is no comparison between God's kingdom and Satan's. It is like comparing a whale to an amoeba, a lion to an ant, the sun to a 5-watt light bulb.

Malachi 4:2

The sun will rise with healing in his wings
A new dawn, a new day, glory coming down
Filling our souls, making us whole
Our candle getting brighter, burdens getting lighter
Thy kingdom coming, thy will being done

May 9

We use the word *God* to represent all that God is, but he has referred to Himself by many names. When he called Moses to lead his people out of Egypt, Moses asked him his name. God answered, "Tell them *I AM* has sent you." Jesus said to the mocking crowd, "Most assuredly, I say to you, before Abraham was, *I AM*." Jesus was declaring himself to be God. God refers to himself as a father when he tells the Israelis that he would treat them as his children. Jesus is called Everlasting Father. He said that he and his father are one. "The words that I speak to you I speak not of myself; but the Father that lives in me, he does the work" (John 14:10). "If you have seen me, you have seen the Father." Jesus came to earth as a man to give his life to destroy the works of the devil, to set people free, and to seek and save those who are lost. He did not come as God, but he was God. The Jewish teachers did not like it when Jesus referred to himself as the Son of Man because this name was a claim of deity according to Daniel 7:13-14. They also had a strong reaction when he forgave the lame man's sin and the woman who had committed adultery; they knew that only God could forgive sins. The people who followed Jesus expected him to rise to the throne and defeat the Roman Empire. They knew he had the power to do so. But when he came the first time, he went as a lamb to be slaughtered. Next time, he will come with power, the Lion of the Tribe of Judah.
(Exodus 3:14; Isaiah 9:6; Luke 4:18-19; 19:10; John 14:9-11; John 10:30).

There are two kinds of people, those who say to God, 'Thy will be done,' and those to whom God says, 'All right, then, have it your way.' -C. S. Lewis

May 10

What do Job, Joseph, and David have in common? They were all vindicated by God. Job was not a perfect man, but he was righteous and tried to please the Lord. When disaster struck his family, his wealth, and his health, his friends accused him of a hidden, unforgiven sin. Job tried to vindicate himself to his friends without success. As he scraped his boils, which may have been shingles, he wished he had never been born. To his credit, he said he would wait for his *chalaph* to come; this word means redeemer, avenger, deliverer, the one who would purchase and ransom him. He wasn't awaiting death, but a divine intervention. He had faith in the middle of the crisis. God did show up and ask Job seventy-seven questions. Job responded with humility and awe. "I know that you can do all things; no plan of yours can be thwarted. Surely, I spoke of things I did not understand, things too wonderful for me to know. My ears had heard of you, but now my eyes have seen you. Therefore, I despise myself and repent in dust and ashes" (Job 42). God rebuked his friends for not speaking truth about God, then commanded them to make an offering of 7 bulls and 7 rams. He had Job pray for them so they would not face judgment. After that, the Lord gave him great prosperity. Job could not vindicate himself; that is God's job. (*Chalaph*, 1350 in Strong's Concordance).

Do not take revenge, my friends, but leave room for God's wrath, for it is written: 'It is mine to avenge; I will repay,' says the Lord. For there is nothing hidden that will not be brought to light. Romans 12:19; Luke 8:17

Joseph was vindicated after 22 years in Egypt, after being sold as a slave by ten brothers. They hated him for his pompous dreams and for being their father's favorite. Years later, a famine forced his brothers to go to Egypt to ask for food. They did not know that Joseph was second in command. He did not know if they still had hearts full of hatred. He did not know if they had treated Benjamin, his full brother, the same way they had treated him. He tested them and then knew that they had sorrow for what they had done. They bowed down, repented, and Joseph blessed them. God did the vindicating. Joseph had to forgive his brothers completely. King David was vindicated after his son Absalom drove him out of Jerusalem, and Shimei pelted him and his guards with rocks and dirt. David commanded his group not kill Shimei, "If he is cursing because the Lord said to him, 'Curse David,' who can ask, 'why do you do this?' Leave him alone; let him curse, for the Lord has told him to. It may be that the Lord will see my distress and repay me with good for the cursing I am receiving today." Later, when David came back to his throne, Shimei repented to the king and was forgiven. David left his vindication to the Lord. When Solomon became king, he told Shimei to stay in Jerusalem, that if he ever left, he would be killed. Three years later, he went to chase down a slave. Vengeance finally came to him because of how he treated the king of Israel. We must not seek vindication nor vengeance for ourselves; let God do his job.
(Genesis 37,39; 2 Samuel 16:5-14; 19:14-23; 1 Kings 2:36-46).

Vindication means to be proved right when one has been right all along.

May 12

"Look at the heavens and count the stars-if indeed you can count them. So shall your offspring be" (Genesis 15:5). This was God's promise to Abraham before he became the father of Isaac. Abraham and Sarah did not believe God's word, so Abraham took a slave girl to bear him a son. Ishmael and his mother were sent into the desert after he had mocked Isaac, the promised son. An angel told Hagar that Ishmael would become a great nation, "too numerous to count." God gave Abraham another promise. "I will surely bless you and make your descendants as numerous as the stars in the sky and as the sand on the seashore" (Genesis 22:17-18). After Sarah died, he remarried and had six more sons. The sand represents all of the offspring of Abraham. With eight sons and thousands of years, his offspring are now innumerable. "The people of Judah and Israel were as numerous as the sand on the seashore..." (1 Kings 4:20). Abraham has two kinds of offspring, physical and spiritual. Jesus talks about building on the sand of ignoring that we are spiritual beings with an eternal existence. We must build on the rock, Jesus, to have eternal life and to be able to endure the storms of life. "Do everything without complaining and arguing, that you may become blameless and pure... shining as stars in the world" (Philippians 2:14-15).

Foolish in Greek is Moros, from which we get the word moron, meaning someone who does not pay attention.

May 13

Exodus 28 and 29 detail the instructions for the priestly garments Aaron and his sons were to wear. There were six different parts to this outfit: a breastplate (intercession), an ephod (seeking God's will), a robe (holiness), a tunic (purity), a turban (authority), and a sash (readiness to serve). The specifics given for the creation of each piece are extensive. After sacrifices were made, oil and blood were used to anoint each garment. These beautiful coverings were splattered with blood and oil! They went to the trouble of making these stunning garments, only to be commanded to soil them. Why is that? It was more than keeping high officials from becoming prideful; it mirrors the spiritual process we enter into when we become New Testament priests of God. The splashes of blood represent the blood of Jesus that cleanses us. The oil is the Holy Spirit anointing that must be on our lives if we are to minister to others. This dedication was serious, so is ours. Two of Aaron's sons died after thinking they were important enough to offer an unauthorized sacrifice before the Lord. With all they had been anointed to do, they forgot about obedience. "Then the Lord said, 'Among those who approach me I will show myself holy; in the sight of all the people I will be honored'" (Leviticus 10:1-3).

Now if you will obey me and keep my covenant, you will be my own special treasure from among all the peoples on earth;...and you will be my kingdom of priests, my holy nation. Exodus 19:5-6

THEN AND COMING SOON

Exodus 19, Revelation 8-11

For two days, they purified themselves
(For two thousand years, we have too)
On the morning of the third day
(At the beginning of the three thousandth year)
Exactly two months after leaving Egypt
(Exactly two thousand years after Messiah's resurrection)
A dense cloud came on the mountain
(The glory over the Mountain of the Lord's Kingdom)
The mountain shook violently
(The last days shaking of the earth)
The sounding of the horn grew louder and louder
(The seven trumpets blown by angels)
God called Moses to climb
(God calling his remnant home)
"If you obey me, keeping my covenant
You will be my special treasure
A kingdom of priests, My holy nation"

We are given six garments to wear, mirroring those of the Old Testament priests. In Ephesians 6, the belt of truth is first, because Jesus is the Truth, and we can only come to truth through him. The belt of the Roman soldier was what all of the other armor could hook onto, especially the sword. Then the breastplate of righteousness must be in place. Not our own righteousness but the righteousness that grace and forgiveness that Jesus brings. Our feet are fitted with the readiness that comes from the gospel of peace. Then we hold onto the shield of faith. The Roman's heavy shield covered the entire body and was overlaid with animal skin. They were kept wet, so a fiery arrow hitting it would be extinguished. These shields could be linked together for protection. We use our faith and join with the faith of others to quench the fiery darts of the evil one. The helmet of salvation keeps our minds and thoughts centered on Christ, keeping us on the right track. And finally, the sword of the Spirit, which is the word of God, is used against the attacks of the devil. Jesus did this when Satan tempted him in the wilderness; he exposed the enemy's lies by quoting Deuteronomy. "He had in His right hand seven stars, out of His mouth went a sharp two-edged sword" (Revelation 1:16).

Do you think you are capable on your own to be righteous?
Do you believe Jesus gave his life for you?

May 15

We are commanded to pray in the Spirit after we are clothed in the armor of God. Praying in the Holy Spirit means praying in tongues. Apostle Paul thanked the Lord that he spoke in tongues more than anyone else (1 Corinthians 14:18). Paul was beaten with rods, stoned, suffered a shipwreck, was imprisoned and accused by false brothers, fasted, faced sleeplessness, was cold, suffered nakedness, and yet cared deeply for the Lord's people. He needed to pray in tongues (2 Corinthians 11:23-28). But do we? We are told that in this life we would suffer tribulation, persecution, and pressure (John 16:33). Jesus told his disciples not to do anything but to wait until they had been baptized in the Holy Spirit. "You shall receive power when the Holy Spirit has come upon you; and you shall be witnesses to me...to the ends of the earth" (Acts 1:8). If you have not had this encounter, ask him to fill you; he promises he will! We need the Holy Spirit to pray for long periods. "We do not know what we should pray for, but the Spirit himself makes intercession for us with wordless groans" (Romans 8:26). Jesus groaned in the spirit. The word "groan" in Greek has to do with anger and indignation (John 11:33). "Learn to pray in the power and strength of the Holy Spirit" (Jude 20). "If parents who are sinful by nature give good gifts to their children, how much more will your heavenly Father give the Holy Spirit to those who ask him?" (Luke 11:13). Being full of Holy Spirit is being full of love. "God's love is poured into our hearts by the Holy Spirit" (Romans 5:5).

God was appalled that there was no one to intercede. Intercession is a serious, intense type of prayer for a person or a country in crisis. Isaiah 59:16

May 16

Holy Spirit is our helper in our walk with God, giving us guidance, knowledge, wisdom, understanding, the fear of the Lord, and power (Isaiah 11:2-3). Ask him daily, "What do you want me to know?" When in a trial, "What do you want me to learn?" You are his temple; he sits on the throne of your heart. Expect his voice to rise within you because that is where he dwells. "If you stray to the right or to the left, you will hear a word that comes from behind you saying, 'This is the way, now follow it'" (Isaiah 30:21). Walking in the Spirit is not for the complacent, apathetic, or lethargic; it is for the warrior who is dedicated to God. Time spent in worship, thanksgiving, studying his word, confession, repentance, prayer, speaking in tongues, and contemplation are ways to come near the Father through Holy Spirit. If you have not yet spoken in tongues or have not in a long time, ask him to fill you, and submit your tongue to him, saying the foreign-sounding words that you feel coming from your spirit. It may be just a few syllables at first, but do not stop. Yes, it will seem foolish, but aren't we told to be fools for Christ? (1 Corinthians 4:10). "He who prays in tongues edifies himself" (1 Corinthians 14:4). "Beloved, build yourselves up in your most holy faith, praying in the Holy Spirit..." (Jude 1:10). "The person without Holy Spirit doesn't accept the things coming from the Spirit of God but considers them foolishness and cannot understand them, because they are discerned only through the Spirit" (1 Corinthians 2:14).

God has two thrones from which He rules and reflects His glory. One throne is in heaven, where God permanently dwells, and the other is on earth, in the believer's heart. -Guillermo Maldonado.

May 17

The Bible tells us that every man is right in his own eyes, but the Lord sees the heart (Proverbs 21:2). The heart is tricky above all things; who can know it? (Jeremiah 17:9).

Our desire is to be proven right; we think we are always right! How can we discern our own heart's intentions and motives? The Lord knows, and if we ask him to search our hearts, then listen, he will speak to us when we are in error. "If we bring our offering to the Lord and there remember that someone has something against us, we must go and make it right with them" (Matthew 5:24). "If we have something against our brother, then we must also go to him and tell him his fault just between the two of you" (Matthew 18:15-17). We are not to quarrel but are to be completely humble, gentle, and patient, bearing with one another in love (Ephesians 4:2).

Call upon me in the day of trouble; I will deliver you, and you will glorify me. Psalm 50:15

God's Greatness
The depths of God cannot be dug
Cannot be excavated
Trying only scratches the surface
The depth and width of his thoughts and ways
Are as tall as the universe, deep as the sea
His beautiful will hangs down in golden ribbons
A lattice of glorious interwoven intricacies
Connecting the details of humanity
To His heavenly will on earth

May 18

Paul, King David, Solomon, Moses, Noah, and Mary Magdalene needed forgiveness; the Lord pardoned them (Psalm 103:12). The problem with condemning someone for their sins is that we do not know what is in their heart, or whether they have received the Lord's forgiveness. We do not want to call null and void the cleansing blood of Jesus. We forget that our own sins have been forgiven. There is a song from the 70s that says, "He paid a debt he did not owe; I owed a debt I could not pay." (Alton Howard Singers-*Glory*). We have all sinned; when we accuse others, we are insisting that we are more righteous than they are, that they have sinned to a greater degree than we have. Thinking that another's sin is much worse than mine, that mine is justified because of my own righteousness, is arrogant. The actual equation is that my sin equals their sin. Theirs is not greater than mine, and mine is not greater than theirs. If the Lord has forgiven and forgotten, then we must also forgive. "For whoever keeps the whole law yet fails at just one point is guilty of breaking it all" (James 2:10). "Above all, love each other deeply, because love covers a multitude of sin" (1 Peter 4:8).

Nor height, nor depth, nor any other creature, shall be able to separate us from the love of God which is in Christ Jesus our Lord.
Romans 8:39

A Church

Favors, a form of currency, a motive with a hook
Serve instead with love, no expectations in return
Using people with gifts and ignoring those who hurt
Dangling a carrot is belittling, manipulating for a profit
Encourage and qualify the humble to be a part
Help them find their place, salt and light, deployed
An anointing of love's healing method of serving
Putting on an apron, kneeling, washing feet
A minister with the servant-heart of God

Elijah Stream, Barry Wunch, June 27, 2025

Isaiah 14:24

The Lord Almighty has sworn
'I have planned, so will it be,
I have purposed, so will it stand
I will crush the enemy in my land
I will trample him on my mountains
The yoke will be taken from my people
The burden from their shoulders'
This is the plan for the whole world
His hand is stretched over all nations
Who can turn it back?
For the Lord has purposed
Who can thwart him?
His hand is stretched out
Who can turn it back?

May 19

Have you ever thanked God for you and for the way he created you? How about for your disabilities and personal challenges? God can heal you for his glory, or he may lead you into your purpose through doors of opportunities because of your handicap. Can you thank him for failures, bad habits, sins, or trials? When we accept that we are sinners incapable of fixing ourselves, we can receive the grace of God to help us overcome. When we see failures and sins as an impossible mountain, we see only defeat. When we try to be a better person on our own, our failure to succeed makes the mountain seem larger; we feel demoralized and doomed. Trying to climb the mountain of perfection is exhausting, and we may want to quit the "Christian" life. In shame, we wonder if God loves us, especially when we read, "Whosoever is born of God does not commit sin" (John 3:9). The word "commit" here in Greek means a behavioral pattern, a way of life, rather than a single action. Sin is no longer our nature; we have new desires and inclinations. But we do what we don't want to do! Tell God the truth about your faults; let him speak to you about how to overcome. Focus on him, and the mountain will seem like a molehill to step over. When we are weak, we are to acknowledge our weakness, then he can become strong within us (2 Corinthians 12:9-10). Since we belong to him, he can fix us, heal us, and deliver us. Then we can boldly say to the mountain we face, "Be cast into the sea" (Mark 11:23). "He who overcomes shall inherit all things, and I will be his God, and he shall be My son" (Revelation 21:7).

He who is forgiven much, loves much. Luke 7:47

EMOTIONS

Do not let the sun go down on:

Anger, fury, hostility

Cast these burdens on Him:

Fear, anxiety, stress

Love one another without being:

Disgusted, irritated, annoyed

There is no condemnation, be rid of:

Shame, guilt, remorse

Love must be sincere and full of:

Acceptance, devotion, adoration

Be curious about others and God with:

Wonder, awe, amazement

Enjoy the life God has given you with:

Joy, contentment, gratefulness

"Deliver us from evil," Paul tells us, we are not to give the devil a foothold in our soul or body, which we do when we participate in the traps he sets before us (Ephesians 4:26-27). He tempts curious ones to peer into his dark culture, ensnaring them to delve deeper into the tantalizing CGI of his kingdom. The consequences can be seen in our bodies through evil spirits of affliction, infirmity, or even death. The result of meddling in Satan's so-called deep secrets is that our souls become darkened (Revelation 2:24); we lose connection with our Father and no longer hear his voice. Repent and submit to him (Revelation 12:11), then resist the devil's temptation and do it verbally. "I submit to you, God, and I resist fear" (or whatever you are facing). "Spirit of fear, be gone." What if there is damage to the soul or body because of meddling in unclean things? We clean our house by getting rid of everything that attaches us to the evil kingdom of darkness, asking Holy Spirit what those things are. Then we sever, by the blood of Jesus, all unholy emotional-soul connections to those items and to people we have had sinful relationships with. "In Jesus name, I take back what was stolen from me and send away from me the evil attached to me through those items and people." It is time for God's people to experience their own D-Day, a day of deliverance! "Do not bring a detestable thing into your house, utterly abhor and detest it" (Deuteronomy 7:26).

The word of God is powerful and effective; it is sharper than any two-edged sword, and it divides between the soul and spirit, the joints and marrow of the deepest parts of our nature, exposing and sifting and analyzing and judging the thoughts and purposes of the heart. (Hebrews 4:12 AMPC).

Deliverance

The evil spirit is gone; the house is swept
clean
Empty and in order, but seven more arrive
They come to dirty the house
Controlling emotions and destroying joy
Fill the empty house with God's Word and
Spirit
When they try again to sneak in
Resist them in Jesus' name, they will flee
 (Matthew 12:43-45)

Vindication

The need to prove I'm acceptable
In bondage to past injustices
Bitter from unfulfilled revenge
Judging and feeling judged
Suspicious of gossips and
Liars, trusting no one
Being cheated out of a happy life
Rejecting others, self, and God
Time for healing and maturity
A path of humility and self-denial
A complete overhaul of the past
Deliverance!

May 21

Some families have iniquitous sins stuck in their bloodlines from past generations. Acts of perversion, murder, idolatry, addictions, or witchcraft can affect us even if we have never participated in these sins. They lie dormant until the enemy gets a foothold through deception or from our own sinful actions, then we become caught in Satan's net. Breaking generational curses and past iniquities is essential and should be done when a child is born or even before. Things to break off of you and your children are false religions, freemasonry, enslavement, perversion, broken covenants, racism, and antisemitism (Exodus 34:6-7). Break off superstitions, religious oaths and rites, spiritism, words of decay, hurtful wounds, and disappointments. Trauma is a coffin of torturous thinking; open it up, clean it out, and refuse negative self-talk. How many paradigm shifts need to be shifted in your thought patterns? We must win this war to receive peace. Submission, repentance, and speaking to the things in our lives that have a grip on us will drive these evils away. These entities are like parasites, not to be feared but to be ousted. A mature believer can help with this. Psalm 91 is an excellent prayer for continued protection against what the enemy tries to throw at our family and us. We do not walk in fear but are vigilant and discerning about his plans and snares. "Finally, whatever things are true, honest, just, pure, lovely, and of good report, if there be any virtue and praise, think on these things" (Philippians 4:8). "Let the words of my mouth and the meditations of my heart be acceptable in your sight, Oh Lord" (Psalm19:14).

Call to me, and I will answer you and tell you great and unsearchable things you do not know. Jeremiah 33:3-4

May 22

Shrek describes himself (in the movie *Shrek*) as an onion with many layers. We can become an ogre by ignoring our own layers. Deep inside are hidden secrets, traumas, regrets, shame, foolish acts, evil acts, and all the condemning self-loathing connected to memories. We feel weak, inferior, and unacceptable. Then we cover it all with layers of smelly self-protective barriers. We put on an act, a persona that isn't really who we are, a false identity–a bombastic party person or a shy doormat. We become protective of our flawed beliefs. Rejection drives others away, and then we blame them. An eruption occurs, something triggers a response from deep within the locked-up places of the soul, and with a volcano of shouting, cussing, slamming–all that is hidden pours out. Our inner abused child becomes the abuser with a desire to control and manipulate others. There is a solution to the onion dilemma, and it isn't a perpetual numbing by drugs or other calming methods. Ask God what false identity you believe about yourself, write it down, confess, and repent. Ask him what your true identity is, then listen. Some believers are trained to do deliverance, or you can do it yourself. Symbolic acts are not silly gestures when done by faith. Here is one: cup your hands in front of you, then speak the pain, regrets, and mistakes into them, and lift them to God. He receives these as a gift. It is his reward for the sacrifice he bore on the cross. You may need to do this often until all the rejection, self-rejection, rejection of others, and hatred of self are gone. He will say, "Thank you, my child."

He that covers his sins shall not prosper; but whoever confesses and forsakes them shall have mercy. Proverbs 28:13

May 23

Most people go through life comparing themselves to others. They see life as a competition to be won. They compete with siblings, parents, spouses, and friends. The goal is to win at games and arguments, and they love the feeling of well-being and superiority when they are better than others. Can you see a few problems with this? Pride, conceit, and haughtiness are not beautiful character qualities but flaws. There is something insidious about believing that we are better than others. It becomes the foundation for life. I am not better than others; they are not better than me. We have different gifts and identities because we complement each other. I am grateful for how God made me and for how he made you. "Those who compare themselves to others are unwise" (2 Corinthians 10:12). "Each one must carefully examine his own work, actions, attitudes, and behavior, and then he can have the personal satisfaction and joy of doing something commendable without comparing himself to another" (Galatians 6:4 AMP).

Hear a just cause, O Lord, attend to my cry; give ear to my prayer, which is not from deceitful lips. Let my vindication come from Your presence; let Your eyes look on the things that are upright.
Psalm 17:1-2

May 24

Are people deceived because they sin, or do people sin because they are deceived? Both are true. Children raised in a false religion are fooled into believing its concepts. If they then follow the ideas that oppose God's innate laws, they sin. Those who adopt a philosophy or religion that condones their sin will end up searing their conscience. A blistered conscience feels nothing except offence, bitterness, and hatred against the Bible and those who disagree with the path they have chosen. If we let God heal our conscience, two things happen: we become happy, and we do not have to face judgment when all unconfessed sin is revealed (1 Corinthians 11:32). Eve was deceived and failed. Adam was not deceived but failed by choosing to follow his wife's example. Whether sin or deception comes first, God seeks out those he can save.

There is an ocean called the Sea of God's Forgetfulness. There is a river that washes away our transgressions. There is a fountain for sin and for uncleanness, the cleansing water washing away our past sins, mistakes, traumas, and defeats. The tide carries them away, and they are sunk to the bottom of the ocean. Dick Mills and Zechariah 13:1

Have you ever watched competitive surfers enter the pipeline of the curled-over wave? They disappear, then usually reappear unfazed. This is how we are to face the problems and dangers of life; we stand on the foundation of the surfboard of our faith and let the raging waters do their thing while we sail on through. Yes, sometimes the surfer does not make it, and a rescue boat rushes in to rescue the fallen wave rider. We all have our waves to ride in life. As long as we keep standing on the Lord and his promises, we will be fine. What if we drown? Paul said, "For to me to live is Christ and to die is gain" (Philippians 1:21). The fear of death is the greatest enemy of faith. It lies to us about God and his power to protect us. It keeps us from surfing, from living the life God has for us. He knows what we are capable of. If you have a desire, a crazy, outrageous thought, it could be the Lord calling you into deeper waters. Take the step, paddle into the deep, stand in faith, and sail on through the wave!

Let the morning bring me word of your unfailing love, for I have put my trust in you. Show me the way I should go, for to you I entrust my life. Psalm 143:8

Contradictions

To live is to die; To lose is to gain
To give is to receive; To forgive is to be forgiven
Joy in sorrow; Thankful in pain
Worship in sadness; Rejoicing in persecution
A light in darkness; The greatest–a servant

Paul uses Christ and his church to explain the relationship of marriage. (Ephesians 5:22-30). As head of the church, Jesus gives us gifts and encourages us to step out in faith to accomplish our destiny. He is not controlling but loves it when we do difficult things in his name. He takes great joy in our successes and only asks for our love. He alleviates fear and ministers to us in our pain by washing us with his word. He is patient and does not get irritated when we make mistakes. His bride admires and praises him and takes joy in serving him. His heart is her heart. What he loves, she loves. When he is sad, she weeps with him. They work together to bring new baby believers into the fold. The husband likewise loves and encourages his wife to pursue her dreams and callings. He provides what she needs to make her feel bold and secure when taking risks. They share their feelings, their sorrows, and joys. They are on the same team, with no competition between them. They bring babies into this world with the intention of raising godly offspring. He speaks kind words of encouragement, washing away the shame and trauma of her youth. The wife respects and honors her husband, appreciating all that he does to make the home a refuge from the darkness of the outside world. They are one. God's purpose for marriage is a partnership, not dominance on either side. (Malachi 2:15)

If God gives us a gift...He does not take it away. That does not imply that everything else about us is right. -Dr. R.T. Kendall in *God Meant It for Good.*

God's gifts and His call are irrevocable. Romans 11:29

May 27

The Holy of Holies in God's temple is where the Ark of the Covenant was placed. It was the physical manifestation of God's presence. It contained three things: the Ten Commandments, a jar of manna that God provided for 40 years, and the rod of Aaron that miraculously produced almonds, proving that Aaron was indeed the high priest. The Ark was made of acacia wood, meaning thorny; it was overlaid with gold, and on top was the mercy seat, which was sprinkled with the blood of the sacrifice once a year to atone for the sins of the nation of Israel. Facing each other, golden angels were on each end of the mercy seat, their wings touching. Long poles were attached so the Ark could be carried. When Jesus died, and the temple curtain to this most holy place was torn from top to bottom, his people became the ark. We are fleshly thorny vessels covered by his golden grace and mercy. The law is written on our heart—the Bread or Manna of Heaven, Jesus, by his Spirit dwells in us. We, like Aaron's rod, are the holy priesthood interceding for others. By his sacrifice of blood, we have the mercy and forgiveness needed to enter the holiness of his presence. He has given the host of Heaven to watch over and protect us, and he carries us through life. The ark was seen once a year, a solemn time of the fear of the Lord, when the priest would offer the yearly sacrifice for sin. Jesus died, the perfect sinless Lamb of God, and now we have permission to enter into his presence to offer our loving sacrifices of praise and worship. (Isaiah 46:4).

We are the carriers of his presence wherever we go, and that is a tremendous responsibility. He sees what we see, goes where we go, and leads us in his Most Holy Way

"The boundary lines have fallen for me in pleasant places" (Psalm 16:6). The first boundary line was Eden. It was a beautiful provision for Adam and Eve, filled with perfection, no conflict, hunger, sickness, or death. There was one law, one boundary line, "Don't eat of that tree." The following boundary line was Noah's ark. It was uncomfortable, smelly, confining, but safe from the flood. The next one was the slavery of the Jews for 400 years. They faced hard labor, ate leeks and garlic, were abused, but were kept intact as a people group. Bondage kept them from debauchery. Next came the strict laws of God through Moses to keep the evil of the surrounding tribes with their idol worship and human sacrifices from infiltrating God's chosen people. Jesus' death and resurrection secured the next boundary line, his law now written on our hearts. "Everyone who does what is right has been born of him" (1 John 2:29b). The fruit of this boundary includes self-control. External controls are what religion uses to control its followers, but they do not experience freedom, and it does not make them holy. Internal controls give God's people freedom to resist temptation. We choose to stay within the boundary of his word, or we choose to disobey. "Stay always within the boundaries where God's love can reach and bless you" (Jude 21).

Look at the roots. If the roots are evil, the fruit is not good, so do not partake of it.

If the root is holy, so are the branches. Romans 11:16

What lie do you believe about yourself? It is time to break those curses that you have thought or said following the words, "I am..." Remember that God revealed himself to Moses as "I Am." This is His name, do not profane it by calling yourself, his creation, other than what he calls you. Break curses others have spoken to you, like ones that said, "You will never be..." Then believe the blessing of what God says about you and your life. You are a child of God. He created you; he loves you; he has a fabulous plan for your life. Break thoughts, past or present, of suicide and depression. Replace the negative scenes of your past with new pictures that include Jesus standing over you and sharing your pain. Remove Satan's legal rights, break inner vows and judgments you have made against your parents and others. Confess, repent, and be a new creature, full of the Spirit of God, ready to face the world with new purpose and joy. Regret leads us to repent or change; it does not mean sorrow or condemnation, but "God help me, I want to change, and I will change!"

If the earth-living pain points us to the cross, then so be it; the worst day on earth is better than the best day in hell and should be avoided at all costs. Suicide is not an escape; it is a trap.

https://elijahhouse.org

May 30

Why did Jesus die for you? Was it only to give you eternal life when you die? His eternal will on earth "as it is in Heaven" begins now, not his will when we die. We start preparing to meet him so we can be a bride without spot or wrinkle. Our salvation is now; our eternal relationship with Jesus begins now, made possible by the Holy Spirit connecting us with the Father. We do not belong to ourselves; we belong to Him, now! We do not perish because we have already begun our eternity. When we meet face to face, we will recognize each other because we started a relationship the day we gave control of our lives to Jesus. We shed the useless baggage that weighs us down and pick up the things the Lord graciously hands over to us. Jonah's revelation after being in the whale's belly was profound: "He who clings to worthless idols forfeits the grace that could be theirs" (Jonah 2:8). Forfeiting God's grace is giving up on joy, peace, and destiny. As we walk in this our eternity, we slowly shed the unimportant, the useless, the weights and sins that easily entrap us (Hebrews 12:1).

Jesus never talked people into following him. He did say, 'I will make you fishers of men.'

Dust
The serpent bit the dust, cursed by God for eternity
We are made from dust, we return to dust
Our carnality, gone in eternity
Satan feeds on carnality, wash it off!

Jezebel was the wicked wife of King Ahab, the seventh King of Israel, who ruled for 22 years. She had certain character qualities that made her especially evil. She was of Phoenician descent and worshiped the gods of her fathers. She hated the one true God. Her weak-willed husband, Ahab, agreed to implement her witchcraft worship of idols and did not speak up when she had the prophets of God murdered. She was a temptress and did whatever it took to become the ruling queen. Her name appears in Revelation 2:20 because there are men and women in churches with a spirit of Jezebel, and Jesus warns us not to tolerate them. Tolerate in Greek means to leave them alone, allow what they do without reproving or examining them. A person under this influence will have a controlling, seductive, greedy nature and will lead people into idolatry and adultery. In these last days, we must guard our hearts against this crafty spirit. The end of times will be difficult, and like the Israelis in Egypt who suffered through three plagues, we will also have tribulation. They were rescued from the last seven, so will we be. "In this world you will have tribulation, but be cheerful and daring, I have overcome the world," Jesus said, asking whether he would find faith when he returns to earth. Let's not disappoint him! (1 and 2 Kings; John 16:33; Luke 18:8).

Lives based on having are less free than lives based on doing or being. -William James

June 1

After Jesus was baptized, Holy Spirit sent him into the wilderness to be tempted. We see this wilderness-type experience in the lives of Noah, Moses, and Joseph. We have wilderness experiences caused by health issues, relationship conflicts, or money problems. God promises that it won't last forever, and while waiting, we learn to surrender complete control to him. Often, wilderness times are God's way of transitioning us into the future. Things we wouldn't consider before the wilderness, we welcome like a job change or move away from family, a new ministry opportunity, or a change in what we believe. It may be that God is pointing to something or someone he wants us to give up. "He that suffers in the flesh is done with sin" (1 Peter 4:1). In 1940, at the age of twenty-eight, Catherine Marshall contracted tuberculosis and spent two years bedridden. She discusses her experience in her book, *Meeting God at Every Turn*. One Sunday morning, she prayed a prayer of relinquishment. She told the Lord that if he wanted her to be an invalid the rest of her life, she wouldn't argue. She said she wanted Him more than health. From that moment, she began to recover. She learned that prayer cannot demand, command, or insert self-will. The prayer of trust says, "I accept whatever my loving Father sends." Wilderness times are times of suffering. Have you passed your wilderness testing? This season will end; joy will come in the morning.

We must keep an open mind; we cannot be rigid, structured, religious, or traditional; we have to embrace change. He does what He wants, when He wants, where He wants, how He wants, and with whom He wants. Guillermo Maldonado; Isaiah 46:10-11.

"You blind guides strain out a gnat and swallow a camel!" (Matthew 23:24). Jesus spoke this in frustration to the nitpicky, proud, and abusive religious leaders who burdened the people with rules and laws while hypocritically breaking God's law. They worried about their appearance and how much honor and respect they received, rather than addressing their character flaws. The gnats were that they criticized what Jesus ate, who he ate with, his parentage, that he didn't wash his hands before eating, and that he healed and cast out demons on the Sabbath. His response was, "It is lawful to do good on the Sabbath." The "swallowed camels" represent their own opinions held higher than God's word. They wanted control of the people and their money. What a rotten bunch they were! Wait! Do we see this kind of religious control in our modern age? We do. We call gnats camels, the unimportant, the utmost importance. We could go through a litany of religious rules and regulations that churches require. Those who break the rules are judged harshly. Some say that if you do not believe the way they do, you are condemned to hell. These are burdens Jesus never put upon his church. He said his burden is light (Matthew 11:28-30). The first-century apostles gave four laws to the Gentiles: do not eat food offered to idols, do not eat blood or meat from strangled animals, and abstain from sexual immorality—three laws to do with food and only one concerning a sin issue. "Don't let anyone condemn you for what you eat or drink, or for not celebrating certain holy days, new moon ceremonies, or Sabbaths. For these rules are only shadows of the reality yet to come, and Christ himself is that reality. You have died with Christ, and he has set you free from the spiritual

powers of this world. "So why do you follow the rules of, Don't handle! Don't taste! Don't touch! Such rules are mere human teachings. They may seem wise because they require strong devotion, pious self-denial, and strict discipline. But they provide no help in conquering a person's evil desires."
Luke 11:38-42; Matthew 12, 23; Romans 14:1-10; Colossians 2:16-23

For the love of money is a root of all kinds of evil. Some who are eager for money have wandered from the path of faith and have encountered many griefs. You cannot serve both God and money.
1 Timothy 6:10; Matthew 6:24

Times of Abasing

Buy some chickens, eat the eggs, hatch a few for leaner days
Plant a garden, can some fruit, think of Joseph, follow suit
Even the ant will store up food, even the bird will feather its nest
Have no regrets in days to come, when floods and droughts
And debts end fun. Fill the shelves, think about sharing
Don't be greedy, remember the needy, this kind of love is rare

Pigs

Jesus cast demons into pigs; the pigs ran off the cliff and perished
The wayward son squandered all his inheritance on loose living
He ended up eating the pig's food, wallowing in the mud, despondent
Supping with demons is an unhappy meal, trapped in a pen, dirty and alone
Behold, Jesus is knocking, open the door and sup with him
Then run to the Father, receive clean clothes, new shoes, and a ring of belonging, all things becoming new!

June 3

Jesus never made excuses or justified himself. When John baptized people, it was to acknowledge their sins. Jesus had no sin, yet it did not bother him that people would think he was sinful, needing to be baptized. When he stood before his accusers, he did not retaliate or justify any of his words or deeds. He knew who he was and what he needed to accomplish; we need to follow his example. Our lives can be filled with the striving to justify ourselves or a desire to take vengeance on those who have hurt and offended us. Ask the Lord to show you the places in your life where the world named you, and write down those names. Then ask him what he names you, your true identity. Ask him where the hurt came from, what you are afraid of, and where the hatred of self came from. Confess these to the Lord, repent for wrong thinking, and God will transform you into what he has intended for you from your beginning. Be real about who you are, be open and honest, and let God tell you what is true about yourself. Satan hates the truth, and that is how we beat the Liar. When we speak the truth, Satan moves away because we are submitting to God. Confession is telling the truth. (Lessons from *Living Fearless* by Jamie Winship)

If I were still trying to please men, I would not be a servant of Christ. I am a slave to all, that I may win some for Christ-Paul. Galatians 1:10; 1 Corinthians 9:19

June 4

The great sculptors chipped away at stone blocks for years. Michelangelo's *Angel* took a few years to complete. In our impatient society, how many people take time to paint beautiful paintings, write symphonies, or carve intricate life-like statues? We must become more patient, especially in our prayers. We should never give up or quit. Sometimes our prayers are like missiles that shoot out and hit the target straight away. Sometimes they are like the sculptor's hammer and chisel, slowly chipping away at the block of stone of someone's heart, when millions pray for the same thing, a quick work is accomplished. "If two or more agree as touching anything that they ask for, it shall be done for them of my Father which is in heaven" (Matthew 18:19). The word "agree" in Greek is *sumphoneo,* meaning "with sound," where we get the word "symphony." When we pray together in unity, he hears and answers. This is a beautiful, faith-building promise that encourages us to pray together.
We are called to pray in our private "prayer closets," to fast and pray, to pray daily, and to pray for all people and for our land. Prayer takes time. We are addicted to speed and are irritated when standing in lines or waiting for family members to get in the car. Take those irritating moments and praise, worship, and pray (and repent for impatience). See it as chiseling out a beautiful kingdom for the Lord. Your prayer has been heard; the answer is on its way. It is a most unusual answer, coming from the most unexpected source (Isaiah 28:21).

Prayer is a transparent, unedited conversation between you and God. -Pastor Landon Mauricio

Understanding words and their meanings is essential. "Do not let any corrupting talk come out of your mouths." "Evil words destroy." "Cutting words maim." "Don't use foul or abusive language. Let everything you say be good and helpful." "The tongue can bring death or life." "If you claim to be religious but do not control your tongue, you are fooling yourself; your religion is worthless." "I tell you this, you must give an account on judgment day for every idle word you speak, for by your words you will be justified, and by your words you will be condemned." "But now you yourselves are to put off all these: anger, wrath, malice, blasphemy, and filthy language from your lips." "There is one who speaks like the piercing of a sword, but the tongue of the wise promotes health" (Proverbs 12:18). Sarcastic speech pierces like a sword, damaging its victims, but wise words mend and build up. Look up what euphemisms, swear words, and certain profane, blasphemous, and expletive words mean. You might be saying something you will be held accountable for when facing Jesus. "You have wearied the Lord with your words. 'Wearied him?' you ask, 'how have we wearied him?' By saying that evil is good and it pleases the Lord. Or by saying that God won't punish you, that he doesn't care" (Malachi 2:17).
(Ephesians 4:29; Proverbs 15:4; Proverbs 10:19; Proverbs 18:21; James 1:26; Matthew 12:35-37; Matthew 15:18-20; Colossians 3:8)

Judge ourselves, so we will not be judged, humble ourselves, so we will not be humbled, discipline ourselves, so we will not be disciplined, restrain ourselves to avoid being restrained.
1 Corinthians 11:31

June 6

Do you have a victim spirit from a soul wound? A person feeling like a victim will not be grateful; nothing will be good enough to quell the injustices they have endured. They feel privileged; the world owes them. They cannot see others' pain or identify with their suffering. They won't apologize. They won't easily say "thank you" or acknowledge the good things in life. They become dependent on addictions to help them escape. They have a heart of bitterness and unforgiveness, and when they have a chance to erupt in an angry outburst, they will take it. This will affect the character of their children, who will also feel they are being preyed upon. When Jesus washed his disciples' feet, he was showing us that as we walk through life, the world will make us dirty, it will cling to us like dust from those first-century roads. This dirt must be washed off, or it will begin to corrupt us and our relationships. Jesus said, "A person who has had a bath needs only to wash his feet; his whole body is clean." We have taken the bath of salvation; now we need cleansing from the daily dirt. Are you a victim of abuse, bullying, a crime, unfairness, disease, slander, or loss? Guard against the buildup of caked-on dirt, confess and repent for seeing your pain as being worse than others' or than Jesus' pain of the cross. He carried our pain as the ultimate victim who willingly became one, so we could be free. We don't want to be stuck in the mud, let's wash our feet!

If...you have been hurt by being falsely accused, God feels more deeply about it than you do, but if you try to defend yourself, He will back off...Be quiet, say nothing, and do not try to manipulate the situation. God will be moved, and He will act. -Dr. R.T. Kendall in God meant It for Good.

June 7

"There is one body, and one Spirit, just as you were called in one hope of your calling; one Lord, one faith, one baptism; one God and Father of all, who is above all, and through all, and in you all" (Ephesians 4:4-5). Paul is reminding us that there is only one church, the body of Christ, and he is the head. There is one God, the three-fold cord of the Godhead, who has chosen to represent himself in three persons and yet is one. The one baptism is interesting because Scripture mentions three baptisms: water, Spirit, and fire. But perhaps they are similar to the three-in-one God. Water baptism is for dying to the sinful parts of who we are, the Spirit baptism is for empowering us to serve, and fire baptism is that which creates divine holiness in us. "I baptize you with water into repentance (or towards repentance, to repentance-Greek translation), but he who is coming after me is mightier than I, whose sandals I am not worthy to carry. He will baptize you with the Holy Spirit and fire. His winnowing fan is in his hand, and he will thoroughly clean out his threshing floor, and gather his wheat into the barn; but he will burn up the chaff with unquenchable fire." -John the Baptist (Matthew 3:11).

Sergio Scatalingi, a great holiness preacher, says that we cannot think that if we are 98 percent holy, we will be where we need to be with God. Two percent poison will still kill us. We need to be 100 percent holy. Reformers Arise, page 237

Holiness is genuine happiness. -Dr. R.T. Kendall

June 8

There is an argument in a logic textbook written for Christian students that, at first glance, seems untrue. It goes like this: "If you love God and others, you can do as you please. I love God, and I love others; therefore, I can do as I please." First, we must define terms. Apostle Paul defines love in 1 Corinthians 13. Restate this passage to read: If I am patient, then I will not sin by being impatient. If I am kind, then I will not sin by being unkind. If I do not envy, then I will not sin by desiring another's property, status, or riches. If I do not brag and boast about my own achievements or possessions, then I will not sin by being prideful and arrogant. If I do not sin by being selfish and self-centered, then I will not sin by being rude. If I am not easily angered, then I will not sin by losing my temper and becoming violent, abusive, or destructive. If I forgive others immediately, I will never keep a record of wrongs. If I do not delight in the evil of the world, then I will not be enamored and tempted by its decadence. If I always protect others, then I will refuse to rejoice when they are brought low. If I trust God to keep his promise, then I will let him take revenge, and I will not seek my own. If I always hope in his faithfulness and persevere when trials come, then love will not fail. If I am this kind of person, then yes, I can do as I please. I will not sin because every sin is a sin against love. No sin exists that is not against others, God, or self. Love does not attack others, does not kick someone who is down, and never rejoices when people get their just desserts, no matter who that person is.

Some people embrace unbelief because they think faith sounds arrogant. But faith is simply believing what God says.

June 9

Defining terms can be the key to stopping an argument before it begins. Here is one: If you believe God wants you to prosper, then you are a greedy person who thinks only of your own selfish desires. The definition of the word "prosper" is to be financially successful, strong and healthy, to thrive and flourish both materially and spiritually. Wanting to prosper doesn't mean having a greedy heart. Greed is not determined by what a person owns. Being wealthy is not a sin; greed is. So, must we take our brother to court, where a jury will find him guilty of greed based on method, opportunity, and motive? Do we assume the worst by assigning motives when motives are hidden in the heart? Have we forgotten to give our brothers the benefit of the doubt? "Why not rather be wronged? Why not rather be defrauded?" (1 Corinthians 6:1-8). We recognize false believers by the fruit of their contrived doctrine and self-focus (Matthew 7:16). Good fruit are character qualities that the Holy Spirit develops within us and are clearly seen by those closest to us. Most social media judges do not personally know the leaders they are accusing. Nor are they ordained to be the accuser of the brethren. There is only one with that title, and we should not work for him. (Matthew 7:16-20).

Of King Uzziah it says, 'As long as he sought the Lord, he prospered' (2 Chronicles 26:5)

June 10

God's requirement for the noble task of being a church leader is that they are to be blameless, the husband of one wife, self-controlled, sensible, not affected by emotion or passion, respectable, hospitable, able to teach, not addicted to alcohol, not a bully, not greedy for money, but gentle, not argumentative, not covetous, but one who manages his own house well; his children are to be respectful and well-behaved. He should not be a new believer, or he might become puffed up with pride and fall into the same condemnation as the devil. He must also have a good reputation among those who are outside the church (1 Timothy 3:1-7). These are qualities for every born-again believer! Take leaders off a pedestal and pray for them, covering them with the Lord's much-needed protection. When they get off balance, God will work on them. When last did you pray for your leader?

Happiness comes from winning battles, not emptying bottles.
-Dick Mills

Sober in Greek from 1 Timothy 3:3 means clear-minded, self-controlled, and abstaining from excessive wine. It also implies being watchful and alert, both physically and spiritually. The opposite would be frivolous, superficial, shallow, a partier.

June 11

The opposite of greed is generosity. "Give generously and do so without a grudging heart; because of this, the Lord your God will bless you in all your work and in everything you put your hand to." "He who gives to the poor will never have need." "Give, and it will be given to you, and people will pour into your lap a good measure; it will run over. For by your standard of measure it will be measured to you in return." (Proverbs 28:27; Luke 6:38). Judas had issues with Jesus over money. He was upset with Mary for pouring expensive perfume onto Jesus, "Why wasn't this perfume sold, and the money given to the poor? It was worth a year's wages." He did not say this because he cared about the poor, but because he was a thief, and as the keeper of the money bag, he would help himself to the money (John 12:1-6). Jesus' rebuke to Judas over his comments about Mary wasting the perfume most likely humiliated and angered him. He may have been disgruntled when Jesus drove the money changers from the temple. Both occurred shortly before Jesus' crucifixion. If someone is generous, they are probably not greedy. Envy of what others have, jealousy, idolatry, drunkenness, swindling, and gluttony are signs of greed. (Luke 12:15). God generously gives good things for our enjoyment. We are not like those "whose god is their stomachs and who think only of earthly things but are citizens of heaven where our Lord Jesus lives" (Philippians 3:19-20; Romans 16:18).

You will be enriched in every way to be generous in every way, which will produce thanksgiving to God. 2 Corinthians 9:7

June 12

"Give us a measure of revival in our bondage" (Ezra 9:8). This is the bondage of the world's negative, unhappy attitudes that surround and hound us. It is a heavy feeling in our souls that cries out for justice, joy, and truth. When we hear sick jokes, vile stories, complaining, slander, gossip, and profanity, our spirit begins to shrink. Your gut will let you know if what you are hearing is "a tasty morsel going down into the inmost body" (Proverbs 18:8); it is gossip. There is something pleasurable yet evil when you feel joy at hearing of others' flaws, sins, or embarrassments. It takes courage to speak up and defend those who are being smeared humbly. A barrage of cursing and slimy conversations from co-workers, peers, media, and entertainment grieves the heart, which can easily become hardened by accepting these as usual. Strongholds may develop from the tainted entertainment we choose to be involved with; what we find entertaining may end up entering us. If we love what he loves and hate what he hates, then our desires will be his desires. "Lord, give me a measure of revival!" Start praying for this, claiming salvation for hostile co-workers, sarcastic peers, and antagonistic family members. Carry the life of Jesus with you, stay cheerful and sensitive with a soft heart, and believe God for revival. "Stoutly defend the unchanging truth that God has given us" (Jude 1:3).

Don't criticize, look at the mirror, and examine yourself.

June 13

There is purpose in prosperity. God blessed Israel because he wanted to bless the whole world. God blessed Solomon because he did not seek riches but wisdom. Jacob never did receive an inheritance from trading Esau's birthright for a bowl of stew, or from receiving the blessing from his father, Isaac, when he tricked him into thinking he was his older brother. He received his wealth from God. "It is God who gives the power to gain wealth, that he may confirm the covenant that he swore to your fathers" (Deuteronomy 8:18). Today, we would not consider 12 children, cattle, sheep, or wells to be a sign of wealth. Now, a big home, a yacht, a plane, or a multi-billion-dollar business are considered riches. Should we be bothered when the world or believers have such things? In the near future, I will have a mansion, walk on streets of gold, and be surrounded by the expanse of the wealth of God. Are we not praying that God's will be done on earth as it is in Heaven? A greedy heart envies the wealthy. Let God be the judge. Let him decide the purpose of each individual and the purpose of their status on earth. "I will be content with my portion on earth for it has fallen for me in pleasant places" (Psalm 16:6). If our brother or sister is doing something we believe is going to bring God's judgment, our first response is to fall on our knees and pray for them. That is the definition of love.

In my Father's house are many princely mansions. -Jesus and *Psalm 49*

Paul Learned

I have learned to be content in all circumstances
I know what it is like to be in need and to have plenty
I know the secret of being content in every situation
Whether well fed or hungry, having much or nothing at all
I do everything through him who gives me strength
Only one church helped me out when I was in need
Not that I am seeking a gift, but I am looking for that
which can be credited to your account, a fragrant offering
An acceptable sacrifice, one that pleases God
And my God will meet all your needs according to his
Glorious riches in Christ Jesus.

Philippians 4

Opulence

Cadillac and Rolex
Six full baths
Hobbies and collectables
Cruises on the Nile
Ski trips to the Alps
Gucci, Armani, Louis Vuitton
Prada, Chanel, and Dior
A second home in France
Sailing the ocean blue
Is there time for Jesus too?

June 14

What do we compare our standard of living with, a third-world country or Heaven, luxury or poverty? He gave up the glories of Heaven to live in the lowliest, a birth in a stable, eating grain from a field, sleeping on the ground. His disciples then continued what he began. Now, some disciples live in luxury to reach the wealthy, while others live in poverty to reach the poor. It is not more spiritual to be poor, but some are called to leave their riches to minister to those who need help. God has many people in every circumstance, so all corners of the planet may be reached. We are commanded to condescend to men of low estate so that His light will shine in abasing situations. Sometimes the Lord calls us to sell all and follow him. God desires that all would be saved, rich and poor. Would you be willing to sell all if God told you to? "He gave them their request but sent leanness to their soul" (Psalm 106:15). What you think you desire may not be a good idea.

Daron Babcock left a great job and moved to a poor neighborhood in Dallas, Texas. He loves the poor and helps them plant vegetables, grow fruit, raise goats and chickens, and tend bees. They have their own restaurant, sell their produce, and now have 50 acres of land full of crops. They hire people coming out of prison. He is making a difference!
https://bontonfarms.org/our-story/

June 15

Repent of the sin that caused a curse, whether it is your own or your forefathers'. Take authority and break it. How to recognize a curse? Sickness that cannot be cured or has no known source, financial ongoing lack, ongoing mental and emotional distress (confusion and depression), barrenness, marriage breakdown, family alienation, being accident-prone, suicidal thoughts, or premature deaths. Then have faith, the expectation of good things, which is the opposite of fear, which is expecting and envisioning the bad to happen. Anxiety is the emotion of fear; removing hooks from the past will delete future anxiety. A trauma loop relives a moment over and over and is a tool of Satan. Agree with me, "I silence the voice of the enemy. I silence my own thoughts and bind my mind to the mind of Christ, my heart to Father's heart, and my feet to the path Holy Spirit has mapped out for me." Then ask the Lord the question, "Are there any open doors or past generational sins that have given the enemy a foothold in my life?" After you receive your answer, take time to confess, repent, and renounce those things. Then ask God to release his vengeance against those demonic structures of torment. Stop describing the problem, describe the promise instead. Agree with God about what he says about you.

We are either slaves to sin, which leads to death, or to obedience, which leads to righteousness. Just as you used to offer the parts of your body in slavery to impurity and wickedness, so now offer them in slavery to righteousness leading to holiness. What benefit did you reap from things you are now ashamed of? Romans 6

June 16

The word "submission" makes us want to recoil. It is a word that has been misunderstood. Submission is based on a close and trusting relationship; it is a choice one makes. You cannot enforce submission from a spouse; it is willingly given. "Submit to one another out of reverence to Christ" (Ephesians 5:21). Being submissive means being humble, asking questions, listening to the answers, wanting to know the other person's opinions and preferences, and desiring to please him or her. We should not make demands, always insisting on getting our own way or being a controlling taskmaster, not even when we are the head of a nation, company, church, or family. Was Jesus submissive? Yes. He submitted to being baptized, to being led into the wilderness, to his mother's request to turn water into wine, and to dying on the cross. When he knew what he had to do or say, he did it in a manner of complete submission to his Father. When we marry, we agree to a partnership built on submission, with communication as the key to an honest, loving relationship. Neither the husband nor the wife can claim rights to every decision. Marry someone who can be trusted, but we are warned not to put confidence in man. If we think he or she is perfect, we are setting ourselves up for disappointment. It is not good to be naïve about the frailty of human nature. Most people do not walk in the Spirit all the time, even though the Spirit dwells in them.

When they begin to admire someone too much, they are in for a keen disappointment. -Dr. R.T. Kendall.

June 17

Burnt offerings were required by God as described in the book of Leviticus under the Old Covenant. Now, in Romans 12:1, we are to "present our bodies a living sacrifice, holy and pleasing to him, for this is our reasonable service." This is the sacrifice of obedience. A sacrifice of praise is not only praising the Lord when we don't feel like it, but it is also denying ourselves, complaining, and self-pity. Grain offerings were thank-offerings and a first-fruit tithe given to the Levites. We support ministries as we cheerfully give. The fellowship offering is when we feast together and share what we have with others. The guilt offering is paying back someone you have offended; it makes amends and repairs relationships, including our relationship with the Lord. Drink offerings are the offerings of our joyful and sacrificial service to the Lord. Paul said, "Even if I am to be poured out as a drink offering upon the sacrificial offering of your faith, I am glad and rejoice with you all" (Philippians 2:17). These offerings in the Old Testament point to relationships, for that is what God loves most.

The wave offering of the breast of the animal was waved from side to side, the heave offering of the leg of the animal goes up and down, making the sign of the cross. The goat offering was for sinners, the calf and bull offerings were for Israel, and now the Lamb is Jesus for everyone. Numbers 18 KJV

Flip Wilson was a comedian in the 60s and 70s who is best known for his line, "The devil made me do it." This may have some truth to it when considering the demoniac who lived among the tombs, cut himself, and was strong enough to break all shackles. He did not want that lifestyle, but was demon-owned. When Jesus arrived, the true man buried inside his demon-controlled body ran to Jesus, his last hope. The man still had a choice, and he chose to run to Jesus. The demons cried out in protest, but the man wanted freedom, and he received it (Mark 5). Flip, you were wrong. We always have a choice. We can cry out to the Lord for freedom, no matter how much ground the enemy has taken from us. What did that man in the tombs do to be so demonically controlled? We don't know, but the Bible is full of warnings about stepping into the evil territories of Satan. Divination is witchcraft, and it uses prophecy and fortune-telling as a means of financial gain, self-exaltation, and control. This deception can entrap God's people. Satan wants your will, but he can't do anything without your permission. God must be your greatest desire, or your own desires will have preeminence. When you have a choice whether to please God or to cave to temptation, which will you choose? If you have given in, deliverance is needed. No matter how much you justify your actions, the enemy has you in his grip. Have a minister pray with you; the vortex of control needs to be broken. Be set free!
Hammon, Frank and Ida Mae. *Pigs in the Parlor.* August 1990.

All who hope in the Lord will not be disappointed. Isaiah 49:23

June 19

Has the thief stolen from you either physically or spiritually? Proverbs 6:31 says, "When he [a thief] is found, he must restore sevenfold; though it cost all the wealth of his house." We know who the thief is, for he comes to steal, kill, and destroy. Much has been stolen from families; so many lives ruined. Heaven has a court; "God presides over Heaven's court..." (Psalm 82:1). Present your case before him, make sure you enter his court guilt and sin free with thanksgiving and humility, then appeal to the Judge for what you want returned. We know who the ultimate cause of our personal losses is. "Father, Judge of the universe, Satan is found out; he has stolen from me. He must restore sevenfold according to your word, in Jesus' name." What do you think the host of Heaven working on our behalf is for if not to defeat the thief and make him pay up? Here is another promise to believe, "Return to your fortress, you prisoners of hope, today I declare that I will restore double to you" (Zechariah 9:12).

Evil is a parasite that can only exist in contrariety to holy and good. Evil was not created; it should not exist–it is a conscious personal force with will and intent. Evil is an inversion of the truth of the reality of existence. -Jonathan Cahn from The Dragon's Prophecy.

"JESUS"

His name is power, His name is holy
Speak it out over family, shout it out over nations
His name is healing, cry it out in pain
Whisper it in devotion, say it on your knees
The name above all names, Jesus!

June 20

Do the one thing. A depressed, discouraged, and hopeless man spoke of his breakthrough. The Lord told him to make his bed every morning, and he obeyed; then his life turned around, and he became successful. God didn't ask the man to do a difficult task, just a simple one. That was all it took for him to be set on the right path. Could this work for you? Ask the Lord what he wants you to do, then do it. King Joash was told by the prophet Elisha to pick up a bow and arrow and aim it out a window. Elisha then put his hands upon the king's hands and commanded him to shoot to signify the defeat of the Syrian army. Then he told him to take the arrows and hit the ground. He didn't tell him how many times, so the king struck only three times. The king knew that these acts represented his victory in war, yet he lacked the conviction and belief that they were significant; he should have struck many times, knowing this act had actual consequences. He lacked zeal. He wasn't desperate enough, and Elisha was angry. He hit the ground three times and only received three victories. When God speaks, take his words seriously and passionately do what he says. (2 Kings 13:14-19).

Conviction is from Holy Spirit and is about a specific act or thought, condemnation is a broad feeling of guilt and shame. 'There is therefore now no condemnation for those who are in Christ Jesus.' Romans 8:1

June 21

There are times when God advances us by having us do things we do not feel qualified for. The assignment seems too difficult. This is when we are to step out in faith and trust that when we are weak, then he will be strong. Realizing our weakness is a signal to God that we are completely humble and ready for his assistance. "Finally, brothers, be strong in the Lord and in the strength of His power" (Ephesians 6:10). Noah had to build an ark; Moses had to lead a nation across a desert; Esther had to save her people; Joshua had to lead the Israelis to victory; Paul had to spread the gospel. We forget that these people were just like us, yet they accomplished these daunting tasks. The Lord may lead us into times of fasting and prayer for the release of bondages, for starving unbelief, for removing obstacles, and for moving us into an alignment with God's will. Isaiah 58 outlines the purpose of a fast: "To loose the bonds of wickedness, to undo the heavy burdens, to let the oppressed go free, and to break every yoke." Many need us to cry out to God on their behalf. Will we do the hard things and trust that he can help us in areas of our weakness? Whether it is fasting, a missionary journey, writing a book, meeting a neighbor, or going back to church, be strong and take the first step.

You don't have to be talented, educated, or clever; you have to start the journey, and the talents will become evident.

June 22

"Your Word is a lamp to my feet and a light to my path"
(Psalm 119:105). This lamp keeps us from stumbling on the
dark path filled with demonic perils and traps. One can
easily lose the way by veering off in the wrong direction.
Sticking to the righteous, narrow path that God has
designed needs a guiding, constant light, not a sporadic
one. It needs to be kept lit to avoid stumbling. The Word of
God, with Holy Spirit's enlightenment is that light (John 1:1-
5). Our time reading or listening to the word needs to be
daily because the pitfalls are many. Leaving the narrow way
finds us on a smooth, wide path heading toward the
downhill trend of fitting in with the wide-path crowd. King
David exclaimed in Psalm 119:97, "Oh, how I love Your law!
It is my meditation all day." Taking time to quiet your soul
and mind, and focusing attention on the Lord, will allow you
to hear his quiet voice with the answers and
encouragements you need. Daniel did this three times a
day, David did it seven times, and early church believers
prayed at specific times. Connecting to the Lord throughout
the day will keep our steps firm and on the straight and
narrow. (Psalm 119:164, 37:23; Acts 3:1; 10:9; Daniel 6:10;
Proverbs 3:6).

His commandments are not burdensome. 1 John 5:3

June 23

"The thief comes to steal, kill, and destroy." Do you see thievery in your life or the life of your family and friends? Are they being robbed of joy, peace, and Holy Spirit's leading? The enemy of God is pursuing them. Is death chasing you with sickness, accidents, threats, or thoughts of suicide and depression? It is the thief. Is your business, health, or future being destroyed? We cannot let this happen. John 10:10 says that Jesus came that we might have an abundant life full of joy and purpose. According to Merriam-Webster's dictionary, abundance means existing in large amounts or being amply supplied. Synonyms include plentiful, copious, crowded, bursting, and packed. There are Christians who push this verse into the Heavenly realm to be experienced after death. But that is not what this is referring to. It is declaring, "Thy kingdom come, thy will be done on earth as it is in Heaven." If you are accepting anything less, then it is time to tell the enemy that his plan and purpose for your life are over in the name above every name, the Lord Jesus Christ! With his blood, he purchased for himself a victorious church, full of the Spirit of God—the same Spirit who raised Jesus from the dead. The thief's days of killing, stealing, and destroying are over!

Our physical body mirrors our soul; a sick soul produces a sick body. Peace and joy produce health. Detox the soul, detox the body.

June 24

You cannot be a better Christian. You are a Christian, which means you are following him; you belong to him. Confession and repentance are not just for the beginning of your life with the Lord; they are about permitting God to intervene when we feel we cannot change, always recognizing our need for his forgiveness. Repentance is the greatest gift from God, a choice to stop displeasing him, turning to him wholeheartedly, and doing the opposite of the wrong we have been doing. It is visible–if change hasn't happened, then neither has repentance. "Therefore, bear fruit worthy of repentance" (Matthew 3:8). When the Lord looks at us, he sees us clean and forgiven. He smiles at the progress we are making. Babies do not walk the day they are born, and some of us are still toddling around, yet he smiles. He wants us to grow and calls us to spend time with the fertilizer and water of his word, the encouragements of his saints, and the refreshing of thanksgiving, praise, and worship. Look back and take joy in how far you have come! We stumble rarely, our words have more grace, and our focus is less on the world and more on the things of God. Quit being impatient and enjoy the journey of life; focus on Jesus, not on imperfections. Please enjoy your life. He paid for it!

When we can forgive others totally, asking the Father not to hold their sin against them and to bless them, then we are becoming like Jesus, and that pleases the Father.
Ricky Scaggs in *God Meant It for Good* by R. T. Kendall

June 25

A wise youth accepts his father's rebuke, a young mocker doesn't.

The good man wins his case by careful argument; the evil-minded man only wants to fight.

Self-control means controlling the tongue. A quick retort can ruin everything.

Lazy people want much but get little; the diligent prosper.

A good man hates lies; wicked men lie constantly and are shamed.

Some rich people are poor, and some poor people have great wealth.

The good man's life is full of light; the sinner's road is dark and gloomy.

Pride leads to arguments; be humble, take advice, and become wise.

Wealth from gambling quickly disappears; wealth from hard work grows.

Crushed hope makes the heart sick, but when dreams come true, there is life and joy.

Despise God's Word and find yourself in trouble; obey it and succeed.

A wise man thinks ahead; a fool doesn't, and even brags about it.

An unreliable messenger can cause a lot of trouble. Reliable communication permits progress.

If you refuse criticism, you will end in poverty and disgrace; if you accept it, you are on the road to fame.

Be with wise men and become wise. Hang out with evil men and become evil.

Curses chase sinners, while blessings chase the righteous.

A good man leaves an inheritance for his grandchildren; a sinner's wealth goes to the godly.

If you refuse to discipline your son, you do not love him; if you love him you will be prompt to punish him.

The good man eats to live, while the evil man lives to eat.

(Proverbs 13)

June 26

One of the major enemies of Christ is religion, because it is not interested in compassionately winning the lost, "being all things to all men in hopes that some may be saved," it is harsh, cruel, and tries to prove its own rightness. It persecutes and looks down on those who think and worship differently from themselves. It doesn't win converts; it uses manipulation and control to badger people, then, with fear and intimidation, traps them. It says, "If you leave us, you are going to hell. We are the only ones who will make the cut and get to Heaven." Its greatest tools are guilt and fear. Religion shuts the door on and locks out its thinkers and questioners; it hates to be challenged. Religion looks great on the outside; its rules and rituals make people feel good about themselves, but it avoids a relationship with God. Buried deep is guilt because religion cannot wash sins away and make one holy. Religion has its own Bible, and it is very thin. It is like two fathers living in the same house. One rules by the law, runs a tight ship, is cold, hard, and legalistic, has no joy; he never smiles. The other Father loves and enjoys his children, works on their character from the inside out, not from the outside in. He is warm, friendly, and full of peace and goodness. He runs out to meet the prodigal when he comes home from a failure, then throws a party in his honor.

Religion is now seen in unexpected places. The world political system has become a religion with all the earmarks of a cult. It will eventually demand your worship.

The Evil Kingdom

Satan has a three-fold cord: poverty, infirmity, and religion

The religious spirit hates joyful praise, opposes healing, and preaches poverty

Its worship is icy cold, somber, joyless, and unsmiling

It twists God's word to execute its own will and does not have the heart of the Father

Its only concern is money and power while looking piously righteous

Legalism, religion's offspring, is the narrow interpretation of God's law without its heart of love and mercy

Infirmity keeps us sick and running to doctors, our focus always on pain and fear

It leads the conversation with all things disease, sorrow, and loss

A spirit of poverty forever keeps us in the red, trying to catch up, shuffling bills and paying fees; never a break, in debt

God wants us to enjoy life! Break that cord of misery!

God has for us a "promise of entering his rest," which is not resting for a day, but an inner state of awareness. Hebrews 4 warns us that we should fear falling short of entering into this rest. "You can choose to hear His voice daily, do not harden your hearts. There is a rest for the people of God. For the one who enters His rest has rested from his own works, as God did from His." Paul is not telling the Gentiles to start following the law given to Israel to "keep the Sabbath day as an eternal symbol and reminder of the covenant between them." (Exodus 20:8, 31:12-17). Not working every day of the week is important to God; it shows we trust him. But "God's rest" is daily listening to him and submitting everything to him, rather than being agitated, worried, and stressed; this is an act of faith, not duty. It is being at peace, after our troubles, betrayals, and burdens are laid at his feet. The world may be in turmoil, but we can be at rest. Today, if you hear His voice saying, "Come to me right now, and I will give you rest," do it, and do it often.

I would not have known what sin was except through the law. Apart from the law, sin is dead. As a slave to sin, I do what I don't want to, and what I do not want to do, I do; it is the law of sin proving that the law is good. I delight in God's law, but my sinful nature is a slave. The law is powerless because of our sinful nature, but God sent Jesus to be a sin offering, so that the righteous requirements of the law might be fully met in us who live according to the Spirit. Thanks be to God, through Jesus Christ, I am rescued from the downward spiral of death! Romans 7 and 8

https://www.ou.org.
https://www.franknelte.net/article.php?article_id=208 What is 'The Rest' of Hebrews Chapter 4?
https://answersingenesis.org God's Rest in Hebrews 4:1-11

Day of Rest

Sabbath rest from work and hurry
Decisions, pressures, and worry
Forget obligation and technology
Be joyful with wonder, and delight
Enjoy the sun and nature's beauty
Call on friends, talk to family
Pretend there's no electricity
Light candles, play a board game
Stop, be still, centered, and let go
Focus on Father, Son, and Holy Ghost
Listen in the silence, do nothing
Contemplate, meditate, pray
Sing a Psalm, worship the Lord
Once a week, or three times a day

Rest

God worked for 6 days, then his rest began
We have worked for 6,000 years, our rest is coming
A thousand years of rest from enemies, evil banned
Jesus on his throne, ruling with a rod of iron
The number of man is 6, completion number is 7
New beginning number is 8
New Heaven, New Earth, we will meet Him at the gate!
Hebrews 4:3

June 28

Mormonism holds beliefs different from those of Biblical Christianity. It believes that god, who was once a man, came down and borrowed Joseph's fiancée to produce Jesus. Some Mormons believe that Jesus was married to Mary and Martha. They think that good Mormons will be gods áfter death, having many wives. They believe that Adam and Eve did not sin, that eating the forbidden fruit was a blessing, and that being driven from the garden was essential to mortality and to leading to exaltation. They believe that the queen of heaven is god's wife, and even if he does wrong, he is not wrong. They hold to the belief that Jesus and Lucifer were brothers. The Bible is considered valid if it is interpreted correctly; reading it is not encouraged. Mormonism is a false religion that puts burdens on its people and is selective about who can be in its temples. A Mormon must give tithes and offerings, attend their neighborhood ward, and be baptized for the dead, or they are excluded. Joseph Smith said that if you do not pay your whole tithe, you will burn at the time of the second coming. He also said that the Mormon church is the only true church, and all others are an abomination.

Without a "temple recommend," you will not dwell in heaven with the father; you will live in a lower kingdom. In their *Doctrine of Covenants*, "Abraham received concubines and had children, and it was counted unto him as righteousness." The Bible says that it was faith that made Abraham righteous. "The Lord commanded Abram to take Hagar to wife" (Doctrines and Covenants). That is not what the Bible says. Their way of life may look good on the outside, but it has many contradictions and non-biblical teachings. Reading the Bible will help shine a light on the truth for those who desire it.

They have a zeal for God, but not according to knowledge. For they, being ignorant of God's righteousness, have not submitted to the righteousness of God but seek to establish their own righteousness. For Christ is the culmination of the law so that there may be righteousness for everyone who believes (Romans 10:2-4).

https://www.utlm.org Utah Lighthouse Ministry

DOOR OF HOPE

He tricked me and brought me into the wilderness
It was to pull me out of my slumber
But he did not abandon me
He provided vineyards in the wilds
"Stay here, listen, I am bringing deliverance"
Suddenly, I see a way in the wasteland
Rivers running through the desert
Recompense for all that has been lost
"Ishi," my husband, "Achor," a door of hope
A pavilion in the valley of trouble
Psalm 27:5

June 29

Parents love it when siblings get along, and God loves it when his children get along. He loves unity. "Don't have anything to do with foolish and stupid arguments, because you know they produce quarrels; the Lord's servant must not quarrel; instead, he must be kind to everyone" (2 Timothy 2:23). "You desire but do not have, so you kill. You covet, but you can't get what you want, so you quarrel and fight. You don't have because you do not ask God. When you ask, you do not receive, because you ask with wrong motives, that you may spend what you get on your pleasures" (James 4:1-3). Jesus tells us to love our enemies. A man asked Jesus to settle an inheritance dispute, but he rebuked the man and exposed his greed. Paul urges us to accept being wronged or defrauded rather than sue one another (1 Corinthians 6:7). Jesus Christ has one Church; the walls of division must come down through the love we have for one another, for other denominations, and for the world's inhabitants. Paul condemned sectarianism, "For we are God's fellow workers; you are God's field, you are God's building" (1 Corinthians 3:9-23). "As much as possible, with everything in us, let us strive to stay in love, unity, and peace" (Romans 12:18).
(1 John 4: 20-21; Matthew 5: 21-23; Luke 12:13).

When a man's ways please the Lord, He makes his enemies be at peace with him. Proverbs 16:7

He can turn your enemies into friends.

June 30

Our Lord's Sermon on the Mount in Matthew 5, 6, and 7 starts by saying that he did not come to abolish the law but to fulfill it. He fulfilled the laws about animal sacrifices that covered the sins of Israel when he offered himself for the sins of the world. Jesus also says that if anyone breaks one of the laws and teaches others to do the same, they would be called the least in the kingdom of Heaven. He said that if your righteousness does not exceed the righteousness of the Pharisees and the teachers of the law, you will not enter Heaven. These were the greedy, controlling hypocrites who rejected Christ. So, a righteous saved-by-grace person who is off in his doctrine will go to Heaven, but the unrighteous person, no matter how pious or how high up in the church, will not. Righteous living for the Christian is important to the Lord. Do not be angry with your brother and call him a fool. Do not commit adultery by lusting after a woman. Divorce is to be taken seriously. Swearing comes from the evil one; say yes or no. Be gracious to those who attack you or want to sue you, or who force you into conscripted service–instead, when asked, give and lend. Love your enemies and pray for them. He tells us to give to the poor and to do these acts in secret. Don't pridefully pray in public to be seen for your eloquence. When fasting, don't let others know how miserable you are; just be your usual, cheerful self. Store up treasures in Heaven, keep your eyes from looking at evil, and don't live for and serve money. Don't worry about anything, and finally, don't judge, or you too will be judged. These are Jesus' words!

Enjoy people, even if you don't agree with their views. -Rick Renner

July 1

God tore the temple curtain leading to the Holy of Holies at the time of Jesus' death. Under the Old Covenant, only the high priest could enter the Holy of Holies. The priest could not be king, and the king could not be the priest. The priesthood began with Aaron, Moses' brother, and continued through his bloodline. Jesus was not of that bloodline; he was high priest and king through the lineage of Melchizedek. Melchizedek had neither father nor mother, was the "King of Righteousness and the King of Peace and remains a priest forever. He has no beginning and no ending. He is like the Son of God", which means he was not Jesus appearing before he was born (Hebrews 7:3). Who is Melchizedek? Perhaps Melchizedek is a physical representation of the Holy Spirit, who also took the form of a dove at Jesus' baptism. The Holy Spirit conceived Jesus, was raised from the dead by the Spirit, and as priests, the Holy Spirit and Jesus intercede for us. (Romans 8:26-27,34). Jesus is king and priest after the lineage of the Holy Spirit, God's eternal Spirit.

Jesus became a priest not by his ancestry but by the power of an indestructible life. He is a priest forever in the order of Melchizedek. Hebrews 7:15-17

July 2

"A living dog is better than a dead lion" because "as long as there is life, there is hope" (Ecclesiastes 9:4). On a podcast, two men discussed psychopaths who, they said, are people with little or no conscience, who lack empathy and guilt, and tend to be antisocial. The specialist didn't have hope for these people, saying they couldn't change. He said that the cause was either genetic or from trauma during childhood. But anyone who cries out to God can be saved, and a person submitted to the Holy Spirit's work in them can learn to love and care for others. Many YouTube videos describe how selfish and abusive these people are, saying the only choice is to separate from them. I have yet to find one that tells how we can help them overcome. Genetic damage or a traumatized soul is like a snake caught in a pipe that needs the power of God to shake it out. Bowing in humility to the authority of Jesus and then confessing to having a dysfunctional soul is the first step. Looking at issues from the past four generations may point to what needs to be renounced. Satan is a legalist, and without applying the blood of Jesus, he won't easily let go of who he thinks belongs to him. God's power is limitless; he created us, and he can re-create us. There are those whose conscience is seared and who will never choose salvation, but only God knows who they are (1 Timothy 4:2). "You are wrong because you do not know the Scriptures or the power of God" -Jesus (Matthew 22:29). As long as there is life, there is hope!

Heal me, O Lord, and I will be healed; save me, and I will be saved. Jeremiah 17:14

July 3

The Church, in Greek, *Ekklesia,* is not a walled fortress, a huddle of God's people, nor is it an impressive cathedral. It is a welcoming place of encouragement and ministry. In Acts 2, the Holy Spirit was poured out and drew people to Jesus from 12 countries, Jews, proselytes, Cretans, and Arabs. Three thousand were saved and added to the church, then they dispersed to their own nations where they listened to the Apostle's teaching, took communion, and prayed together. They provided for the needs of the poor and met in homes. The beginning of the church was marked by community, a deep feeling of connectedness, and love. We are the Ecclesia (church), a family, the house of God, the army of God, the body of Christ. We honor one another, each faithfully administering the gifts Jesus gives us, a corporate "one." Jesus prayed that we would be one as he and the Father are one. A church may have people of a different culture, age group, or music style that yours, but when you walk in, you will know it is family, that you are home. Community–Come unity!

The church or 'Ekklesia,' means a called-out assembly, a gathering for a purpose. It was a Greek term for when a body of male citizens made policy, heard appeals in public court, or took part in the election of chief magistrates. The Greek word 'kurikon' is related to the word 'kurios', meaning Lord, and 'kurikon oikia' means 'the Lord's house.' During the Middle Ages, it was shortened to 'kurkon.' West Germanic used 'kirika' and eventually Old English used 'cirice.' Old Norse used 'kirkja' and the Scottish, 'kirk.' We say church, but 'Ecclesia' is often used to broaden our perspective that the Church is a governmental entity and with Jesus Christ as the head, imposes his will and purpose on earth.
https://www.britannica.com/topic/Ecclesia-ancient-Greek-assembly

July 4

The progression of the Israelis after they departed from the slavery of Egypt began with the Passover meal, then the Red Sea crossing, 40 years of wilderness wanderings, battles, the Promised Land, and then many continuing skirmishes of victory and defeat. This was also similar to the beginning of the foundation of the United States of America. We began as slaves to a religious system, then escaped on ships sailing through the Atlantic Ocean. The wilderness time marked the end of one life and the beginning of another. Then came the battles, the Revolutionary War, and the Civil War, unsettling times of trials and testing. As individuals, we too follow this pattern. We leave the carnality of the world (Egypt), are baptized (Red Sea), and are trained for war. Our prayers, praise, and declaring the Scriptures are our weapons. We have leftover hidden hooks of Egypt in our souls that connect us to slavery with its smelly leaks and garlic. The Lord gives us a strategy to resist and win those battles. As the Lord continues his miraculous work of healing our history, we faithfully trust him. But we must not relax because the enemy is lurking about and will try every scheme to bring us down. Each day, we pick up the sword and shield and, with full armor on, we fight for truth, righteousness, and justice. "He will make your righteousness shine like the dawn, the justice of your cause like the noonday sun" Psalm 37:6. "Remember how the Lord your God led you in the desert these forty years, to humble you and to test you to know what was in your heart, whether or not you would keep his commands" (Deuteronomy 8:2).

I have come to bring fire on the earth, and how I wish it were already kindled! -Jesus (Luke 12:49)

July 5

Ezekiel had a vision of a river. The angel measured off a thousand cubits; it was ankle-deep. This is the faith of God's people to go where God sent them between 2000 B.C. to 1000 B.C. During this time, Abraham, by faith, obeyed and left his home, and Moses led his people out of Egypt to the Promised Land. The next thousand feet were measured, and the water was knee deep, a new demand on faith. This was the time of Solomon's Temple, and of the 17 main prophets. The people had to believe and obey the prophets. Malachi was the last one around 400 B.C. Israel did not heed the prophets, and they fell to the Greeks in 323 B.C., then to the Egyptians. In 204 B.C., Antiochus the Great of Syria captured Israel. He and his successor, Antiochus Epiphanes, persecuted the Jews and desecrated the Holy of Holies in 171 B.C. Then Jesus came, bringing his waist-deep water of faith, salvation through his shed blood on the cross. Then, around 1000 A.D., God began aligning the world to make ready for the culmination of all things (1 Peter 4:7). The next 1,000 years began with the Crusades, the Black Death, and then the printing of the first Bible in the year 1450. Mankind entered the Age of Exploration, the industrial Revolution, and two world wars. Then Israel was recognized as a nation in 1948. Now have all we need to have faith to be in the middle of the river, the faith to go where he sends us without the security of the riverbed under us, because we have God's promises, Holy Spirit, God's Ecclesia, and with full trust we can say, "Whether I sink or swim, I will believe you, God!" (Joel 2:28; Ezekiel 47).

https://www.gotquestions.org/400-years-of-silence.html. Got Questions. *What were the 400 years of silence?* January 4, 2022.

A Prayer

Pour out your favor, for you are our Savior
Rise up in fury, you are not bound
To save by many or by few
Fight for us now, come, do not tarry
You are the same, you never change
Please save us now, color the earth with your glory
We give you honor, for this is your story

Heaven

Heaven coming down, compressing the atmosphere
Demons going crazy, God's kingdom rising
It seems to be getting worse, but it is getting better
Evil's heyday, a clash of good versus evil cut short
The conflict is prodding people to repent
The invisible yet tangible Reformation is here!

Nations Under God

A nation has boundaries, faith, language, and history
A one-world government has none of those things
Only domination, control, poverty, and affliction
Obedience or prison, complaining means death
Thought crimes, word crimes, anarchy ruling
Guard the boundaries, keep the Faith

July 6

What is Wrong with the World?
G.K. Chesterton (1874-1936)

"Babies need not to be taught a trade, but to be introduced to a world. To put the matter shortly, woman is generally shut up in a house with a human being at the time when he asks all the questions that there are, and some that there aren't. It would be off if she retained any of the narrowness of a specialist. Now if anyone says that the duty of general enlightenment...is in itself too exacting and oppressive, I can understand the view. I can only answer that our race has thought it worthwhile to cast this burden on women in order to keep common sense in the world. But when people begin to talk about this domestic duty as not merely difficult but trivial and dreary, I simply give up the question. For I cannot with the utmost energy of imagination conceive what they mean. When domesticity, for instance, is called drudgery, all the difficulty arises from a double meaning in the word. If drudgery only means dreadfully hard work, I admit the woman dredges in the home, as a man might drudge at the Cathedral of Amiens or drudge behind a gun at Trafalgar. But if it means that the hard work is more heavy because it is trifling, colorless and of small import to the soul, then as I say, I give it up; I do not know what the words mean. To be Queen Elizabeth within a definite area, deciding sales, banquets, labors and holidays; to be Aristotle with a certain area, teaching morals, manners, theology, and hygiene; I can understand how this might exhaust the mind, but I cannot imagine how it could narrow it. How can it be a large career to tell other people's children about the Rule of Three, and a small career to tell one's own children about the universe? How can it be broad to be the same thing to everyone and narrow to be everything to someone: No; a woman's function is laborious, but because it is gigantic, not because it is minute. I will pity Mrs. Jones for the hugeness of her task; I will never pity her for its smallness."

To make one pound of honey, it takes 560 bees, 2 million flowers and 55,000 miles of travel. To make one godly man or woman it takes just as much work, but the result is so sweet!

July 7

There are six famous valleys in the Bible. In the Siddim Valley, a war broke out when four kings from the east attacked Sodom, Gomorrah, and three other towns. The eastern kingdoms captured and plundered the valley towns. Abraham rescued his nephew Lot, and all that was stolen was returned (Genesis 14:19). Then Sodom and Gomorrah were destroyed by fire; they were arrogant, gluttonous, haughty, and unconcerned; they did not help the needy and did detestable things before God (Ezekiel 16:49-50). Twelve men of Israel spied on the Eschol Valley and carried back heavy clusters of grapes. It was their first taste of the riches of the Promised Land, which they ended up not pursuing due to their fear of giants (Numbers 13). The Valley of Achor means trouble. It is where Achan took some of the forbidden loot from the Battle of Jericho. He tried to bury his sin but because the small army of Ai defeated Israel, his sin was discovered (Joshua 7). In the Valley of Elah, David killed Goliath, a victory for Israel (1 Samuel 17). In the Jezreel Valley, Jezebel helped Ahab steal Naboth's vineyard after having him killed (1 Kings 21). In the Valley of Jehoshaphat, also named Valley of the Son of Hinnom, meaning lamentations, and Gehenna, meaning grief, is where children were offered to Molech, and is the place of the final judgment, Megiddo or Armageddon (2 Kings 23:10; Jeremiah 19:6; Revelation 16). We have our own valleys of captivity, injustice, fear, sin, grief, temptations, failure, warfare, trouble, and judgment. The answer then and now is confession, repentance, faith, and courage.

Even though I walk through the valley of the shadow of death, I will fear no evil, for you are with me. (Psalm 23)

VICTORY!

Praise the Lord of Hosts who is victorious from coast to coast

Bind the thoughts and naughty deeds coming from evil hosts

Cancel hexes, vexes, voodoo; expose the cheater, thief, hacker

That conniving devil of deceit

No weapon formed will ambush the righteous crew

"Cease! Desist!" Judgment is coming

We push back against the gale. Justice will prevail!

The trap they craftily set, they are now caught in their own net

The Spirit cries, "Repent!"

Arise, Oh Lord, pick up your sword, deliver us today, we will obey!

CHANGE

Hurt enough, so you have no choice but to change

Learn enough so you have hope for change

Receive enough love, so you have the power to change

When your wound is not comforted

You have an inner torment of pain

Go for the root, forgive and be forgiven

July 8

Don Gossett's School of Faith teaches that to walk with God, we must agree with him (Amos 3:3). Our words can weary God (Malachi 2:17). Agree with God and disagree with the devil. Never say I can't (Philippians 4:13), I lack (Philippians 4:19), I am afraid (2 Timothy 1:7), I doubt (James 1:6), I am weak (Joel 3:10), Satan is more powerful than I am (1 John 4:4), I am defeated (Romans 8:37), I lack wisdom (James 1:5), I am worried and frustrated (Philippians 4:6-7), I am in bondage (2 Corinthians 3:17). If you speak the truth long enough eventually you will believe it. "I believe, therefore, I speak" (2 Corinthians 4:13). Faith believes, and faith speaks. Words work wonders or blunders. You will not rise above your own words. YHVH, Yehovah, is God's name in Hebrew. Y is Yod, meaning "in Him." Hei means "we live, we move." Vav means "and." In Him we live and move and have our being (Acts 17:28). We must agree with Him if we expect to live and move "in Him" (John 15:5-7).

Say what is good and true, and soon your thoughts and feelings will follow.

Biblical covenants mark the history of God's relationship with mankind. The first one was the Adamic Covenant. Eden and the Tree of Life were their provision; the commands were: be fruitful and multiply; fill the earth, subdue it, have dominion over every living thing. One law to obey, when it was broken, blood was shed to provide new coverings to replace God's lost glory covering. The sign of the Noahic Covenant was the rainbow; the command was to be fruitful and multiply. Blood was shed when Noah's family gave an offering to the Lord after leaving the ark. The Abrahamic Covenant was a blessing to Abraham's offspring, promising blessing to those who bless them and a curse to those who curse them. The sign was the ram caught in a bush sacrificed in place of Isaac–a test of Abraham's faith. The Mosaic Covenant set Israel apart through the priestly covenant, sacrifices, and God's laws. The Davidic Covenant emphasized worship; the promise was that his throne would last forever through a coming royal descendant. Jesus, fully God and fully man, implemented the New Covenant of Grace by shedding his blood, sealing the promise to all who would accept him as Lord. This covenant has stood for 2,000 years, and blood sacrifice is no longer needed to reinforce it. We are to "eat his flesh and drink his blood," by taking communion and remembering what he has done for us. "Is not the cup of thanksgiving for which we give thanks a participation in the blood of Christ? And is not the bread that we break a participation in the body of Christ? There is one loaf, we, who are many, are one body, for we all share the one loaf" (1 Corinthians 10:16-17).

A promise is a test until it comes true.

July 10

The church in Ephesus had some unique problems. Gnostic influences combined with the local Artemis cult, the belief that Eve, the power force and teacher of knowledge, was created and gave life to passive Adam. Paul addressed a particular woman in the church who was teaching that Eve was formed first and that Adam was the one who was deceived (1 Timothy 2:11-14). Notice in this chapter the difference between the word "women" and "a woman." This particular woman was told to keep quiet and learn the truth and to be in subjection to the governmental rule of the church. Paul says that this woman was not permitted to teach or have authority, she must be silent. This word "authority" in Greek is only used one time in Scripture and it means "dominate, usurp authority over" (#831 Strong's Concordance). "Let a woman learn in silence with all subjection" (1 Timothy 2:11). "Silence" here is the same Greek word used in 2 Thessalonians 3:12, "Such people we command and urge to settle down [to be silent]." This also can mean stillness or quietness or agreement. It is used in Acts 22:2, "When they heard him speak in Aramaic, they were all silent." It is not the same word as 1 Corinthians 14:34 "...women should remain silent in the churches," the word here for silent means "to hold peace." (Concordance #2271). "Then all the multitude kept silent [held their peace] and listened to Barnabas and Paul" (Acts 15:12). "But if there is no interpreter, let him keep silent [hold peace] in church [don't give a message in tongues if no interpreter is present]" (1 Corinthians 14:28). Women or wives were told not to interrupt in the church setting.

Deborah, the leader and prophet of Israel, led Israel into battle, and the enemy was defeated by a woman, Jael (Judges 4).

"Then Miriam, the prophet, took a timbrel in her hand, and all the women followed with timbrels and dancing" (Exodus 15:20).

https://www.margmowczko.com Adam and Eve in Ancient Gnostic Literature
Strong's entries: 5292, 1396, 5293, 5293 *Subjection, submission, slave*

RED LIGHT
Red light, green light
Simon says, dodgeball
Chutes and Ladders
Games for children
Watch for God's lights
To stop or continue
Do what God says
And you will dodge tragedy
Through all the ups and downs
You will score a 100!

Flying Standby
The plane was empty, a perfect opportunity
Police cars and ambulances all along the way
Coming to the checkpoint, my ticket is on my phone
I left the phone at home, drove back to retrieve it
Still lots of police and lights, feeling funny inside
Getting to the checkpoint, where is my phone?
I left it in the car! Walking the distance
Grabbing the thing, got on the empty plane
Made it to Los Angeles, pilots go on strike
Two full nights in airports, needing to learn a lesson
And listen!

July 11

There are many symbols and mysterious groups in Bible prophecy: the 10 virgins in two separate groups, those believers who are ready for him and those who are not, and the watchmen who give the cry, alerting them of the groom's arrival. Elijah and Moses (or Enoch) are the two witnesses proclaiming repentance in Israel, and the Jews who accept Christ after the rapture, kept safe in the wilderness of Jordan for 42 months. During this time, 144,000 servants of God from the 12 tribes of Israel will proclaim the Lord's salvation. Then saints, clothed in fine white linen, descend with Christ. "And then He will send His angels, and gather together His elect from the four winds, from the farthest parts of earth to the farthest parts of heaven" (Mark 13:24-27). He gathers his elect from three different places: the four winds–all the angels (Psalm 18:10; Hebrews 1:7 ESV); the ends of the earth–those who refused to bow to the evil ruler; and the ends of the heavens–the saints coming down on white horses. All will be gathered to see the victory of the Great King (Isaiah 11:10-12). In Heaven, we see 24 elders on thrones seated around God's throne, martyrs under the altar, multitudes of people standing on a glassy sea, and the angelic host of Heaven. The devil's kingdom is Satan the dragon, a wicked woman seated on a beast, a false prophet deceiving people into worshipping the beast, and the city of Babylon, the center of evil and corruption. After the chaos, Jesus establishes his earthly kingdom, as seen in Ezekiel 40-48. (Ephesians 1:9-10, 2 Thessalonians 2:1-2)

The most overlooked sign that Jesus is ready to catch up his church (the rapture), is that 'He might present her to Himself, the glorious church who will be without spot or wrinkle, holy and without blemish.' Ephesians 5:27. *He will come when the church is glorious, and he says we can speed up that process.* 2 Peter 3:12. *When He appears, we shall be like him...All who have this hope in him purify themselves, just as he is pure.* 1 John 3:3.

End time verses to study in the New Testament: Matthew 24; Mark 13; Luke 21; 1 Timothy 4:1-3; 2 Timothy 3:1-13; James 5:1-8; 2 Peter 3:3-13; 1 John 2:18-20,28; 1 Thessalonians 4:13-5:10; 1 Corinthians 15:35-58; Philippians 3:20-21; Colossians 3:4; Titus 2:11-14; Hebrews 9:27-28, 10:25,37; 1 Peter 1:3-7; 1 John 3:2-3; Jude 14-18; Romans 11:25-26.

WINNING
Take the initiative, the offensive stance
Instead of resisting doubt, vanquish it
Not repelling fear, conquering it
Not rejecting poverty, defeating it
Not just renouncing sin, subduing it
Overcoming the flesh, the world, and the devil
Pulling down the strongholds
Demolishing fortresses, go in for the win
Inspired by Dick Mills

July 12

Before day one, darkness ruled, the earth was formless and void, *tuhu-wa-bohu,* in Hebrew, means in chaos and empty–a wreck and a ruin. Then God said, "Let there be light; and the Spirit of God hovered over the face of the deep." Four thousand years later, the light of the world came to earth. Mary was with child by the Holy Spirit who hovered over the deep of her dark womb, and Father spoke, "Let there be light." And there was light—the light of the world. The Word became flesh and dwelt among us. "In the beginning was the Word [Jesus], Jesus was with God, Jesus is God, he is the Word of God. This same Jesus was in the beginning with God" (John 1:1). The true light came into the world, steeped in darkness. "Now the light of Christ is within us" (Galatians 4:19). Because Jesus passed the torch to us after his resurrection, he said, "You are the light of the world" (Matthew 5:14). "The night is nearly over; the day is almost here. So let us put aside the deeds of darkness and put on the armor of light" (Romans 13:12). Avoid doing the things that are against God's character.

Like the discordant elements of the primeval earth, because of our sin we, too, were without form, and void, and darkness covered us completely. Our discordant life took on form, shape, symmetry and beauty. -Dick Mills

July 13

Jesus cryptically said in the middle of his discourse on the end of time, "Where there is a dead body, the eagles will gather" (Matthew 24:28; Luke 17:37). Some translations say vultures, but the Greek word is eagle. "...Two women will be grinding grain together; one will be taken and the other left." 'Where, Lord?' "Where there is a dead body, there the eagles will gather." Translation from Greek: "...one will be taken because of intimacy in their relationship [with the Lord]. The other will be sent away and be left alone to cry for being forsaken and abandoned, but they can be forgiven." The disciples asked where they would be sent. The Lord answered, "Where the lifeless, fallen, dead body is, the one enslaved spiritually because of sin, the eagles will gather to deliver, protect, and heal. The body will be made holy and will endure and tolerate what is coming and will be permitted to receive a pardon and forgiveness." "And you were dead in your trespasses and sins" (Ephesians 2:1). This death is like Adam and Eve's, a spiritual death, "...for in the day you eat it you will certainly die" (Genesis 2:17). "...you have a reputation of being alive, but you are dead" (Revelation 3:1). "Then will appear the sign of the Son of Man in heaven...For as lightning comes from the east and flashes to the west, so will be the coming of the Son of Man." The flash of Jesus' coming will be seen for a split second at the rapture, and many will know what they have missed. This seems to be a message to those who must endure the tribulation and to the Jews who will escape to Jordan's desert (Matthew 24:27,30; Revelation 12:6). He continues by telling them that the persecution of those days, for those left on earth, will be followed by the darkened sun, moon, and stars. Then, at last, he will appear

in the clouds, and all nations will see him arrive with power and great glory, and the final gathering will take place (Matthew 24:29-31).
(Strong's 3880 *Taken*; 4430 *Carcass*; 4883, 4982, 5020 *Body*; 4863 *Gathered*)

Don't you understand this riddle of the eagles? The king of Babylon came to Jerusalem, took away her king and princes, and brought them to Babylon. He made a treaty with a member of the royal family and forced him to take an oath of loyalty, then he exiled Israel's most influential leaders so Israel would not become strong again and revolt. Keeping her treaty with Babylon helped her survive. Ezekiel 17:12-14. Fleeing to Petra will help the Jewish people survive.

BREAKTHROUGH

Intense times of war and disaster, days of tears, alarming news
Uprising among criminals, volcanic eruptions, fires, floods and fears
Trying to mask us again, then BREAKTHROUGH, be astounded
"Behold, I am doing a new thing." He is coming to save you!
He is coming with recompense! A surprise intervention
Trading sorrow and grave clothes for joy and festive liberation
Monumental and explosive JOY of the Lord, Justice Of Yahweh! Check Mate!
Fireworks and streamers, Mercy for an hour, believing is seeing, FREEDOM!
(Sept. 18, 2024, Joseph Z, Amanda Grace, Tim Sheets)

July 14

"You must be quick to listen, slow to speak and slow to get angry. Human anger does not bring about the righteous life that God desires" (James 1:19-20). Elijah was a forceful and fearless prophet whose faith was militant and amazing. Why then did he fearfully run from the threats of Jezebel after his victory against the prophets of Baal? (1 Kings 18:3). For whatever reason, fear gripped his heart, he fled to Mount Sinai, the same mountain where Moses had received the law and the first five books of the Bible. Moses was in a cave, and now so was Elijah; it may have been the same "cleft of the rock." They both experienced wind, earthquake, and fire, but God was not in these violent things. Instead, they heard a voice, to Elijah it was a still small voice-a whisper. Both men had anger in them. Moses struck an Egyptian and killed him, then, in anger, disobeyed and struck the rock. After the cave experience, Elijah's confidence was restored. They both began to understand something about God's character, that he is a God of grace and gentleness, and they needed to learn that lesson. "I am slow to anger and filled with unfailing love and faithfulness. I lavish unfailing love on a thousand generations. I forgive iniquity, rebellion, and sin. But I do not excuse the guilty." (Exodus 19:16-20; 34:6-7; 1 Kings 19:8-18).

He is not safe, but he is good. He is the king, I tell you! -Father Christmas in *Chronicles of Narnia*

July 15

Julia Bolton Holloway of the University of Colorado studied the history of Saint Patrick. She found that the earliest legends about his life held that his Jewish forefathers fled to Britain after Roman Emperor Vespasian and his son Titus led the campaign against Jerusalem, conquering it in 70 A.D. Patrick, in 387 A.D., was a rebellious young person who was sold as a slave to the Irish Chieftain Milchu. God convicted Patrick and spoke to him, telling him to escape Ireland and return to England to study the Bible. God then had him return to Ireland to be a minister in 433 A.D. While there, he trained a group of Irish believers who went to Iona, then to Scotland, to Holy Isle, then to Whitby. Druid paganism ended, and the Celtic Church thrived. During Patrick's time, 33 people were raised from the dead. He celebrated Passover, married, and had children. This was 200 years before Catholics came to Ireland. In 325 A.D., Constantine abolished the Passover, and in 665 A.D., the Whitby council submitted to pressure from the East, and the Celtic movement slowly died out. In 717 A.D., King Nechtan drove the Christians out of Iona. Now, satanism and witchcraft are popular in these isles. Catholic historians do not claim that he was Catholic. The Celtics had the New Testament church model. They had 24/7 prayer and praise for 200 years. The Valley of the Angels is in Bangor, Ireland, where Patrick had a vision of angels.

Miracles are not contrary to nature, but only contrary to what we know about nature. -St. Augustine

Information from teacher Robert Heidler from Glory of Zion Ministries https://stujakblog@wordpress.com *Vale of Angels*. By stujak74. March 23, 2016

July 16

Because the Lord said, "The evening and the morning" during creation week, the Jews always start their day at sundown the night before. Passover always occurs on the 15th of Nisan; it is always a full moon, and on the Essene calendar, it was on a Wednesday. "For as Jonah was three days and three nights in the belly of a huge fish, so the Son of Man will be three days and three nights in the heart of the earth" (Matthew 12:40). In Exodus 12, the Passover meal occurred on the evening of the fourteenth, the first meal eaten with unleavened bread. This would have been on Tuesday evening when Jesus ate with His disciples. That night, he was betrayed and arrested. Early on Wednesday morning, the decision was made (6:00 A.M.) to crucify Jesus. He was crucified on the 3rd hour (9:00 A.M.). From the 6th to the 9th hour, it was dark (12:00-3:00 P.M.), at the 9th hour, Jesus died (3:00 P.M.). Jesus hung on the cross for 6 hours, an hour for every thousand years from creation to the return of Christ. Joseph of Arimathea asked for the body and Jesus was buried on Wednesday night; this was the first night in the tomb. Thursday was day number one, a High Sabbath, the first day of the feast of unleavened bread, the day after Passover. Jesus could not have been crucified on that day; Thursday night was the second night. Friday (the Feast of Unleavened Bread) was the second day, and Friday night was the third night. Being a feast day, he would not have been crucified then either. On Saturday, Jesus rose at the end of the third day, before twilight (to make it exactly 3 days and nights, he would have risen at 3:00 P.M.). On Sunday morning the women came to the tomb, and it was empty. "The Son of Man must be delivered into the hands of sinful men, be crucified and on the third day be raised again" (Matthew 17:22-23, Luke 24:7). All seven feasts are Sabbaths, and it is an incorrect assumption that they are all celebrated on Saturday. There were two Sabbaths that week, and the women brought spices after the Sabbaths (Greek is plural), which would have been Sunday at dawn. Wednesday was the preparation day of the Passover celebration held on Thursday (John 19:14,31). They had to bury him before sundown on Wednesday, when the High Sabbath Day began on Thursday. The Feast of Unleavened Bread was on Friday, and the regular weekday Sabbath was on Saturday (Leviticus 23:3-8). "By the seventh day God had finished his work so he rested. He blessed the seventh day and made it holy" (Genesis 2:2). Jesus rose on the seventh day, on Saturday night before nightfall, and he rested from his work. John 2:19-21; 20:1; Exodus 12; Numbers 28

Tetelestai, It is finished. - Jesus (John 19:30). *This Greek word was spoken by a servant who was returning home after being sent out on a mission. The counterpart word in Hebrew was spoken by the high priest the moment the blood of the sacrifice touched the mercy seat. In the business world, this word was stamped on a debt that had been paid off. Jesus went back to his home after completing the mission of his blood being poured upon the mercy seat, and if we receive him, our debt of sin will be paid in full.*

https://renner.org/article/it-is-finished/ *It is Finished!* Rick Renner. 2025
https://www.bible-truth.org/WhatDayDidChristDie.html
https://christianity.stackexchange.com. Was Jesus Christ crucified on the 14th of Nisan?
See Josh Peck in the Bibliography for his book on the Essenes
https://thoes-sphragis.info/essene_passover_dates.html.

*If you disagree with this research, it does not matter. Please continue anyway!

July 17

The word "prodigal" in Greek means "wasteful extravagance" or "reckless." It describes behavior that lacks restraint, disregards consequences, is low in self-control, and is excessively indulgent. This is the son who asked his father to give him his share of the inheritance, not wanting to wait until his father had died. He then left his father's house to live a life free from rules and constraints. These are the ones who leave the heart of God and seek other ways to find happiness, living for this life rather than the next heavenly one. But it is also a beautiful picture of our Heavenly Father, who is waiting in anticipation for that one to return and say. "Father, I have sinned against heaven and against you. I am no longer worthy to be called your son." But what a glorious day! The angels in Heaven are rejoicing, the heavenly witnesses are cheering, but one person is not: the older brother. Here, this reckless son wastes Father's inheritance, yet is given his ring, his best robe, and shoes–and he, the good son, receives nothing. "I have slaved in the hot, miserable field for years. How dare this kid waste his inheritance on a vacation, then come home and expect a party!" The older brother is furious. He can't forgive. Father never gave him a party. He has served faithfully, and for what? He won't receive his inheritance for a long time. Father interrupts this older son's grumblings and tells him that he can have a party whenever he wants one, then invites him to the one occurring in the house to rejoice that a son who was dead is now alive. This is precisely how our Heavenly Father treats us when we come back home to him!

There are co-laborers, encouragers, mentors, teammates, and family in God's kingdom. -Pastor Landon Mauricio

"Step up to the plate, get ready to swing, expect to hit and be ready to run. The obstacles will be blocked, and I will bring you home. Soon, the game begins; it is warm-up time. You see how it works, you know the rules. Prepare yourself, train rigorously. Open your mouth, and I will fill it. Forget the past and lay aside the weights. Run with faith and focus on me. I need willing vessels whom I can clean up and polish and make ready for use." Kintsugi, or "golden joinery," is the Japanese art of taking broken pottery and repairing it with lacquer, then dusting the cracks with powdered silver, gold, or platinum. This highlights the piece's history rather than hiding it, often making it more beautiful and giving it a second life. Seeing beauty in the imperfect, regretting that something may be wasted, and accepting change are all Japanese ideas. They are also God's. We are made more beautiful when the Lord repairs our lives; he does not want them to go to waste; we must be willing for his loving process to make the changes in us. "To console those who mourn in Zion, to give them beauty for ashes, the oil of joy for mourning, the garment of praise for the spirit of despair; that they may be called trees of righteousness, the planting of the Lord, that he may be glorified" (Isaiah 61:3).

In the year King Uzziah died, I saw the Lord sitting on a throne (Isaiah 6:1). Isaiah received three visions: He saw the Lord in His majesty, He saw himself in his misery, and the world in its malady. Then he saw the answer. -Dick Mills

https://mymodernmet.com/kintsugi-kintsukuroi/

The Day of the Lord is mentioned 21 times in the New Testament. It is a day of judgment before the 1,000-year reign of Jesus on earth. "The great day of the Lord is near and coming fast, a bitter day of wrath, distress and anguish, of ruin and devastation, of deep darkness and gloom, a day of a trumpet blast and a battle cry. The stars and moon will not give out light, and the sun will be darkened. The pride of the cruel and the arrogant will end." Bible scholars believe that Jesus will return during the Biblical Feast of Trumpets, a two-day holiday in the fall. Jesus compares the end of days with the times of Noah. "As it was in the days of Noah, so it will be at the coming of the Son of Man. Days before the flood, people knew nothing about what would happen until the flood came and took them all away." The ark safely sailed away, and the others were swept away. Jesus describes himself as a thief in this event, where "Two men will be in the field; one will be taken and the other left. Two women will be grinding with a hand mill; one will be taken and the other left." "If the owner of the house had known at what time of night the thief was coming, he would have kept watch." "But you are not in darkness so that the day should surprise you like a thief" (1 Thessalonians 5:4). "Stay spiritually prepared, clothed in righteousness because in the twinkling of an eye you will be stolen away, my bride who has made herself ready" (Revelation 16:15 AMP, 19:7; 1 Corinthians 15:52; Zephaniah 1:14-16; Isaiah 13:9-11).

Time will tell the truth. Luke 8:17

https://www.openbible.info/topics/day_of_the_lord What Does the Bible Say About Day of The Lord?

July 20

"And this gospel of the kingdom will be preached in the whole world as a testimony to all nations, and then the end [of the age] will come" (Matthew 24:1-14). There are two "comings" of Jesus. The first will be like a flash of lightning when the dead in Christ rise and meet Jesus in the air, then believers who are alive rise to be "forever with the Lord" (Matthew 24:27). Soon after is the Second Coming when Jesus comes back to earth with his own and stands upon and splits the Mount of Olives. The Gospel will be preached until the very end of the age. This is not just the gospel of salvation but the gospel of the kingdom—a government being transferred to his shoulder. The late Reinhard Bonnke and now Daniel Kolenda have been reaching all of Africa for the Lord since 1967. There are more Christians in Africa than anywhere else. David Herzog travels the world and sees millions saved in his meetings. Christian broadcasting networks like Sid Roth's "It's Supernatural" reach many people worldwide. Marilyn Hickey and her daughter ministered to the Arab world; world evangelism is exploding. Are we getting close to Jesus' return? One last revival and awakening, a pouring out of God's glory, the early rains plus the latter rains, the church made ready! (James 5:7). We must work while it is day (John 9:4). We are "waiting for His Son from heaven, Jesus, who rescues us from the coming wrath" (1 Thessalonians 1:10). He could not judge Sodom until Lot had left; he could not send the rain until he had shut the door of the ark. We must preach to the Ninevehs of this world. "Know this, that in the last days a perilous, dangerous, stressful, violent time will come with furious and hard-to-deal with people." (2 Timothy 3:1; "perilous and fierce" Greek translation *chalepos*)

Abraham asked the Lord to save Sodom if there were ten righteous people in the city. Lot, his wife, his sons, daughters, sons-in-law, and daughters-in-law equaled ten people. Only three were able to escape; the other seven were not godly (Genesis 19:12-14). 'If you can find but one person who deals honestly and seeks the truth, I will forgive this city.' Jeremiah 5:1

Coming Home

I have sinned, I am not worthy
Make me a servant, I bow low before you

*Here is my robe; Here is my ring
A new pair of shoes to cover your feet
Now come, my son, let's party!*

Zephaniah 3:2 & Psalm 27:5

*Seek the Lord, all you humble of the land,
You who do what he commands
Seek righteousness, seek humility
Perhaps you will be sheltered
On the day of the Lord's wrath
For in the day of trouble
He will keep you safe in His dwelling
He will hide you in the shelter
Of His sacred tent
And set you high upon a rock.*

July 21

"Curiosity killed the cat," is what many of us were raised hearing. It kept children from wanting to know and do things that they shouldn't. But is it true? A desire to learn, explore, and discover comes from curiosity. A mind filled with nothing but technology and entertainment, without curiosity, becomes robotic. Break away from scrolling and notice details, wonder again about nature. Take a trip to the zoo, read the plaques at the museum. Care about the details. When with people, see them as the fantastic creation of God that they are. Ask them questions, listen to their heart. Ask God questions, wonder about him, his opinions, and his desires. Become intrigued by the stars, scientific discoveries, historical moments, and the heroes in them. The lack of curiosity killed the cat. "Amazement seized them all, and they glorified God and were filled with awe and said, 'We have seen extraordinary things today'" (Luke 5:26). "I praise you, for I am fearfully and wonderfully made. Wonderful are your works; my soul knows it very well" (Psalm 139:14). Thankfulness opens the gates of Heaven over us. Psalm 100:4

After three days, Jesus was found by his parents. He was sitting in the temple with the teachers, listening to them and asking them questions. Luke 2:46

July 22

"When you are about to go into battle, do not be terrified, or panic before them. For the Lord your God goes with you to fight for you against your enemies so you may have peace" (Deuteronomy 20:2-4). When you are dragged into court, Jesus said, "Do not worry about how or what you should speak; for it will be given to you in that hour what you should say; for it is not you who speaks, but the Spirit of your Father who speaks through you" (Matthew 10:19-20). What if this battle is against the unseen world? James says, "Resist the devil, and he will flee" (James 4:7), assuming you realize that it is the devil attacking. We experience problems because we never consider an unseen, demonic force as the cause. When strange ailments strike us, or we feel discouraged and depressed, it may be because we are unaware and ignorant. Say it aloud, speak submission to God, and then resist what is attacking. He is called the prince of the power of the air, so we must speak into the air to defeat him. We do this boldly, with confidence and faith, not faint-hearted or afraid, but with the authority that Christ purchased for us on the cross. When in war we are to pray as if there is no tomorrow, whether it is a literal war or a spiritual one, then you will begin to see miracles. You will realize that the two-edged sword, (one edge being God's word, the other, us repeating what he has said), is powerful and defeats what is keeping us in prison of bondage and torment.

Miracles effect people in two ways, they encourage faith and praise for those who love truth, but for those who don't, they are a source of skepticism and antagonism. The same sun that melts wax, hardens clay. -Dick Mills

Aggressively pursue healing. The Greek word for "salvation" is *Sozo*, and it encompasses the complete package of healing, health, safety, reconciliation, rescue, freedom, and eternal life. Salvation and healing go together: "He forgives all your iniquities and heals all your diseases" (Psalm 103:3). When Israel left Egypt after the Passover sacrifice of the lamb, there was not one feeble among their tribe. We take communion to remind us of this: Jesus' blood for our salvation, his stripes for our healing. Believe him, quote healing verses, take communion, and have others pray for you. "They will lay hands on the sick, and they will recover" (Mark 16:18). Believe that God does want His Heaven to be on earth, that he is the "Great Physician." There are no diseases, pains, clogged arteries, broken bones, gout, unusable limbs, or cancer in Heaven. They do not exist. If we know what God's will is, then it is easier to declare it to be so in our lives. He gave us authority over the works of the devourer when he died, and now we can crush these leftover snakes and scorpions, from the bothersome irritations to the major afflictions, and put them underneath our feet. "The word is near you; it is in your mouth and in your heart" (Romans 10:8). Craving is the lust of the flesh; submitting to it can affect health. The lust of the eyes darkens the soul, a spirit of pride damages the spirit and hinders God's Spirit (1 John 2:16). Time to be healthy in mind, body, soul, and spirit!

Jesus, the Bread of Life, said, 'Take, eat, this is my body.' He said that healing was his children's bread. He healed bodies, and he healed a wedding by turning water to wine; he healed lack by a coin found in a fish's mouth, and twice by filling a net with fish.

July 24

Jesus tells a parable in Matthew 20. "For the kingdom of heaven is like a landowner who went out early in the morning to hire laborers for his vineyard. He agreed to pay the laborers the usual wage of a denarius a day, then he sent them into his vineyard. He went out the third hour (9:00 A.M.) and saw others idle in the marketplace, and said to them, 'You also go into the vineyard.' So they went. Again, he went out about the sixth and the ninth hour (12:00 P.M. and 3:00 P.M.) and did likewise. And about the eleventh hour (5:00 P.M.) he found others standing idly by, and said to them, 'Why have you been standing idle all day?' They answered, 'Because no one hired us.' He said, 'You also go; work in my vineyard.'" At the end of the day, he gave each one a denarius, starting with the ones who were hired last. That angered those who had been there since early morning; they complained and felt cheated, calling it unfair. They wanted higher wages. The master made all of those men equal, those who had worked the hardest to the ones who worked for only an hour. The master reminded them of their agreement and rebuked them for their evil opinion of his goodness. Then Jesus said something confusing. "So the last will be first, and the first last. For many are called, but few are chosen." The last ones choosing to serve him at the end of times will be the first to be honored. Could the last ones be the ones snatched away before the tribulation, and the ones with the bad attitude, the ones left behind? The complainers are much like the prodigal son's brother, who hated that his brother came home to a party.

How is it that you don't know how to interpret this present time? - Jesus, Luke 12:5

July 25

We are called to be watchmen on the wall. In the Old Testament, these men stationed on the walls warned of dangers approaching their borders and announced when messengers were nearing the gate. God sometimes appoints us to intercede as watchmen. Have you felt an uncomfortable feeling that something is not right? That is a call to prayer. Do you wake up in the middle of the night, unable to fall back asleep? It is because someone, somewhere, needs your prayers. From 6:00 to 9:00 in the evening is a watch for meditation, unburdening, and communing about the day, praising the Lord and settling the soul (Lamentations 2:19). The watch from 9:00 to midnight is when God reveals to us the plans of the enemy (Psalm 119:148). At midnight, God deals with the enemy and gives us a strategy to overcome. (Acts 16:25-26). From 3:00 A.M. to 6:00 A.M. is when to acquire the authority for the new day (Exodus 14:24-25; Mark 1:35; Mathew 14:25; John 20:1). We, as servants of God, carry his burden for others. We remind the Lord of his truth and his promises, appealing to his heart of compassion. We stand in the gap against impending threats and crises, known or unknown, near or looming in the distance. We feel pain as if it were our own, their problems–our problems. It is most deeply felt in matters of life and death. "On my bed I remember you. I think of you through the watches of the night" (Psalm 63:6).

Watchmen are aware of the news, of what is happening in their own country and the world. Then they take what they have learned and present it to Heaven's courtroom to hand it over to the Judge of the universe.

(This is from a teaching from the Glory of Zion intercessory team) www.collegeofprayer.org. The Four Watches of the Night

July 26

"As I move more and more in your midst, the demands of my Spirit grow. I do demand of my servants obedience to my word, purity, and holiness. Compromised lives won't have the rush of my Spirit coming from them and flowing out to others. This is the day to be sober and watchful, seeking me wholeheartedly. My Spirit will not always strive with man; call on me while I am near, and I will show you great and mighty things you do not know. Advance my kingdom, I am calling out the guards, the troops, the watchmen, the eagles, and the scouts. Everyone has a place, a purpose in my army. The battle has been raging over souls and will become even more intense, but my violent ones will take my kingdom by forceful prayer and by their Spirit-led declarations, and the enemy's gates will crumble. Forge ahead, look up, your redemption draws near. Few will put aside the norm and step out into the unusual. Harsh judgers come and go but when my favor rests on my people, the mouth of the enemy will be shut. Battles can be fought in the heavenly realm over misery, pain, sorrow, grief, sickness, fear, troubles, and conflicts. One of you routs a thousand because the Lord your God fights for you just as he has promised. One word out of your mouth, 'Jesus,' has the power to defeat. For everyone who calls on the name of the Lord will be saved. Revival is coming. My people will experience great favor." (Joshua 23:10).

We walk in obedience and sometimes do not realize that our words are coming from him; it seems natural. We are not aware that the supernatural is taking place. It keeps us humble.

"The refiner's fire is burning hot among my people. It is to prepare them for what is at hand. Only vessels of righteousness will be filled with the new wine and the purposes of God. Worship will speed this process as will fasting, praying in tongues, and time spent with me. Time has come for the rattling of bones as they come together. Those outside of my communion will not see, hear, or be involved. The prophets must speak, they must hear; distractions must be few. Marching orders are already being handed out. Intensify, groan, weep, cry out, my burden in you to give birth to a new vision and purpose with boldness and faith. The youth are important; they are sparks that ignite the old and dry to burn up. Sacrifice, lay it down, receive your orders, and run. Prophesy to the nations, to leaders—I will lead as you read my word, watch, and pray. Turbulence causes ships to toss and roll. The work of my Spirit calms the storms and mends broken vessels. I have done mighty repair work in your life so far. You have submitted to my hand, and you have found joy in the knowledge that I restore what the enemy has tried to destroy. Be on guard against new attacks on you and your family. When the storms begin to brew, speak to them with my authority. When you see damage that has been done, with the leading of my spirit and with gentleness, mend and repair. I will lead you in this, for I have called my people to walk in health and to minister health to one another."

Don't be wise in your own eyes: fear the Lord and depart from evil. Turn your ears to my words, for they are life and health to your whole body and to your bones. Proverbs 3:7-8, 4:20-22

July 28

We have a built-in alarm system: inner red flags that alert us to danger, temptation, or evil. This sensitivity can be instilled into our children. Make them aware of a change in atmosphere when entering an evil place or a sudden physical pain. Ask them, "Do you feel that?" They need to know that there are consequences for disobedience and for ignoring red flags. This internal warning system is different than fear. The response to fear is in a different part of the brain, preparing the body to either fight, run, or freeze. We are told throughout scripture not to fear. Self-protection may keep you from obeying the leading of the Holy Spirit when he says, "Come, let us go on an adventure together!" When you feel a red flag, ask, "Is there something you want me to know or do right now?" He will let you know. Don't doubt the love and protection of the Lord, trust him! "You are my hiding place; you will protect me from trouble and surround me with songs of deliverance" (Psalm 32:7). "I haven't given you a spirit of fear, but one of love, power and a sound mind" (2 Timothy 1:7).

Learn; Unlearn; Relearn

https://www.smithsonian.com/science-nature/what-happens-brain-fear
https://my.clevelandclinic.org/health/body/24894-amygdala

Myth to bust: "God doesn't cause bad things to happen, he only allows them." What about these verses, "I form light and create darkness, I bring peace, and I create disaster; I the Lord, do all these things" (Isaiah 45:7). "If there is disaster in a city, has not the Lord caused it?" (Amos 3:6). "Take warning that your hearts are not easily deceived, and you turn away and serve and worship other gods, or the Lord's anger will burn against you. He will shut up the heavens so it will not rain, nothing will grow, and you will perish quickly from the good land the Lord is giving you" (Deuteronomy 11:16-17). "When your judgments are experienced on earth, the inhabitants of the world learn righteousness" (Isaiah 26:9). "Disaster comes from the Lord" (Micah 1:12). Twice, Jesus took a whip and drove the greedy moneychangers out of the temple. Deuteronomy 14:26 and Leviticus 14:30 allow poor people to buy doves for offerings or trade animals for silver instead of sacrificing them if the journey to the temple is too far. What it had become in Jesus' day was a fleecing of the people of their money, taking advantage of the poor, and making the temple more like an auction block of sellers and buyers rather than a place of prayer. Money became the focus, not God. God's justice comes from his heart of love; a land full of injustice is dangerous.

Devote yourselves to prayer, being watchful and thankful.
Colossians 4:2

July 30

Eve was not kicked out of the garden; Adam was, but she chose to follow him. God told her that her desire would be for her husband, and she walked out. It is in the choosing that we are hindered, not when tricked or deceived, but every trick or deception leads to a choice. The only two things cursed in the garden were the ground and the serpent. Adam and Eve suffered the consequences of choosing to believe the serpent. Satan tried to deceive Jesus, but Jesus made the right choices. Wrong choices affect our thoughts and actions and lead to death, a total separation from his love, his family, his heaven. Eve looked at the fruit and wanted its worldly wisdom. The sin you see and take in changes everything; it soils the soul. All have sinned, but not all will perish; those who believe that Jesus is God and who repent of past sins will be saved. To appreciate this good news, we need to know the bad, that hell is a real place. He wants us to choose him rather than eat from the tree of our desires. God does not want robots, so he gave us a choice. Choose his love. "Clothe yourselves with the Lord Jesus Christ, and do not think about how to gratify the desires of the sinful nature" (Romans 13:14). Jesus did nothing independently from his Father. He received instructions and never sought to do his own will or pleasure. He was God in action, and he taught us to ask our Father what we should do in every circumstance. (John 5:30).

We are made right with God by placing our faith in Jesus Christ. And this is true for everyone who believes, no matter who we are.
Romans 3:22

Sci-fi movies seem predictive. We are hearing disturbing reports: strange flying objects, the creation of new species, an uptick of natural disasters, and new weapons. Now we are flooded with sightings of UFOs (now UAPs). Does the Bible have anything to say about what is going on? In Genesis 6:4 and Numbers 13:33, we learn that there were giants, or Nephilim, in the land. They were a mixture of humans and fallen angels, created through some form of genetic manipulation. The Book of Enoch, mentioned in the Bible, has information about the mixing of genomes by the fallen ones. When more people report seeing Bigfoot, claiming to have been abducted, seeing flying objects, and other bizarre things, people will become either fearful or curious. Satan's end-time plan is to distract, deceive, and lure people into looking into his "deep secrets" (Revelation 2:24). Prophecy points to a time when God's people will be fooled into worshiping a false entity with power to perform miracles (2 Thessalonians 2:9-12). We must be aware of his devices (2 Corinthians 2:11).
(LA Marzulli on YouTube)

In 2013, Mark Armitage, a researcher and scientist at California State University, Northridge, discovered the largest triceratops horn at the Hell Creek excavation site in Montana. Under a high-powered microscope, Armitage found soft tissue on the sample. The biology department was shocked; he was fired. It was proof that dinosaurs roamed the earth only thousands of years ago, not 60 million years ago.

Lawsuit: CSUN Scientist Fired After Soft Tissue Found on Dinosaur Fossil. July 24, 2014. KCAL News).
https://cbsnews.com/amp/losangeles/news/scientist-alleges-csun-fired-him-for-discovery-of-soft-tissue-found-on-dinosaur-fossil/

August 1

It is interesting to look at the locations of the seven towns in Turkey whose churches received letters from Jesus in the book of Revelation. There were other towns with churches, but he chose these, and we can learn from them how to be and what not to do. They map the history of the Church both prophetically and chronologically. Each letter is addressed to those who have an ear to hear what the Spirit is saying to the churches, plural, those first churches and those throughout the ages. According to the historian Edward Gibbon, the early church gained between five and six million converts in a single generation. The gospel had spread to the whole world as Jesus had commanded, and the mythological pagan religion of the gods began diminishing.

The church at Ephesus was established by Paul, John, and Timothy; Mary, Jesus' mother, was also there. As predicted in Revelation 2:5, the lampstand of that first apostolic church in Ephesus was eventually snuffed out, and historically, the early church model ended in 325 A.D. It represents a church that had lost her first love.

Smyrna is now Izmir, where the apostle Polycarp served and was martyred in A.D.168. When told to renounce his faith, he said, "Eighty and six years have I served Him, and He never did me wrong, how then can I blaspheme my king, who[se] bath [baptism] saved me?" Thousands of Christians died there for the next 200 years. This church represents the persecuted church from the time of Diocletian to Constantine. The Turks captured it in 1424 and in 1922, killing most of the Christian population. Even though this Smyrna church had compromises, it still exists today and is the headquarters of several mission enterprises.

Pergamum, now buried under the town of Akhisar, was built and named by the Aeolian Greeks soon after the fall of Troy. It is one of the oldest cities in the world. It was built on a high hill and had natural defenses. It was an educational center and had the second-largest library in the world. Historically, it represents the 250 years of the imperial church, ruled by Emperor Constantine and ending with the reign of Justinian the Great, who made the popes the successors of the Caesars. It is a church marked by compromise, idolatry, and the exalting of leaders over the people.

Thyatira was a trade center and is the first of the letters to mention Christ's return. It represents the papal church, which continues to this day. This is the longest letter, a representation of the thousand years of church history.

Sardis was a wealthy city that crumbled into ruin. This church was overconfident and dead spiritually. Historically, it represents the reformation church of the 16th, 17th, and most of the 18th centuries, which began strongly but crumbled due to formalism and disunity. Until the time of John Wesley, many ministers in this established church are said to have been "drunkards and libertines and were among the lowest of people." The Wesley brothers, Whitfield, the Puritans, and the Pietists began to protest these actions, which led to the modern revival and missionary period, mirrored by the church in Philadelphia. "Wake up, or I will come like a thief...You have a few who have not soiled their garments; they will walk with me dressed in white" (Revelation 3:3-4).

Philadelphia, brotherly love, is now the town of Alaşehir, built by King Attalus of Pergamum for his brother. This church has little strength but depends on God. It is the

Church that sends out missionaries to establish God's kingdom, and it escapes the wrath of the tribulation time.

Lastly, Laodicea may be the most impressive church on the outside, but it is the most troubling on the inside. It has great wealth and pride; they need nothing, but the Lord says they are poor, blind, and naked. It represents the end-time church, which is interested in money and prestige. They are in danger of having to suffer through the time of tribulation.

If you do not repent, I will come to you and remove your lampstand from its place. Revelation 2:5

https://www.diggingfortruth.org/digging-deeper The Seven Churches Of Revelation. 2002-2025
https://www.khouse.org Koinonia House YouTube Channel

Words of Advice
You can change no one
When you change, everyone around you changes
Be the message before you speak the message
Forgive all authority, make restitution
Renounce ungodly beliefs
Show gratefulness to all who have helped you grow
Show them honor and respect

August 2

Giving goes against our lower nature; it is an act of leaving the earthly domain with its curses and coming into the heavenly domain with its blessings. Generosity produces supernatural miracles from God's hand. "Give and it will be given to you abundantly" (Luke 6:38). Those who lack need a generous spirit to avoid grasping onto the small amount in fear, like the servant who had one coin and buried it. For those who have an abundance, greed can be a problem, like the rich young ruler whom Jesus told to sell all and follow him. God had an amazing calling and gifting for that young man. What he would have received from the Lord would have been a promotion and an amazing destiny, but he had to go through the door of obedience, selling all and giving to the poor. He refused. What are you holding onto that the Lord is calling you to part with? What is your "precious"? In *The Lord of the Rings*, by J.R.R. Tolkien, it was a ring. What is God calling you to let go of? It may be an attitude, a false identity, a high-paying job, a character quality, a person who is hindering your walk, or a symbol of your self-worth. If something replaces our need for God, we will no longer depend on him.

Because your love is better than life, my lips will glorify you. Psalm 63:3

August 3

In Joshua 9, the Gibeonites, descendants of Ham's son Canaan, put on raggy clothes, packed moldy bread, and then proceeded to lie, telling Joshua that they had come from a far-off place to make a pact with Israel. Joshua believed them and agreed, but it turned out that the Gibeonites were indeed the enemies of God that Joshua was to drive from the land. Joshua was stuck. What could he do? He made these enemies of God their slaves. King Saul and his sons violated this covenant hundreds of years later by murdering some of the Gibeonites. He planned to kill them all. This brought a three-year famine upon Israel, which was atoned for when seven of Saul's sons were hanged (2 Samuel 21). Before we make vows, deals, covenants, pacts, or agreements, we need to seek God's opinion. This is much better than living a life of regret. Samson was another one who was defeated, like the strongest of Christians who ends up tempted by a woman, has an anger problem, a drinking problem, and ends up spiritually blind and a slave to sin. Joshua needed to investigate and pray before making an alignment. Saul should have honored that pact. Kings and the leaders of countries bring misery and destruction to their people with a simple signature. Pray for them! "I raise up kings, and I remove kings" (Daniel 2:21). "It is on account of the wickedness of these nations that the Lord is going to drive them out before you. It is not because of your righteousness or integrity" (Deuteronomy 9:4-6).

The Lord is with you as long as you are with Him. If you seek him, he will be found by you, but if you forsake him, he will forsake you. (2 Chronicles 15:2)

August 4

"Not one of all the Lord's good promises to the house of Israel failed; everyone was fulfilled" (Joshua 21:43-45). There are thousands of promises in the Bible. They aren't automatic; you must claim them like Israel claimed their Promised Land. You must read them, know them, then receive them aloud. Then you must fulfill your side of the bargain. If the promise is, "Trust in the Lord and you will be saved," then you must trust to receive the promise of rescue. Israel's stipulations to receive God's promises were to walk in his ways, obey his commands, and serve him heart and soul. Jesus made it simple: fall in love with God and love him more than anything or anyone else, and love others. Loving God is knowing him, his likes and dislikes, reading his book, sharing his burden, and having the same opinion. Loving others is carrying the heart of Father God, a heart of compassion and servitude. We can be this kind of person by spending time with him and letting his personality rub off on us. Promises given, promises kept!

'No weapon forged against you will succeed, and you will refute every tongue that accuses you. This is the heritage of the servants of the Lord, and this is their vindication from me,' declares the Lord. Isaiah 54:16-17

August 5

It will always take a step of faith to become parents. "Children are a gift from the Lord. They are a reward from Him" (Psalm 127:3). The responsibility of raising godly children can be overwhelming. In the Old Testament, very few righteous parents had righteous children. Good kings had corrupt offspring, and some terrible kings' sons brought redemption. Samuel, the first judge of Israel, had a pure heart and was the one God spoke to, but none of his sons served God. Prophet Eli was disobedient because he would not excommunicate his foul sons; he loved them more than he loved God. After the Ark of God was captured, Eli fell to his death. "The Glory has departed from Israel, for the Ark of God has been captured," are the last words of Eli's daughter-in-law as she gave birth, naming the boy Ichabod, which means "the glory has departed." Eli's passivity blocked his ability to make a difference (1 Samuel 4:22). We can make a difference by honoring God in our homes and by taking time to teach children how to have a relationship with Father God through Jesus and how to be Spirit-filled and led. Teach them that we serve a supernatural God who has the answers to all of life's problems. Discipline them so they learn to be self-disciplined. There are no limits to how much we can trust and believe God for, and godly children are one of them. "I will show you lessons from our history, ones handed down to us from former generations, to reveal truths to you so you can describe the glorious deeds of Jehovah to your children" (Psalm 78:2-3). "As a man disciplines his son, so the Lord your God disciplines you" (Deuteronomy 8:5).

The days of Ichabod over the church are coming to an end. The glory is coming back. -Nate Johnston

August 6

Our faith and unconditional love for the Lord will be tested; that is a promise. During those times when we feel abandoned, we are to pray more often, worship longer, and trust harder. In those times we wait patiently knowing that God has promised never to leave us, that if we keep hoping in him, we will not be disappointed (Isaiah 49:23). He may give us a dream, or show us a small cloud in the sky, or someone may call us out of the blue to encourage us (1 Kings 18:44). Those are the steppingstones God lays out to keep us moving forward. God's eyes are always on us, seeing if we have the faithful heart needed for his next great plan. "I will instruct you and teach you in the way you should go; I will counsel you with my eye upon you" (Psalm 32:8). Fight the good fight of faith, run the course; if you fight and run, you may win, but you will never win if you don't compete. Do not settle for the loop of the defeat of self-pity and grumbling, but believe for victory, healing, and freedom. Sometimes he will say, "It is done, the battle is over." Sometimes he will say, "Having done all, stand, and do not bow to the pressure of societal compromise" (Ephesians 6:13). Always trust, always hope, always praise, always fight!

Hebrews 13:5; Romans 5:5; 1 Samuel 3:1; 1 Corinthians 13:7-13

I lead, guide, and steer you as you move.

A NEW ERA

An era of the supernatural, a blitzkrieg of the Kingdom
Affecting the natural realms, swift strategic maneuvers
Activated through the Ecclesia to scatter lewd pollutions
Striking suddenly and boldly with your words and Heaven's armies
God's advancing kingdom, truth shall be their buckler
Demon doctrines by blind leaders shattered
The avalanche of evil plowed under
Original intent and order proclaimed
A renaissance of never-before-seen occurrences
A rapid, energetic strike, a concerted effort
Unique leaders ordained for the cause
God's word and angels tearing down strongholds
Enemies becoming unbalanced, staggering
Swift victories seen, not one promise will misfire
A supernatural church era. He never lies; how can we lose!
(From a word to Tim Sheets. Oasis Church Online 2/23/25)

August 7

John Kralik wrote an amazing book about hitting rock bottom at age 53. He was getting a divorce, was estranged from his children, and his law firm was failing. He lived in a tiny apartment where he froze in the winter and sweltered in the summer. He was forty pounds overweight, and his girlfriend broke up with him. His dreams of being a judge were fading. He had a thought one day that he should stop focusing so much on his misery and try to be grateful for what he did have. He had received a thank-you note from someone who had encouraged him, so he decided to start sending out thank-you notes, one per day, to everyone in his life, past and present. His life turned around. The book is *365 Thank Yous: The Year a Single Act of Daily Gratitude Changed My Life*. His life really did change. Gratitude is sometimes all we need for a breakthrough, not just for our circumstances, but for our character. "But I, with the shouts of grateful praise, will sacrifice to You; what I have vowed that will I do. Salvation comes from God alone!" (Jonah 2:9).

There are 38 parables of Jesus. Try to read one a week until you can understand what he is saying. There are 31 Proverbs, one for each day of the month!

Bless the Lord, O my soul, and do not forget his benefits. He forgives all your iniquities, heals all your diseases, redeems your life from the pit, crowns you will love and mercy, satisfies you with good things, so that your youth is renewed like the eagle's. Psalm 103:2-5

August 8

Andrew Klavin wrote the story of his life in *The Great Good Thing*. He was raised in a Jewish home where his father always told him that he was smarter than his teachers. This led to the wrong belief that he did not need to study or read any assigned books, even in college. He purchased every book he was supposed to read but didn't. He was only caught once for this by a professor; no one else noticed. One day, while lying on the floor, so sick that he could barely move, he moved his hand, and it touched one of the many unread books he had stacked around his small apartment. He read it. Realizing that he wasn't all that smart after all, he vowed to read every book he was supposed to have read, which he did. He went on to write nearly fifty books and was a screenwriter for Hollywood. He is also a believer in Yeshua. Andrew can now say, "I have more insight than all my teachers, for I meditate on your statutes" (Psalm 119:99). We cannot be proud and think we can't learn from others. The belief that we only need the Bible for our spiritual life is not true. The word of God is indeed our foundation, but the Lord wants to build upon that foundation, and he does it by using people, their sermons, books, essays, advice, gifts, and their failings. "You are our letter, written on our hearts, known and read by everyone, a letter from Christ showing the result of our ministry. This letter is written not with ink but by the Spirit of the living God, not on tablets of stone but on tablets of human hearts" (2 Corinthians 3:2-6).

Aladdin: *People like me don't get anything except by pretending.* Genie: *The more you gain by pretending, the less you will actually have.* (from the movie *Aladdin*)

August 9

Leaders cannot cave to criticism, death threats, fear-mongering, or hate. If you have a great need for the adulation and accolades of men, then step aside and be a follower. God wants people who do not care what others say or think of them, they are to care what God thinks. David's first "church" consisted of men who were outcasts, distressed, in debt, and discontent. It didn't bother him; he was happy to have people he could lead. They rose up against David and wanted to stone him after returning from a battle to find that the Amalekites had stolen all of their possessions, wives, and children. After expressing his grief, David prayed and received God's "green light" to go and take back everything and everyone that had been stolen. He didn't give up and quit (1 Samuel 30). Jesus taught us to be humble servant-type leaders who are willing to stoop down and get dirty for the sake of others. Leaders lead because they love and desire to protect people; God is always willing to help them. "Son of man, do not fear them or their words. Don't be afraid, even though their threats surround you like nettles, briers, and stinging scorpions. Do not be dismayed by their rebellious dark scowls; give them My message, whether they listen or not. Just make sure you do not join in with their rebellion" (Ezekiel 2:6-8).

The worst thing that can happen to a man is to succeed before he is ready. -Dr. Martin Lloyd-Jones

August 10

"'Not by might, nor by power, but by My Spirit,' says the Lord of hosts" (Zechariah 4:6). "Might" in Hebrew means military strength; our confidence is in the Lord who is in charge of angel armies. It isn't about the number of troops or the number of weapons; it is about whether or not a nation is trusting God. Our security is in God alone, and he is not bound to save by many or by few. (1 Samuel 14:6). "Might" refers to the army, whereas "power" refers to a superstar or superhero. He will, by the Spirit of God, empower a leader to do great exploits for him. Do you want to do great exploits for the Lord? It will first take time for the Lord to work humility into the soul. It will be a process. It will be worth it.

Warning: What is our motive for wanting divine power? Are we willing to have God's power yet work in secret, being an anonymous bearer of God's gifts? Are we willing to go anywhere in the world to any people group to minister with our gifts? Do we want to heal the sick and cast out demons so our ministry will be deemed "successful?" Jesus did not even promote himself while on earth; neither should we. Our purpose in asking God for his power is to bring him glory and to meet the needs of the suffering.

August 11

"I am bringing you to a wide space with a capacity for great things. Live by faith, not fear. I will provide for you and bring you through the valley to the mountain. Your offspring will be well watered by my Spirit, and their lives will reflect me and my will. My purpose will prevail. Forget the past, look ahead, and be expectant–joyfully expectant. The days ahead will test this, but be encouraged, they are short, and long are the days of my blessing. Do not fear the pestilence, do not fear because of troubled times. Look up, your redemption draws near. My plans are in order, they are exact, and you just need to hear my voice and trust my guidance. Let the enemy mock, for it will not be long before he cowers and flees because of the power of My might. Just as I led the Israelis, I will lead you. Praise me every step of the way. The Promised Land is up ahead. Do not give way to groaning and complaining. The present sorrows are temporary compared to the glory that will be revealed. I am coming soon, and my reward is with me. Perfect love casts out fear; there is no fear in love, and no expectation of punishment. If you fear, you have not been made perfect in love." 1 John 4:18

I will say on that day, 'Thank you that I did not get my way!'

August 12

Socialism became a new faith in 1825. A Welsh industrialist and philosopher, Robert Owen, had a utopian idea. "Human nature could be molded." He bought 30,0000 acres in Indiana from a group of hardworking German Lutheran Separatists who had established the town of Harmonie in 1814. Owen had in mind an experiment: he implemented equal rights, equal education, equal social status, equal personal wealth, and made everything free in New Harmony. The thousand who volunteered for this experiment didn't have the skills necessary for even the smallest tasks. Anarchy reigned, and the farms and workshops weren't utilized. The people didn't like standing in line for salad, and some with harder jobs than others became embittered and quit working. His own sons couldn't endure the rundown town and left. In 1828, Robert moved back to England, and the property was divided among five of his children. They hired scientists who made the town successful. It is now a tourist destination. Fairness means that there are consequences for actions. Receiving something you don't deserve is not fair. Socialism is not fair; it leads to corrupt leaders and conquered citizens. The movie *The City of Ember* is a perfect example of this.

We tend to take Jesus words and turn them into object lessons because they seem unfair. 'Turn the other cheek. If you are forced to go a mile, go two. Do good to your enemies.' But 'To the weak I became weak, that I might by any means possible save some.'
Matthew 5:39-41; 1 Corinthians 9:22; Psalm 9:8; Isaiah 33:14-17

https://www.britannica.com. New Harmony.

August 13

In 167 B.C., under the rule of Antiochus Epiphanes, it was decreed that all people convert to the pagan Greek religion. Mattathias Maccabee, a Jewish priest, refused to offer pagan sacrifices to Zeus on God's altar. He killed the Jewish man who was about to do this abomination. Judah the Hammer, Mattathias' son, rose up with an army, defeated this Syrian enemy then cleansed and restored the Temple service on December 14, 164 B.C. According to the Talmud, this is when the oil in the menorah kept burning for eight days on a one-day supply while the Jews prepared more of this sacred oil. This is the birth of Hanukkah, the Feast of Dedication that Jesus celebrated. His Hanukkah message is in John 10:22-38, after which they tried to seize and stone him.

The Jewish nation has two menorahs. One has seven branches and was placed on the south side of the Holy Place in the Temple in Jerusalem. It was made of pure gold and represents the seven-fold Spirit of God and the seven churches of Revelation (Exodus 25:31-40). The Hanukkah menorah has eight branches with a holder for the taller 'Sammash' or the 'servant' light which lights the others, this servant light is Yeshua. Solomon put a ten branched candlestick in the temple he built, which was not after God's instruction. Ten represents judgment (1 Kings 7:49). After the first temple was destroyed, a single golden candlestick was used in the second temple (1 Maccabeus 1:21), and according to Josephus, a single candle was also placed in Herod's Temple (Josephus, BJ, V, v, 5).

https://www.biblicaltraining.org/library/the-golden-candlestick The Golden Candlestick
https://www.britannica.com/topic/menorah menorah. May 9, 2025

August 14

Lessons from Jack Frost (1952-2007) on love: The United States culture is guilt-based, with many having the identity of unworthiness. The Eastern European culture is empty of family love. The Asian culture is shame-based, with the belief that they are flawed, unworthy, and undeserving of love. It is performance-based; many strive for perfection, seeking to feel deserving of God's and others' love, while fearing failure and rejection. Communist countries have no emotion or affection. Adults in our flawed world demand respect because that is all they think they deserve. A wound is created at the point of a lack of love or an unmet need. Pain seeks pleasure and becomes a substitute for love. Hidden death wishes can create diseases and cause the body systems to shut down. Love heals and brings deliverance. People need 12 touches a day through eye contact, tone of voice, and touch, all to communicate love. Babies learn to believe, have faith, and trust by having their needs met. An unborn baby receives the mother's emotions. Exchanging false identities with the truth of what God calls you is the road to healing love. Know thyself and know God, receive His love and acceptance!

Frost, Jack. *Experiencing the Father's Embrace*. January 1, 2002.
Standford, John Loren. *Healing the Nations*. 2000

You cannot make a list of how a man falls in love. It is not a scientific process. Neither is becoming a Christian. These are both relational. 'Depart from me, I never knew you.' It isn't a series of thoughts or principles but a mysterious relational dynamic. - Don Miller

August 15

History: In the beginning, let there be light–4000 B.C.
Enoch taken up, Noah's flood–2500 B.C.
Abraham was born, then Moses–2000 B.C.
King Saul, David, and Solomon–1000 B.C. (Israel recognized as a nation).
Yeshua (Jesus)–3-6 B.C.
The Crusades; Vikings become Christians and discover America–1000 A.D.
Israel reborn with Jerusalem as its capital–1967 A.D. or 6,000 years after creation.
After 6,000 years, Jesus rules on earth, and we enter the "Day of Rest" for 1,000 years. "A day is like a thousand years." (2 Peter 3:8). "Now after six days Jesus took Peter, James, and John, and led them up on a high mountain and He was transfigured before them" (Mark 9:2). Notice it says after 6 days. This is a prophetic sign that after 6,000 years, the Lord's kingdom would come to earth with power. He takes a remnant of his disciples up the mountain, a type of the taking up of those ready for his return.

There are 6 different Herods in the New Testament. Herod the Great: the Christmas story. Herod Archelaus, son of Herod the Great: Joseph goes to Nazareth instead of Bethlehem because of him. Herod Antipas, another son of Herod the Great: Jesus called him "the Fox." He had John the Baptist killed. Herod Phillip the Tetrarch, another son, ruled north and east of Galilee and married the daughter of Herodias. Herod Agrippa I, grandson of Herod the Great, put Paul in prison and was eaten by worms when he didn't give God the glory. Lastly, Herod Agrippa II, son of Herod Agrippa I: tried Paul and said, "In a short time you will persuade me to become a Christian" (Acts 26:28 literal translation). Jesus warned us of the leaven of Herod, which was fear that he could instill as a political leader through persecution. He also warned of the leaven of the Pharisees: pride, unbelief, greed, and lack of mercy (Mark 8:15). Jesus said, "Go tell that fox [Herod Antipas] that I will keep on casting out demons and healing people today and tomorrow; and the third day I will accomplish my purpose" (Luke 13:32). At the beginning of the third day, or soon, Jesus' purposes will be accomplished.

https://www.icr.org/content/when-did-noahs-flood-happen
https://www.biola.edu/blogs/good-book-blog/2014/how-many-herods-are-there-in-the-BibleHow Many Herods Are There in the Bible? Kenneth Berding. March 3, 2014

Jesus died on April 3, 30, and He rose again around twilight April 6, 30.
https://www.gotquestions.org/three-days.html On what day was Jesus Crucified? March 29, 2024

SEEK, ASK, KNOCK

Seek first His kingdom, be righteous in speech, thought, and deed
And you will find
Ask, for you have not yet asked, ask for revival, for the Bread of Life, for your friends, ask for justice
And you will receive
Knock at the Judge's door, knock at your Friend's door
It will be opened
He is knocking at your door too

August 16

"Freely you have received, freely give," and teach what you have learned. We attend school for 12 to 16 years or more, then think we are incapable of homeschooling our children or taking a leadership position? Our entire life is full of moments of training, every conflict, every challenge, every embarrassing moment, and every failure. We are leaders, beginning with small assignments or small babies. "Do not despise the day of small beginnings for great will your future be." One day, the small will no longer be small. God is working behind the scenes, like in the book of Esther. He is not mentioned, but he took a Jewish orphan girl and had her save a nation. She became a leader with very little training. He uses young and old, "Do not say, 'I am only a child.' You must go to everyone I send you to and say whatever I command you...Today I appoint you over nations and kingdoms to uproot and tear down, to destroy and overthrow, to build and to plant." (Jeremiah 1:7-10; Zechariah 4:10; Matthew 10:8)

Mother by C.S. Lewis

With my mother's death, all settled happiness, all that was tranquil and reliable, disappeared from my life. There was to be much fun, many pleasures, many stabs of joy, but no more of the old security. It was sea and islands now; the great continent had sunk like Atlantis.

August 17

What was sealed in the book of Daniel, Jesus opens up in Revelation 6. First, a spirit of conquest on a white horse is released to achieve world domination. It will cause division among people with differing worldviews and a loss of freedom. One group will welcome this government, and one will be decerning of its nefarious plans. The opening of the second seal exposes the consequences of this evil rule: wars, death, and more division. The horse is red from the bloodshed. War brings famine, seal number three, a dark time of lack. Division between neighbors and communities escalates as starvation drives people to pillage. Death follows famine, and hell follows death. This is seen in the opening of the fourth seal, where sword, famine, plague, and wild beasts cause much loss. This is the worst division, the one that separates people from hope. The fifth seal reveals a multitude of martyrs. Finally, the earth and the heavens divide with a mighty earthquake from the pressure of the innocent blood that has been spilt upon it. There will be 42 months of suffering from man's evil destruction, then 42 months of God's wrathful response. (Daniel 8:26; 12:4).

There have been five earthquakes of 9.0 or greater; two occurred in the last 18 years, and all five occurred since 1948. In 2011, a 9.0 earthquake knocked the Earth off its axis by 6.5 inches, changing the Earth's rotational speed and shortening the days. At least five are mentioned in Revelation.
(Russia-1952, Chile-1960, Alaska-1964, Sumatra-Andaman Island-2004 and Japan-2011).
https://www.livescience.com/largest-recorded-earthquakes-in-history By Tia Ghose. January 27.2023
https://www.iflscience.com/in-2011-a-magnitude-9-0-earthquake-shifted-the-earth's-axis

Psalms 12 and 13

Help! The godly are disappearing, the faithful have vanished
Neighbors lie to each other with flattery and deceit
"We will lie all we want, who can stop us?"
"I will, says the Lord, I see the violence,
I hear the groans of the poor
I will rise up and rescue, as they long for me to do."
His promises are pure, like silver refined seven times
He will protect the oppressed from this lying generation
They strut around as evil is praised in the land
Answer me, O Lord, restore the sparkle in my eye
Give me peace before I die, I will trust in your love
I will sing praises to you, because you are good to me

August 18

Confession is not an apology; it is telling the truth about what has happened. Transformation does not come from saying I'm sorry over and over again. Telling the truth about what you really believe about God, yourself, and others brings transformation. When you tell him the truth, then he can change your reality with his truth. He already knows your heart, but the heart needs to be exposed for God to do his amazing work of bringing us into freedom, emotionally, socially, and spiritually. Knowing and embracing the truth releases freedom (John 8:32). Hiding and covering keeps us in bondage to lies and excuses. Confession activates repentance, the power to believe, think, and act in a new way. Tell him when you feel afraid and insecure. Secrecy and shame is Satan's foothold, bringing those thoughts and past wounds into the light by confessing them to God and to another trusted person brings freedom. If these statements trigger a response in you, then they have a hold on your core beliefs, "I'm not good enough," "Nothing will ever change," "I'm stuck," "God will never use me," "I'm alone," "I'm a failure," "I am unlovable," "I am rejected," "I can't be saved," "God can't help me." It is time to silence these negative voices. Take time with the Lord, confess these beliefs, then write what God says to you about them. Ask him often, "What do you want me to know right now?" "Show me where I am not living in truth." (Lessons learned from Living Fearless by Jamie Winship)

> *It is for the purpose of freedom that Christ has set us free.*
> *Galatians 5:1*

August 19

Passover, the beginning of the Jewish year, mirrors the outer court of the Temple where the sacrifices were offered, and the laver for washing was. This represents salvation through Jesus' death and water baptism. The lamb's blood saved the Israelis from the death angel then they traveled through the parted Red Sea. Three months later was Pentecost, represented by the Temple's Holy Place, where the Bread, the candlestick, and the incense were located. This symbolizes God's provision in Scripture, the body of Christ, prayer, and the Holy Spirit. The Feast of Tabernacles celebration occurs in the seventh month and mirrors the Temple's Most Holy Place, where the Ark and the glorious presence of the Father resided. This holy day celebrates the fact that God tabernacles, or abides, with his people. The priest entered the Holy of Holies on the Day of Atonement to sprinkle blood on the mercy seat to atone for the sins of Israel. We are able, because of the blood of Jesus and his righteousness covering us, to enter our holy times with him. Many believers in Yeshua stay in the outer court; they have accepted the sacrifice of Jesus to atone for their sins and have been baptized in water. The Holy Place is for the pursuers of truth; they read the word, are filled with the Spirit, go to church, and pray. But the Most Holy Place is where we are the ark of God's presence, inside of us the Bread of Life, the constant light of the Holy Spirit, and a heart of worship; it is the Holy Place where we meet with Him! The three parts of the temple of God resemble the process of our redemption: body, soul, and spirit!

Come into the Holy of Holies, enter by the blood of the Lamb.

August 20

El Olam is God's name meaning Everlasting God. He is the God of eternity who deals with the past, controls the new, and takes us into the future. He put eternity in our hearts, an awareness that there is something beyond death (Ecclesiastes 3:11). This brings people to Christ, a hope that this is not the end, that there is purpose and meaning to life. Awakening this hope in someone will revive a desire for God and for Heaven to be true. We do not convict, convince, or badger an unbeliever. Sometimes we plant a seed, sometimes we water, and sometimes we reap the harvest (1 Corinthians 3:6-9). We are to save some on their deathbed, as from the very flames of hell, and others with kindness, hating their sin while being merciful to doubters (Jude 22, 23). The reasons people reject salvation are: a hard, unrepentant heart, rebellion, ignorance, not mixing the truth of the word with faith, hurt, and offence from the church or parents. These hearts can be softened by hearing and seeing the truth through a believer, or through a near-death experience, a tragedy, signs and wonders, conviction, or a prayer that says, "I don't know if you are real, but if you are, I want to serve you. Please reveal yourself to me." The Lord does not want any to perish! (Romans 2:4). I became a follower of Jesus in Sunday School in 4th grade because the teacher spoke about hell. "Let your speech be gracious, seasoned with salt, that you may know how to answer each one" (Colossians 4:6). This does not mean salty speech, which is rude and caustic, but speech that makes people thirsty for Jesus.

Whoever is not with me is against me, and whoever does not gather with me scatters. -Jesus, Matthew 12:30

August 21

There are 7 mountains or pillars of society: family, government, health, business, science/technology, education, and arts/entertainment. Most people put religion as one but "In the last days the mountain of the Lord's temple will be established as the highest of the mountains; it will be exalted above the hills, and all nations will stream to it" (Isaiah 2:2). "I will bring them to my holy mountain and give them joy in my house of prayer" (Isaiah 56:7). His holy mountain is here and now. Churches are either part of the business mountain or part of the Mountain of the Lord, depending on what motivates their hearts. True believers are on the Lord's mountain, but they will also be a part of one they serve, bringing Christ to every part of society. "Go and make disciples of all nations, baptize them, teach them to obey me; I will always be with you even to the end of the age" (Matthew 28:19-20). Some will be involved with more than one mountain because of the many gifts God has placed in them. Many will go to the highest places on a mountain, taking away Satan's authority and rule, transforming it to reflect God's kingdom. God will open doors and give you access to where he needs you; go through those doors without feeling insecure or fearful. Be bold and confident, and support those who are already at the top.
(YouTube, The Lance Wallnau Show).

Wisdom has built her house; she has hewn out its seven pillars.
Proverbs 9:1

August 22

Have you heard the phrase about an elephant in the room? It refers to a controversial topic no one wants to talk about. We are told not to discuss politics or religion; the problem is that this elephant keeps getting larger, and soon we are unable to talk and are forced to be isolated from one another. It is up to God's people to make a difference through prayer and getting involved. We haven't realized that politics and religion greatly affect every mountain of society. We must make sure our children receive a godly education so they can pursue careers wherever the Lord leads them. If we do not have a vision for improvement or an aspiration for change, then we will lose the culture as a result of the hands-off doctrine. A few years ago, hundreds of homeschool parents gathered to present arguments to a panel of local lawmakers aiming to outlaw homeschools. We argued as to why homeschooling is a viable means of educating children. These lawmakers were not engaged; they were on their computers, looking down, not paying attention to the arguments. At the end of the many-hour-long meeting, the panel conceded. Outside, a reporter asked one of the politicians if that was the end of the matter. He replied that, even though they had publicly conceded, they could still outlaw homeschooling. God's kingdom is counter-cultural; we are called to be "a city on a hill" so our God-light of goodness can shine. As leaders, we need to speak up and reveal the emperor's nakedness and his "new clothes," breaking the spell of evil idiocy.

Be careful to live properly among your unbelieving neighbors. That even if they accuse you of wrongdoing, they will see your honorable behavior (1 Peter 2:11-12).

August 23

Years ago, a man had a dream. He saw a cliff lined with people, with large gaps between them; they faced inward toward a crowd of people coming toward them. Some on the line were shouting warnings, but hordes of people fell through the large gaps and went over the cliff. I have listened to stories from people who had been entrapped by cults and, by the grace of God, were able to get out. But they voiced how they couldn't understand why their Christian friends never warned them or revealed to them the truth. They felt betrayed because they were now well aware they had been heading for a cliff. It doesn't matter if they seem to be listening, it doesn't matter if they reject you as a friend, what matters is that when truth is spoken, it goes deep into a person's soul, and it stays there and does its work. "So shall my word be that goes out from my mouth; it shall not return to me empty, but it shall accomplish that which I purpose and shall succeed in the things for which I sent it" (Isaiah 55:11). "Therefore, my beloved brothers, be steadfast, immovable, always abounding in the work of the Lord, knowing that in the Lord your labor is not in vain" (1 Corinthians 15:58).

"With man this is impossible, but with God all things are possible." Matthew 19:26

August 24

The Lord Jesus was misunderstood by his people when he came to earth. He healed the sick, performed many miracles, and they assumed that he would then overthrow the Roman government. They may have remembered Isaiah 9:6 that says the government will rest upon his shoulders. "Of the increase of His government and peace there shall be no end." There is no end to the expansion of his healing-kingdom on earth. It is invisible to the world, but for those who are looking, they will see it. His involvement in our realm is greater than we can imagine. We see from Israel's history that it was the rulers who determined whether the people would leave idolatry to follow God. He has been involved in removing rulers and putting others in their place (Daniel 2:21). He sends his hosts of Heaven out to aid in the battles of war (Psalm 91:11). His involvement is seen in the Old Testament where he stopped the sun so God's enemies could be defeated (Joshua 10:13). He gave out battle plans, he surrounded the enemy with angels, he caused Israel's enemies to fight among themselves, the list goes on (2 Kings 6:8-17). His kingdom is increasing because his people are connected to him, the head of the church, the King of kings, Lord of lords, not in the sweet by and by, but now! "The earth is the Lord's and the fullness thereof, the world and all who dwell therein" (Psalm 24:1).

I have given you authority to trample on snakes and scorpions and over all the power of the enemy; nothing at all will injure you. Luke 10:19

August 25

"Do my will, and I will bless you. You are a warrior, and you will step on people's misconceptions. Don't worry about what they think. You are a spearhead for my Bride. You will cut a path, and others will follow. As a spearhead, you will also have to be the one to do the 'piercing through'. You will pierce through strongholds, principalities, powers, opinions, and others' self-righteousness. Be strong and keep hold of the vision that I have birthed into your heart and proceed with hope." If we endure this hour, no matter how heavy our hearts or how dark our moments, if we can remain calm and quiet though the world crashes around us, being secure in the knowledge that God loves us, if we can keep believing what we know in our heart to be true; that darkness will fade with the morning, then we will have won the battle, finished the race, and will hear, "Welcome my faithful one, you have done well" (Matthew 25:21). Entering into God's rest is like being in a bubble of peace and joy.

Weeping may endure for the night, but joy comes in the morning. Hallelujah for the dawn, Hallelujah for the day! Psalm 30:5. Expressing grief is not complaining if you know that the one you are crying out to is hearing your sorrow, that he is a good Father who cares.

Strongholds

Evil tries to control, seeking to preserve its own devious life

Attaching like a parasitic plant to the soul of man

This entity blocks thinking; confusion takes over when its host gets too close to the truth

It changes the subject, twisting words like the leviathan that it is, pushing suicide, drugs, and sin

When deception becomes threatened, the evil spirit lashes out with denial, flight, distractions, humor, threats, yelling, feigning death–anything to protect its cover

The swirling of the mind, tunnel vision, blinders, not able to see outside the narrow, dark perspective, indecision

Strongholds nullifying God's word to make it irrelevant, "Nothing to do with me!" It says

This hook latched to a demonic stronghold blocks and binds the mind, a muddle, then madness

This is spiritual warfare–be rid of the thing, oust it, plead the blood of Jesus, confess, repent, get help

Be free so the inner soul can be healed, now thinking straight, emotions settled, and seeing the truth

August 26

"Love covers a multitude of sins" (1 Peter 4:8). This challenge is for a person who is sensitive and easily offended. Hurt may turn into offence, which leads to a heart of unforgiveness. We could be living with wounds from our childhood that have restricted our progress. Ask the Lord to show you where the wounds have come from, then tell him how they make you feel, then forgive and release them to him. We forgive with our words, not to a person, but to the unseen world. Say it, "I forgive so-and-so for the hurt they have caused. My love is covering their sins right now. I will not be offended. I submit to God and his forgiveness. I resist the devil, his accusations, pain, and lies. In Jesus name." Say it often, and your emotions will line up and, poof, the hurt will be gone. You may not even remember the incident in years to come. Don't resist this process, or you will become hardened, and your ears will be shut to God's voice in your life. Having a hard time receiving God's forgiveness for yourself could be because you have not forgiven someone else. We need to stop our minds from falling into the vicious cycle of reliving conversations, fantasizing about vindication, or our own clever arguments where we always win. Tell your mind to stop and ask the Holy Spirit to help. When encountering these trials of hurt, unfairness, injustice, mistreatment, or abuse, some shake their fist at God and become bitter victims. Let the love of God enable you to live in freedom from the chains of woundedness.

'Peace be with you! As the Father has sent me, I am sending you.' And with that, he breathed on them and said, 'Receive the Holy Spirit. If you forgive anyone's sins, their sin are forgiven; if you do not forgive them, they are not forgiven.' John 20:21-23

A test to see if you have forgiven:

1. You want to keep the offense against you a secret.
2. You desire to protect the one you have forgiven.
3. You make them feel at ease, like nothing ever happened, and the relationship is fixed.
4. You do not want the person to be angry with himself or to be afraid of you.
5. You make it easy for him to forgive himself.
6. You don't demand respect or act superior because you were hurt.
7. You know that God will work it out for your good.

A common denominator in a fraction math problem is where the bottom number, the denominator, has a shared multiple of several fractions. Fractions in Christianity always have the same common denominator of believing in and accepting the Lord Jesus Christ as the only way to salvation through the gift of his blood sacrifice, confession, and repentance. All denominations of Christianity have that in common: they are fractions, not factions.

August 27

Traditions can be dangerous because they can replace a desire for a relationship with God. Jesus was confronted by Pharisees and teachers of the law because his disciples were eating food with hands that had not been ceremonially washed. They wanted to know why Jesus' disciples did not live according to the traditions of the elders. He replied from Isaiah 29:13, "These people honor me with their lips, but their hearts are far from me. They worship me in vain; their teachings are but rules taught by men." He told them that they were discarding the commands of God for the traditions of men. He rebuked them for taking money that would have supported their parents and giving it to the temple instead. Then Jesus told the crowd that nothing a man eats can make him unclean; it is what comes out of a man that makes him unclean. "For out of the heart come evil thoughts, sexual immorality, theft, murder, adultery, greed, malice, deceit, lewdness, envy, slander, arrogance, and folly." Jesus is declaring a new angle to the law; it is what comes out of the heart that makes us sinners. (Matthew 15:11). "Rise, Peter, kill and eat!" The Lord spoke these words to let Peter know two things: He was changing the laws about food, and the unclean Gentiles could be saved (Acts 10).

Pharisees were the self-righteous teachers of the law and traditions. The Sadducees did not believe in the afterlife, the resurrection, demons, or the observance of traditions. They emphasized the written law alone. The Essenes expected the Messiah's soon-coming, had strict rules, believed the prophecies about the Messiah, and are regarded as the authors of the Dead Sea Scrolls. -Josh Peck

August 28

Jesus is the one and only true vine, and Father God is the gardener. The gardener looks at the branches coming from the vine; if they do not bear fruit, they are cut off. If they bear fruit, he prunes them so they can become more fruitful. We do not belong to the world, and if the world loves us, it shows us that our allegiance is to the world and not to the Lord. Have you noticed that when celebrities declare their allegiance to Jesus, they are no longer popular but are instead slandered? Jesus prayed, "Holy Father, protect them by the power of your name–the name you gave me–so that they may be one as we are one." Are there parts of your branch that have been corrupted by believing and living a lie, or by a corruption in your generational family tree? "And even now the axe is laid to the root of the trees..." (Matthew 3:10). God's axe can destroy the roots in us, even the genetic roots of cancer, alcoholism, stroke, heart attack, emotional disorders, addictions, or any other inherited negative trait. We inherit a thousand generations of blessings but only three or four generations of defects. Say this, "I lay the axe to _____ in my family line. I claim freedom in Jesus name." After we have been pruned, we are transplanted, we "shall be like a tree planted by rivers of water." All things becoming new, believing the truth of who you are according to what the Lord says you are!

From this day forward, I will bless you. Haggai 2:19

"JESUS!"

Invoke His majesty, authority, character, and excellence,
The name of Jesus is not a formula for success or a good-
luck charm
But a power for the demolition of God's forever loser
And his dastardly killing, stealing, and destroying deeds
Soon, the impious hosts will bow down in humiliation
Before the King and Lord of all, acknowledging their forever
loss
The loss at the cross, at the resurrection, and on the day of
judgment
The blood of Jesus carries no sin, defect, or frailty
The pouring out of perfection, washing away our
imperfections, our defects, human frailties, healing our
bodies
Restoring our souls, awakening our spirits
His blood is at our disposal, like a dynamite explosion
Destroying evil's fortresses, blasting them to pieces
Our enemy on the run, his kingdom in chaos
Jesus' blood–a powerful weapon flowing through our veins

Inspired by Dick Mills

August 29

God has ways to keep us on the right path by permitting limitations or disabilities. Some people feel disabled because they are not great at debating or arguing and struggle to find the right words to say; they feel voiceless. Be grateful even for those limitations, "a thorn in the flesh" (2 Corinthians 12:7-10). Keeping opinions to yourself helps you avoid saying things you should not and helps you focus on what others are saying. Then, when you do speak, you will know it is the Lord speaking through you. Convictions are deeper than opinions, and when deep-seated beliefs are challenged, anger erupts, hindering the discussion of truth. It is being adamant about one's own rightness. People may experience a feeling from the demonic realm, convincing them that their belief system is true. "Even Satan disguises himself as an angel of light" (2 Corinthians 11:14). Philosophical and religious ideas have turned many from Truth. Asking questions is a disarming way to broach subjects that may otherwise trigger an angry response. Simply ask, "Do you believe Jesus is God? What do you think about Isaiah 9, 'For to us a child is born, to us a son is given, and the government will be on his shoulders. Will he be called Mighty God? Jesus said, "If you have seen me, then you have seen the Father, the Father and I are one" (John 10:30, John 14:9-10). Even in weakness, with limitations and disabilities, sometimes without knowing we are doing it, we plant seeds of truth. Holy Spirit takes it from there.

August 30

Habakkuk had two complaints and asked God eight questions. He was deeply troubled by the injustice and destruction that were invading Israel, paralyzing the blessings of the law. He accused God of not listening to his prayers. God answered, saying that he was sending a mighty army to execute judgment upon Israel. Habakkuk was upset by this and questioned God about sending a nation against Israel, who were even more wicked than they were. The Lord spoke a prophetic word about the end times we are entering. He first emphasized that the righteous will live by faith, then described an antichrist figure whose plan would be to enslave all peoples by his evil plots and endorsement of crime. The Lord revealed his plan to pour out his cup of vengeance on an evil empire. This judgment is because of the violence done to Lebanon, the purposeful destruction of animals making food scarce, the shedding of blood, and the destruction of lands, cities, and people. But God promised Habakkuk that the earth would be filled with the knowledge of his glory. He was given a vision of the future, much like what John saw in Revelation. He saw God's final deliverance and decided that he could be patient after all. "The Lord is in his holy temple; let all the earth be silent before him" (Habakkuk 2:20). He asked questions, and God answered. We must do this type of listening prayer. Don't be afraid to ask him questions; God will answer, and he can handle your emotional outbursts.

"Faith is the certainty that He is in control and will do all He has promised." Hebrew 11:1

August 31

What is the difference between prayer and talking? Prayer always refers to communication with God. When we pray, we are talking to God. Why is this important? We do not pray to angels, but they can bring answers to prayer as seen in Acts 12:5-10 and in the book of Daniel. They guard us (Psalm 91:11; Luke 4:10), help us win people to Christ (Acts 8:26; 10:3), are given to children (Matthew 18:10), talk to us, and we can talk to them. We can entertain angels and not even know it. This word "entertain" in Greek means to be a host or lodge a guest (Hebrews 13:2). Zechariah asked questions of an angel, and the angel asked questions of him (Zechariah 1; 2; 4). It is important to follow their directives. Zechariah, John the Baptist's father, did not believe and lost his voice for nine months (Luke 1:11-26). Angels give instructions (Acts 8:26; 10:7,22) and are in submission to God (1 Peter 3:22). Even though we do not pray to angels, we are allowed to talk to them. Angels are messengers, and sometimes we can see them, whether in their majestic form or in a human form, but most of the time they are invisible. "Are not all angels ministering spirits sent to serve those who will inherit salvation?" (Hebrews 1:14) Daniel 10, 11; Revelation 5:11-12; 14:6; 12:22; Psalm 103:20; Job 38:7

Daniel faithfully served under five kings in the two kingdoms of Babylon and Persia. He was taken as a slave from his homeland, taught the pagan religion, was persecuted by the other administrators of Babylon, and was tossed in a lion's den. He prayed three times a day and taught the magicians the prophecies God had given him. Five hundred years later, the Magi from the East read Daniel's work, and when they saw the star, they knew the king had been born. They gave Mary and Joseph gifts that provided for them for several years. Daniel's faithfulness blessed Jesus five centuries later.

The gospel of the kingdom will be preached in the whole world as a testimony to all nations. Then the end will come (Matthew 24:14). *The church has this responsibility first, then when we are removed, two witnesses from heaven take over, and the whole world will see them prophesy for 3 ½ years* (Revelation 11:3-13). *The sealed Jewish 144,000 will be the evangelists for a time* (Revelation 7:3-4; 14:1). *Right after the evangelists are raptured, when no one is left to preach, the angels will fly though the skies declaring the gospel, 'Then I saw another angel flying in midair, he had the eternal gospel to proclaim to those who live on the earth–to every nation, tribe, language and people. He said in a loud voice, 'Fear God and give him glory, because the hour of his judgment has come. Worship him who made the heavens, the earth, the sea, and the springs of water'* (Revelation 14:6-13).

Angels

Michael, a warrior angel, God's mighty one, the great prince
Gabriel, a chief messenger, an interpreter sent to Daniel
Hosts of Heaven, ministering spirits, watching over children
Encircling those who fear Him, guarding, guiding, warning
Millions in joyful assembly, "Holy, holy, holy,
The Almighty, who was, and is, and is to come."
At the end, proclaiming the eternal gospel
To every nation, tribe, language, and people
At God's right hand–angels, authorities, and powers
Around the throne saying, "Worthy is the Lamb, who was slain, to receive power, wealth, wisdom, strength, honor, glory, and praise!"

Isaiah 53

Who will believe this message? Those whom God reveals it to:

He grew up like a tender shoot coming from dry ground
He wasn't particularly attractive, so we didn't desire him
He was a man of sorrows, deeply despised and rejected
We considered his suffering to be coming from God
His afflictions, punishments, and wounds, we ignored
But he did it for us! He carried our infirmities and sorrows
He was pierced for our sins, crushed for our iniquities
He was punished so we could have peace and be healed
We all have gone astray; all our iniquity was laid on him
He was silent during his affliction as he was arrested,
Falsely accused, then deemed guilty; He was crucified
He was not violent or deceitful, quite the opposite
But it was God's will to crush him and make him suffer
He was a guilt offering, justifying anyone who would choose Him
He poured out his life, choosing to be counted as a sinner
Bearing the sin of many, he now intercedes for us
He is the greatest and has the name above all names.

September 1

"Seek his face" is in the Bible dozens of times. "Face," Hebrew #6640 in Strong's Concordance, gives the idea of seeking the Lord's favor, having his face turn toward us in acceptance, and to consider our enquiries. Holy Spirit is the Spirit of God, and he is as close to us as our breath. How should we live knowing that God sees our thoughts and motives? "Those who feared the Lord communed with each other, and the Lord listened to what they said" (Malachi 3:16). We must seek his favor, his forgiveness, his pleasure; it will not be long before we will see him face to face.

The only way we sometimes come to feel the presence of God is when God Himself pulls the rug out from under us, and we begin to fall. Then we cry to Him, and possibly for the first time we feel God. God wants us to feel Him. -Dr. R.T. Kendall

CHURCH

We weren't meant to be in a boat, alone, in the middle of the ocean
Our first defense against isolation is our earthly family
The second line of defense is the family of God, the church
Hard to grow alone, the enemy loves to pick off outliers
Those with no attachments or defenses, those who feel rejected
Those whose beliefs are not founded on the solid word of God
God's will is that everyone is connected to a healthy family
Daily contacts, weekly gatherings, constant encouragement
Even more now that we see the Day of the Lord approaching
We need each other; it is time to join a community of believers!

September 2

Alexander Dumas' *The Count of Monte Cristo* is a French tale of a humble man horribly betrayed by his friend and by a government leader. He is thrown into the worst of prisons and is able to escape after thirteen years with the help of a God-fearing priest. The priest gives him a map to a treasure, making him the wealthiest man in the world, and he plans to get revenge. The 2002 film beautifully depicts the moment when he comes back to faith in God and releases his anger and unforgiveness. He does get revenge, not by killing, but by exposing the crimes of the three men who ruined his life. In the end he realizes that God had saved him from prison, and his family and friends saved him from the prison of his traumatized soul. Forgiveness and peace are so much sweeter than vengeance. Is there anyone you would not want to see in Heaven or to receive God's forgiveness and blessing on earth? If you imagine them on their deathbed and have no heartfelt love and forgiveness, then you must seek God to help you forgive. Forgiveness is a decision, not a feeling. It is not saying what they did is right, but it is handing over the job of repaying what is deserved to the Lord. It is releasing yourself from the disease of bitterness. Look at forgiveness as an offering to the Lord, a sacrifice pleasing to Him. When you forgive, He smiles. "Do not be conquered by evil, overcome it with good" (Romans 12:21).

There is a pain that comes from betrayal and rejection. It is the hurt Jesus felt when Judas betrayed him with a kiss, one who sat at the Passover table, took the bread, and drank the cup. It is also the deep sorrowful pain of Jesus, who knew Judas' future regret that kiss would bring.

September 3

For six days, God created and said, "It is good." On the sixth day, after creating animals and man, he said, "It is not good." What was not good? That man should be alone, so he created a woman. How could God say that Adam was alone since they had each other? Man needed his own kind; one he could continue the creation process with (Psalm 102:18). Woman was never alone; when she woke up, God and man were there waiting for her. Solomon said that a threefold cord is not easily broken (Ecclesiastes 4:12). The word in Hebrew for "alone" also has the meaning of "divided fibers," as in a flaxen thread or yarn–a separated threefold cord. Brokenness occurs when we are alone. The Father, Adam, and Eve were that cord until a serpent sneaked in and spoke defilement against the Father. The cord split apart. This threefold cord is seen in the relationship between Father, Son, and Holy Spirit. It is not good to be alone. We weren't created to escape into a cave to avoid having relationships with others. We were created to face pitfalls and trials together with a team. Pray that God will send you a team member, then with God, the cord will be strong.

'For the Lord is our Judge, our Lawgiver, and our King; He will save us.' This is the model for our three branches of government. (Isaiah 33:22).

September 4

Write down your dreams, ask the Lord if they are significant, then ask him to help you interpret them. God has gifted certain Christians with the ability to easily understand the meaning of dreams. Here are a few guidelines. Most dreams will be for you personally unless God uses you to minister to others. Many dream symbols can be found in the Bible. If you see the sun, it could represent God, judgment, fatherhood, or healing, all symbols found in Scriptures. God uses dreams to guide, warn, or bring comfort and hope. Seeing your child fall off a cliff shows what is happening with him, then seeing the child safely land on an outcropping reveals God's protection and rescue. Numbers and colors are significant. A basement represents the soul, and an attic the mind; the backyard or a rear-view mirror is the past; the front yard is the future. Teeth, or lack of them, can represent our faith or maturity, our ability to chew the meat of the word. Animals, jobs, vehicles, buildings, people, relatives, trades, directions, and even metals have meanings. You may not understand your dream in the morning, but if you write it down, pray or confer with a friend, the meaning may become clear, or it may be for future times. The fact that you remember a complicated, detailed dream is a sign that it could be from the Lord. The interpretation usually has a simple, clear meaning, but we can make it too complicated. Turn a dream of warning into a prayer for God's protection. Reject and renounce dreams from the copy-cat enemy inciting terror, bringing defilement, or violating God's character. *Understanding the Dreams You Dream* by Ira Mulligan

When the flesh is in control, the spirit is drowning. Do you have drowning dreams?

September 5

"He raised us up together with him and seated us with him in Heavenly places in Christ Jesus" (Ephesians 2:6). Heavenly places are our position and access to his authority over the kingdom of darkness. Jesus' mission was to destroy the works of the devil; now we have that mission and privilege. "He canceled the charges against us by nailing them to the cross. And having disarmed spiritual authorities, he shamed them publicly by his victory on the cross. You have died with Christ, and he has set you free from the spiritual powers of this world" (Colossians 2:14-15). Jesus took authority away from Satan and put it into our hands. We must believe this transfer of power occurred, or we will live a defeated life with the devil not under our feet but us under his. Ignorance of our dominion will keep us powerless. Battles are never won by taking a defensive stance; we must be on the offensive. We are told to battle our thoughts, taking them captive to the obedience of Christ, and to destroy lofty arguments and opinions and bring them under his Lordship. The word captive means "at the point of a spear." Diligently war against those thoughts with the truth of God's spear to avoid the enemy's destruction (Joshua 1:8; 2 Corinthians 10:5).

Watch out for that which is programmed by man who has turned against God and who is trying to reprogram you.

September 6

"There is a kind of preparation that cannot be found in a university or theological seminary. It is not necessarily found in gaining more experience. It is a specific education God sovereignly ordains for our purpose. It drives us to our knees in surrender and humility. The task to which we are called is unique; therefore, the preparation we need will also be unique" (Dr. R.T. Kendall). This includes the Lord's chastening. When God puts his finger on you, things may get worse before they get better. The training comes suddenly and unexpectedly, and our world is shattered; we are at the bottom of a pit, unable to climb out. Since the "heart is deceitfully wicked above all things," we may think we are in great shape when in truth, we are not. We think we have forgiven but still justify self-pity and personal hurt. Part of the Lord's preparation is to deal with those types of personality defects. We put the blame on our parents for what we have become, but God desires to remake us; we must forgive our parents. God's promise is that all things will work out for the good if we love him, which includes our upbringing, no matter how bad it was. God made you unique, and he has chosen you. Since God can work all things together for good, he can take your history and the dumbest things you, your parents, and your children have done and make them turn out right (Romans 8:28; Hebrews 12:6-12).
(Lessons from *God Meant It for Good*.)

Trials, sorry to say, do not end until we are trial-free in Heaven. They get more difficult and more intense, but our faith has grown so strong that we don't even consider the trials, our mind is stayed on Him. Isaiah 26:3

September 7

Rat fink, snitch, blabbermouth, and gossip are all words meaning tattletale, but is it always wrong to tell on someone? What if they are doing something dangerous, sinful, or harmful? It all depends on what motivates the telling. Are you being self-righteous, desiring admiration, or seeking vengeance, wanting to punish someone? Then yes, it is wrong. What about the words: informant, spy, whistleblower, or collaborator? These can involve someone revealing secret crimes or dangers at their job. Exposing them may save lives. Telling secrets can be good or bad. Judge your own motives and make sure the telling will have positive results. Even if people dislike you and call you names, you must do the right thing. "A gossip betrays a confidence, but a trustworthy person keeps a secret" (Proverbs 11:13). When we see someone sin, we are told to go to them personally and with humility appeal to their conscience (Matthew 18:15-17).

I will make a road in the wilderness...Isaiah 43:19. We can talk about the road, or we can talk about the wilderness. We do not need to worry about the future; just follow the path, one foot in front of the other, with a positive attitude, focusing on God's leading rather than the wilderness of doubt.

What Will It Take?

What will it take to shake us awake?
An earthquake, a fire, or heat turned up higher?
What will it take to stop the scrolling
The inflammatory trolling?
What do we need to be still and to hear
Jesus' voice loud and clear?
Where is our devotion, love's emotion?
The family is scattered, dreams being shattered
What will it take? The hours are wasted
Feeling sad and devastated
No more relationships or funny quips
The sand in the hourglass, Oh, how it slips
What is left except feeling bereft?
What will it take to say that I'm done
And put down the distracting cell phone?

Answers

Praying with desperation, needing answers
But the heart has bitter roots choking faith
Unforgiveness, resentment, malice, and hate
It's like talking to the ceiling, expecting a debate
Wanting God to listen, so confess the feelings
The hurts, the wounds, and the pain of past dealings
Allow the Lord to wash that dirt from your feet
Those deep-rooted cycles of soulish defeat
Feeding on the failures of lost battles and wounds
He always listens, has hope, and he is answering
In the day of pleading and crying, peace comes
The light and glory shine, joy after mourning

September 8

When God gives us a gift that exposes us to notoriety and fame, it appeals to our self-esteem. Self-esteem needs a radical surgery before the Lord will allow us to proceed. Even if God does something in an undeniable way, it does not make us exempt from Satan's subtle temptation to suggest, "You did that, aren't you talented?" God does not share his glory. "Before we can be of any value, he will do what it takes to bring us to the place where we see that God has given us a gift for His glory, for His greater purpose, and for His church. When a person is not being chastened, it is easy for him to think that he is quite ready to conquer the world and Satan. But God is working silently behind the scenes to bring us to full dependence on Him." (*God Meant It for Good*, by Dr. R.T. Kendall). We see the fall of those who have not understood this concept and have refused to humble themselves before the Lord. Jonah was chastened because he did not like the Ninevites and did not want them to be saved. He wanted his enemies to suffer and his prophecy to be fulfilled so he could be validated and vindicated. A minister who has not gone through this chastening process will not be willing to obey when the Lord gives him a message that may make him unpopular with the crowd.

Demas left Paul, who was facing a trial in Rome; Demas loved the world. Diotrephes was in the church, but he was egotistical and ambitious; he loved the honor of men. Demetrius loved the truth and had a good testimony. Love not the world, neither the things in the world. -Dick Mills (2 Timothy 4:9,10; 3 John 9-12; 1 John 2:15)

September 9

"Christian" originated as a term of derision by people in Antioch; it means "little Christs." Before that, believers called themselves "Followers of the Way." The name "Puritan" came from a name-calling insult, implying that these people had a "holier than thou attitude." They were Separatists who wanted to leave Catholicism, but the name Puritan stuck. Richard Baxter said, "I am neither as good nor as happy as the name suggests." We can expect persecution because we make the world feel guilty. The joy of the Lord will be with you when persecuted for believing in Jesus. The joy of the Lord will be your strength (Nehemiah 8:10). You may be ridiculed, humiliated, opposed, criticized, harassed, or fired, but the promise is, "If you are reproached for the name of Christ, you will be blessed" (1 Peter 4:14; Matthew 5:10-12).

To some, we are the aroma of death leading to death, to others the aroma of life leading to life.
2 Corinthians 2:16

www.chritianhistoryinstitute,.org. Richard Baxter and the English Puritans: Did You Know?
www.christianstudylibrary.org. Christian Library. The Name "Christian" 2004

September 10

Despair comes from facing desperate times and despairing is a feeling that there is no hope for the future. It comes in a crisis moment when no foundation of security is left to stand on. A loss of a job, a repossessed car or house, an arrest by police, a divorce, a death, an accident, or any number of tragedies that bring us to the end of our rope. It seems we are backed into a corner, and the only place to look is up. It is out of our hands; there is nothing we can do but get on our knees and pray. Desperate times call for desperate measures. How desperate are you to hear his voice? "Faith sees the invisible, believes the unbelievable and receives the impossible. When I try, I fail. When I trust, he succeeds" (Corrie ten Boom). Then a door opens up, it is not what we may have expected, but we are so relieved that it seems like all of heaven has answered. It may be a move to a foreign country, a job outside your particular field, or any number of escapes God sends because it is the path of change he wants for you. Let's not resist the change we feel is coming. Change isn't easy, but change we must. "Because they do not change, therefore they do not fear God" (Psalm 55:19 NKJ). "But stand here awhile, that I may announce to you the word of God" (1 Samuel 9:27). Samuel had a pause to receive a word from God. Take as many pause moments as you need for the faith to see that there is a light at the end of the tunnel and to hear which way to go. He will lead you through.

Sameness begets tameness, tameness begets lameness. -Dick Mills

September 11

"Rebellion is as the sin of witchcraft" (1 Samuel 15:23). "Rebellion" in Hebrew is connected to bitterness. A bitter rebel's disobedience is not just a spur-of-the-moment act but is an evil that has overtaken the heart and controls the emotions. It has been there a long time, and it feels powerful. The opposite of rebellion is willingness and obedience (Isaiah 30:1,9-10). Rebellion comes against Father God, an earthly father, and against all ruling authority. It is tempting to rebel against parents; it feels empowering to cast off restrictions, but the result is a shortened life. "Therefore, whoever resists authorities resist what God has appointed, and those who resist will incur judgment" (Romans 13:2). "Be subject for the Lord's sake to every human institution, whether it be to the emperor as supreme, or to governors as sent by Him to punish those who do evil and to praise those who do good" (1 Peter 2:13-17). *Pater* is Latin for father, and *pateras* is the Greek word; this is where we get the word "patriot." It represents our forefathers, what they gave their lives for, and the foundation they created with God's help. When we do not honor parents, teachers, country, or our forefathers, we are in rebellion and the rebellious live in a dry land (Psalm 68:6). "He appointed the law which He commanded our fathers, that they should make them known to their children; that the generation to come might know them, that those yet to be born would not be like their stubborn fathers, a rebellious generation that did not have an upright heart, and whose spirit was not faithful to God" (Psalm 78).

...patriotism and bravery in concert with the kingdom of God, the enemy would claim fewer casualties...-Don Miller

LIFE

Psalm 139

Your eyes saw my substance before it was formed
In your book were written the days you fashioned for me,
O God, even before I was created, you knew my destiny
How precious your thoughts are toward me
How great the sum of them, if I were to count them all
They would number more than the sand of the sea
When I awake, you are there, no matter where I be
Search my heart and try me, know my anxiety
And see if there is wickedness lingering in my heart
Lead me in your everlasting way so I may be in your
presence for eternity

STRIFE

The desire for superiority results in conflicts and quarrels
They cut like knives, those bitter disagreements
Within the community, a clash of competition
Bringing up the past as if it were yesterday
A battle over words, wounds, and hurts
Years of seething, finally boiling over
Turn discord, Lord, into harmony

September 12

One's character opens doors or closes them, begins relationships or ends them, pleases God or turns him away, delays a blessing, or expediates one. Navigate relationships wisely. Don't trust secrets to a gossip, step on toes unnecessarily, or tease with words and actions. Pranks may make you laugh, but if they aren't funny for the recipient, you blew it. Caring about others more than you care for yourself was modeled by Jesus. He always did what was best for an individual no matter what the crowd thought. He went to the tax collector Zacchaeus' house for dinner, the most hated among all the Jews. Jesus wasn't worried about his reputation as he went toe-to-toe with the religious leaders. He spoke the truth, and most of them hated him for it. He spoke and did what his Father told him to speak and do. Our script should come from God; being disconnected from the source of wisdom and knowledge makes us the religious leader in need of a rebuke. Be a person of godly character, be interested in others and in what they say, don't be offended by those who disagree, let your conversation ooze with the grace of the salt that makes people thirsty for more. Don't pretend to love others, really love them!
(Romans 12:9, Colossians 4:6)

A soft answer turns away wrath, but a harsh word stirs up anger.
Proverbs 15:1

September 13

My family met a man on a beach who had decided to become a "beach bum." He told us his story of getting a master's degree, but wasn't able to acquire a job that would pay him the six figures he deserved, so he decided not to work at all. It used to be the norm to start at the bottom of a company and work your way up to higher positions. It is certainly God's method for exalting someone. Joseph, the favorite son in a rich family, was sold as a slave, spent years in prison, and then, after twenty-two years, became Egypt's second in command. Moses was well educated in the palace of Egypt, but had to escape to the desert for forty years before God called him to lead. These men were brought low before being elevated. I wonder where the man on the beach is right now. Did he finally decide to start at the bottom? An expensive education doesn't always buy immediate success. Joshua 1:8 says that we can have good success, which in Hebrew means intelligence, wisdom, good understanding, achieving a goal, having discretion (behaving or speaking in a way to avoid offense, able to keep a secret), and prudence (having common sense and shrewdness).

When you have done all those things which you are commanded, say, 'We are unprofitable servants. We have only done our duty' (Luke 17:10). Whether we lead a million people to the Lord or our spouse through holy living and prayer, no one can boast. We do what we are led to do, and He receives the glory. We may be unprofitable servants, but the Lord calls us precious jewels. (Malachi 3:17)

September 14

Have you ever experienced a desert season where your soul seemed dry and starved? Hezekiah experienced this, "God left him, to try him, that he might know all that was in his heart" (2 Chronicles 32:31). Paul exhorts Timothy to be ready in season and out of season (2 Timothy 4:2). There will be dry seasons in our lives to prove we love God, whether we feel His presence or not. Do we love him because of who he is, our loving Heavenly Creator, Father, and Savior, or for what he does for us? Passing the wilderness test means we won't have to go around the mountain for forty years, facing the same old trials. When going through hard things, ask the Lord, "What do you want to show me through this trial?" He is bringing us to the purpose and destiny for which we were created. Battles predict the coming influence. If we have a crack in our foundation, the weight of success can be crushing. Let him fix the cracks and move us toward the greater things he has planned for us. "He led you through the vast and dreadful desert, that thirsty and waterless land with snakes and scorpions, to humble and test you so in the end it might go well with you" (Deuteronomy 8:15-16).

'Good Christians' are those who love more, not those who sin less and try to be more compliant. God's yardstick measures the love we have for him and for others. Matthew 22:37-40

What do you want to show me, Lord?"

September 15

Even though the law didn't arrive until Moses came down from the mountain, people knew right from wrong. Joseph, when confronted with the temptation of Potiphar's wife, said, "How then can I do this great wickedness and sin against God?" (Genesis 39:9). Joseph resisted over and over; he had no escape except to avoid being in the same room with her. All he could do was keep quiet and resist her alluring words. And yet he ended up in prison after all that godly resisting. He was accused of what he diligently avoided. Little did Joseph know at the time, but he was now on his way to becoming the second-highest official in Egypt. Potiphar's wife, on the other hand, had become a crazed, bitter woman who went from wanting Joseph to wanting him destroyed. She couldn't keep from spouting her lies even to her servants. She destroyed his reputation and hers. Vengeance is ugly. It isn't recorded that Joseph was cleared of the charges against him, but it does not matter because God vindicated him. He was an innocent man yet kept silent, just as Jesus did at the cross. We would agree that Joseph seemed boastful about his new coat and his dreams, but God has a way of skimming off those things that our inherited sin nature gives us. Let's take these refinements with a good attitude, "counting it all joy" and keeping our eyes on the prize.

'Dear friends, do not be surprised at the painful trial you are suffering, as though something strange were happening to you. But rejoice that you participate in the sufferings of Christ, so that you may be overjoyed when his glory is revealed. If you are insulted because of the name of Christ, you are blessed for the Spirit of glory and of God rests on you.' 1 Peter 4:12-14. *We share in His suffering, then we share in His glory.*

September 16

The chastening of the Lord does not mean he is punishing us. The chastening of Joseph was not because he sinned but because he needed a time of refining, maturing, and cleansing. By the time he saw his brothers after 22 years, he had reached a place of complete love and forgiveness. It is called sanctification, and it is a process. "He does not deal with us according to our sins, nor repay us according to our iniquities. For as high as the heavens are above the earth, so great is his love for those who fear him; as far as the east is from the west, so far does He remove our transgressions from us" (Psalm 103:10-12). So, he is not punishing us; he is pruning us. He is calling us to take part in his holiness (Hebrews 12:10). Learning to love with his agape selfless love, not based on emotion, feeling, or sentiment, is a choice and is the foundation of everything we do for the Lord. "If I speak in the tongues of men and angels, but do not have love for others, I am only a noisy gong or clanging cymbal. If I have such faith that can move mountains, but do not love others, I am nothing. If I give everything I have to the poor and become a martyr, but do not love others, I gain nothing" (1 Corinthians 13). We must love the Lord more than anything or anyone, or we will fall when temptation knocks at the door. If you aren't sure of how much you love God and people, ask him to increase your love. Then you will know that your love for God is so great that you would not even consider offending him. His chastening moves you closer to him. "The love of God is poured into our hearts by the Holy Spirit" (Romans 5:5).

Every trial is designed to show you something about yourself that you did not know. -Dr. R.T. Kendall.

"How can anyone enter a strong man's house and carry off his possessions unless he first ties up the strong man? Then he can rob his house" (Matthew 12:29). Jesus is prophesying about how he would enter the kingdom of hell at the moment of his death and "tie up" the strongman Satan by removing his authority and robbing him of all the godly ones from the past 4,000 years. Jesus surprised the enemy when he descended with the keys of death and hell and released the prisoners, those who could not enter Heaven until Jesus had purchased their salvation. Before that time, only Enoch, Elijah, and Moses had the pleasure of being in God's Heaven. The others had to remain in paradise, in a place of comfort, but near the torture of the dark place of Satan's rule. (Luke 16:19-31). Moses was buried by the Lord but rose from the dead and was taken up with Elijah in the chariot. We know this because Moses and Elijah were both on the Mount of Transfiguration. Elisha saw them both when he said, "My father, my father," as the chariot left the earth. This is why Satan argued with the angel Michael over the body of Moses. He was accusing and blaspheming God by saying He broke the rules by taking Moses out of Paradise to Heaven (Jude 1:9). God does not obey Satan's rules. (Revelation 1:18, 9:1-2, 20:1-3; Ephesians 4:8-10)

And having disarmed the powers and authorities, he made a public spectacle of them, triumphing over them by the cross. Satan's plan to kill Jesus backfired. Colossians 2:15.

September 18

Self-exaltation is taking advantage of opportunities to advance oneself for personal honor and glory. It is part of our basic human nature to want to be acknowledged and admired. It can lead to stretching the truth on resumes, boasting, or stepping on others as you climb the corporate ladder. God wants to be the one who exalts you. "Humble yourself under the mighty hand of God, and He will exalt you when it is time" (1Peter 5:6). When is it time? When all self-effort fails. The butler finally did remember Joseph; no effort on Joseph's part was needed. It was God who arranged Pharaoh's dream, reminding the butler of Joseph's gift. Secular self-improvement methods are not God's methods. He doesn't want us to think that by our own effort, we are masterful successes. He knows what our best future is, and only he can lead us into it. While waiting for doors to open, be wholeheartedly diligent in the small, unseen tasks and duties. For he rewards those who do "all for the glory of God" (Colossians 3:23). He will give you promises and dreams to help while waiting. "Before the crown comes the cross, and he who exalts himself will be abased. He who desires to come after me must deny himself, pick up my cross and follow me" -Jesus.

May I never boast except in the cross of our Lord Jesus Christ, through which the world has been crucified to me, and I to the world. -Paul (Galatians 6:14)

September 19

Here is a conditional promise from God, "If you confess with your mouth that Jesus Christ is Lord and believe in your heart that God raised him from the dead, you will be saved. For it is with your heart that you believe and are justified, and it is with your mouth that you confess and are saved." (Romans 10:9-10). Jesus said, "Whoever acknowledges and admits to knowing me before men, him will I acknowledge before my Father which is in Heaven. But whoever rejects and disowns me before men, him will I also disown before my Father" (Matthew 10:32-33). "Without faith it is impossible to please God." Following Christ is all about having faith, trusting without tangible evidence, and acting on that trust. After confessing and praying the prayer of repentance to accept Jesus into your heart, there is water baptism and Holy Spirit baptism. It takes faith to step out and use the gifts of Holy Spirit, so does sharing your testimony. Getting married and having children takes faith. The more steps you take, the more faith you will have and the more the Lord will reveal Himself to you. It is an exciting life of adventure. You cannot out-dream God; He has already out-dreamed you! "When I come back to earth, will I find faith in my people?" (Luke 18:8).

But to all who believed in him and accepted him, he gave the right to become children of God (John 1:12). You may have believed in Christ and accepted him, but have you claimed your right to become His child? His children believe, trust, and rely on Him.

September 20

It is no fun getting caught doing wrong, but it is worse not getting caught. Exposed sin is the first step on the road to recovery. When we are ashamed of ourselves, we become fearful, defensive, isolated, and irritable. We make excuses or deny what we have done, pushing it into the backpack of our subconscious. We do not want to face the pain and guilt, so we bury it, then work hard to feel worthy by acts of service and dedication, ways of feeling valuable. Accept that Jesus paid for your sins on the cross, repent, and accept his forgiveness. Jesus has always called you valuable; nothing you do can separate you from that. So no more blaming others or making excuses, pray, "Father, I confess that I have not been able to see my value in your eyes, that you paid a price for my redemption, forgive me for my sin of_____. I repent, show me my true identity. Forgive me for blaming others, for making excuses. Thank you for forgiving me. I give you my life. In Jesus name." Ask him to speak to you about your true identity, who you are meant to be, and what you are supposed to do. Expose your sins and failures to the light of God's forgiving love.

We know that we have the petitions we ask of him (1 John 5:15). Write out a petition to the Lord for what you need and desire, along with the promises in the word that answer those needs.

September 21

Blaming others and self-pity keep us helpless and unable to progress beyond the point of the trauma we have experienced. It feeds on bad news, expects the worst, and craves sympathy. Life becomes very narrow with very few bright spots; self-focus, fear, and paranoia take over. Jesus came to give us an abundant life, and it begins with healing the damage done to our hearts through trauma, making inner vows, cursing ourselves and others, believing lies, and having unholy relationships. People caught in this trap refuse help and become insensitive to others' feelings, wanting others to suffer, be punished, and feel guilty. They feel and need to boost self-esteem and balance the scales by doing things to appease their conscience, such as religious pilgrimages and rites, or through forms of self-punishment. These emotional gymnastics choke out the abundant life Jesus promised. Holy Spirit's job is to comfort you. Forgive yourself and others, be rid of the small demon of pity, it's the cork keeping all bondage in place. Pop that cork, toss it, and receive freedom to be "strong in the Lord and in the strength of his might." Confession is acknowledging the lies, and repentance is an about-face to a complete surrender to Jesus. It is time to pour it out to him and be free.

We prove to God that we love Him by reading his book. -Dr. Kendall

September 22

We cannot relive or redo the past; all we can do is have a fresh beginning and do it right every time we get the chance. He works everything out for our good, so miraculously that we end up praising him for all we have been through and even for our mistakes. Treating those we have hurt with respect, giving up trying to earn our own righteousness, not having an ounce of blame or self-justification, but simply admitting and repenting for sin, are the first steps to a regret-free life. When the blood of Jesus removes our sin, he no longer sees it. He looks at us through his Son and sees us as adopted sons and daughters in his great family. We serve a joyful God who longs to be with us forever. He loves to see us happy. It was for the "joy set before him that he endured the cross." We were that joy. And now, "I reckon that the sufferings of this present time are not worth comparing with the glory which shall be revealed to us and in us, for all creation waits eagerly for when God's sons are revealed. We also groan, longing for God's open acknowledgement of our sonship by the redemption of our body" (Romans 8:18-23). We have much to look forward to in this life and in the next!

When we are born, we come from a place of confinement into air and atmosphere, a vast world to discover. When we are born again, we come into a new life, a new atmosphere, an eternal world to discover, a never-ending adventure that eventually births us into God's Heaven of delights.

How are we to share the Gospel? Be filled with His Spirit, ask for opportunities, and be watchful for them. Be kind and considerate with their time, and never argue over unimportant subjects. Use words they can understand and relate to. Ask questions. If the Holy Spirit gives you a word of knowledge, something the Holy Spirit shows you about them, or an encouragement, gently share it. If they do not receive it, you are just the messenger, and the Holy Spirit will take it from there. Jesus told us that he must go away so he could send the Helper, "And when he has come, he will convict the world of sin, and of righteousness, and of judgment." The Helper is the one who does the convicting; it is not our job (John 16:7-8). It is difficult to admit being wrong about Jesus. It may take years. We do not lead others toward Jesus out of duty or obligation, but out of deep compassion and love. "I am the door. If anyone enters by me, he will be saved and will go in and out and find pasture" (John 10:9). We go in to spend time with him, then we go out to minister to others in the "pasture" of the life God grants us. In Acts 1, there were 120 in the church; in Acts 2, there were 3,120. What a difference one day can make when we are led by Holy Spirit.

Jesus had a word of knowledge when he said of Nathanael, 'Here is an Israelite in whom there is no malice.' 'How do you know me?' asked Nathanael. Jesus answered, 'I saw you under the fig tree before Philip called you.' Nathanael then declared, 'You are the Son of God, the king of Israel.' Under the fig tree in the Hebrew understanding signifies a place of studying the Torah, of receiving wisdom from a teacher, or of studying the messianic prophecies (John 1:48). http://wildbranches.blogspot.com Under the Fig Tree. March 19, 2014

September 24

When you run out of prayers, pray scripture back to Him. God loves to hear his word. Pray the Psalms. You do not need to try to impress him with big words or a pious attitude. Be yourself, be truthful, and humble. Expect him to answer, expect miracles. See your prayers as missiles flying through the air and hitting the mark. Pray for mercy for those needing it. Pray with faith, knowing that he hears you. Pray with excitement and passion. Pray often, not just when you need something. Enter your closet-prayer time by giving thanks, praising him, and by raising holy hands, seeing yourself joining with all of Heaven and earth in worship (1 Timothy 2:8). Pray standing, kneeling, prostrate, or while doing dishes. Pray in the car, with your children, and at night with your spouse. Pray with joy, with sorrow, or with tears. Believe, not like demons, who believe in God and shudder in fear for what is coming, believe with a heart full of trust that he who began his good work in you will carry it to completion (James 2:19; Philippians 1:6). We live in a time when there are people in our world being arrested for praying silently, this tells us that even our silent prayers make the kingdom of darkness quake. Pray for victory, that the increase of his government is occurring, and for more workers to go into the harvest fields. Pray with clean hands and a pure heart, then know he hears, know he answers!

You number my wanderings and put my tears into Your bottle; are they not in Your book? Psalm 56:8

September 25

The word "glory" in Hebrew is *Chabod,* and it means a heavy, awesome presence, or the manifestation of God's power and majesty. It is the visible or felt qualities of God, his holiness, majesty, love, and goodness. After Solomon finished the temple, the musicians, 120 consecrated priests, and all of Israel praised and sang in unison, "He is good; his love endures forever." "Then the temple of the Lord was filled with the cloud, and the priests could not perform their duties because the glory of the Lord filled the temple" (2 Chronicles 5). The glory came down on the Mount of Transfiguration and on the day of Pentecost when a rushing wind was heard and tongues of fire were seen over the 120 who were gathered. God's glory is eternal, powerful, supernatural, and it works miracles and transforms lives. It is when God surprises and amazes us by invading our space, and all we can do is respond in worship. "Lord, I stand in awe of your deeds, renew them in our day, in our time, make them know. Let your praise fill the earth, your glory cover the heavens. Your splendor is like the sunrise; rays flashing from your powerful hand. You come to deliver your people, to save your anointed one" (Habakkuk 3).

Then the glory of the Lord will be revealed, and all flesh will see it together; for the mouth of the Lord has spoken. For the earth shall be filled with the knowledge of the glory of the Lord, as the waters cover the sea. Isaiah 40:5; Habakkuk 2:14

GLORY

His glory covers the heavens, his praise fills the earth
His splendor is like the sunrise, rays flashing from his hand
Plague goes before him; pestilence follows his steps
He stands and shakes the earth and makes the nations
tremble
The ancient mountains tremble and crumble, the hills they
too, collapse
You ride with your horses and your victorious chariots
You uncover your bow and call for many arrows
You split the earth with rivers, the deep roars, lifting its
waves on high
In wrath, you come to deliver your people and save your
anointed one
You crush the leader of the land of wickedness and crush
his warriors
Yes, I will wait patiently for the day of calamity to come upon
the evil
Though the fig tree does not blossom and there be no fruit
on the vine
Though the olive crop fails and the fields produce no food
Though there be no sheep in the pen, no cattle in the stalls
Yet will I rejoice in the Lord and take joy in God my Savior
He is my strength; he makes my feet like the feet of a deer
I am able to climb the heights, let all the world be silent
before him
I stand in awe of your deeds, renew them in our day and in
our time
In wrath, remember mercy

Habakkuk 3

September 26

Jesus was asked whether the man born blind had this disability because of his sin or his parents' sin. Jesus said neither, but that the works of God might be revealed in him (John 9:1-3). He said this when he was about to raise Lazarus from the dead, "That the Son of God may be glorified through it" (John 11:4). After Lazarus was raised, he said, "Did I not tell you that if you believe, you will see the glory of God?" The Glory of God is being revealed today through miracles, deliverance, healing, signs, and wonders. God's glory is also seen through people like Joni Eareckson Tada, who was paralyzed from the neck down from a diving accident at age 17. God redeemed her life, and her ministry to the disabled is profound. She is an author and artist, and she has the longest-running radio show. Nick Vujicic, born without limbs, travels the world to encourage and lead people to Christ. These two people are full of joy and prove that God can turn the worst of situations into an amazing display of his glory. Moses said, "Please show me your glory," and God did (Exodus 33:18). King Jesus International Ministry Church documented over 5,000 miracles in 2022. "Christ is in us, the hope of glory" (Colossians 1:27). "And we have this treasure in our weak earthen vessels, that the excellence of the power may be of God and not of us" (2 Corinthians 4:7). We receive the benefit and God receives the recognition.

And the glory which You gave Me I have given them, that they may be one just as We are one. -Jesus (John 17:22)

September 27

We join with heaven to bring down an atmosphere of glory through worship. God's glorious atmosphere led the Israelis out of Egypt with a pillar of cloud during the day and a pillar of fire at night. When this visible glory moved, they followed for 40 years. We must also follow his glory, or our churches will become stagnant and religious. We are to move from "glory to glory," never staying camped at a certain movement of God, but moving when the Holy Spirit says move (2 Corinthians 3:18). We cannot manipulate the movements of God through our own inventions and programs because God's movements are his appointments. Leaders who want to control every aspect of the ministry down to the minute, becoming nervous when something is out of the prescribed order, need to be flexible and let the Spirit lead. This takes dedication and surrender. "'The latter glory of this house will be greater than the former,' says the Lord of angel armies" (Haggai 2:9). The first glory was visible in the Old Testament; now we are in the latter glory. How do we know? "Once more will I shake the heavens and the earth, the sea and dry ground; and I will shake all nations, and they shall come to the Desire of All Nations, and I will fill this temple with glory" (Haggai 2:6-7). We see the shaking; the latter glory has begun. Jesus is the Desire of All Nations!

Lord, prepare me to be a sanctuary, pure and holy, tried and true.
With thanksgiving, I want to be a living sanctuary for you.
Song by Randy Scruggs and John Thompson

September 28

Stagnation, no longer finding meaning or fulfillment in life, creates frustration, depression, and discouragement. These dry times are calling us to spend more time listening to the Lord and preparing for a change. The raven stopped bringing Elijah food, and the creek dried up; he was forced to move. It is time to move and find water again, or the effects of drought and famine will mean death spiritually. Fear of change, fear of the future, fear of failure, and the urge to fix problems with logic and reasoning are paralyzing. Success becomes elusive. Fight stagnation, not change. Be zealous in seeking the Lord for answers. Keep an attitude of transition, always be ready to move when the cloud moves. Do you want to be useful in this end-time season? Then be flexible. The mistake is believing you have achieved your peak season in life. Don't become dry and stiff, spectators and judges of the outpouring of the Holy Spirit, not liking that the old men are dreaming dreams, the young men are seeing visions, and the children are prophesying (Acts 2:17). Don't become irrelevant during this next outpouring, embrace change, be a new wine skin!

In the book of Acts, three thousand were added on the first day when foreigners heard God's works being glorified in their own language as 120 disciples spoke in tongues. The Ethiopian eunuch received Christ because Philip was translated to his chariot. The jailer and his family were saved because an earthquake released the prisoner's shackles. Paul became a Christ follower because Jesus spoke to him, then blinded him for a time. Cornelius and his household accepted Christ because of an angel's message. Signs, wonders, and miracles happen because believers step out and obey, causing the kingdom to expand. Miracles follow obedience.

Holy Spirit and His Great Reformation Day

Omniscient, All-knowing; Omnipresent, Everywhere
Surges of the King's Omnipotent Power
God's strong arm revealed, warrior's rising
An artesian pure river springing up
A spring of living water ready to flow
Ankle deep, knee deep, now swimming
Prepare for the atmospheric river of life to flow
It will never run dry, a continual flow
A mega-outpouring of former and later rains
The seven times greater latter rains
Soaking then moving by His great power
Streams, springs, and rivers, oil, fire, and wind
Over every region, nation, and territory
The waste places and badlands of the world—new
purpose!
Historic winds blowing with good news and
deliverance
Blowing away confusion, addiction, brokenness, and
fear
Pointing prodigals toward home
You can feel it, love springing up in the heart
You can see the effects; demons are trembling
A supernatural era bursting forth
A continuous flow to ripen the harvest
A billion-soul harvest, the threshing floor piled high
Restoring what the grub worm has devoured
From faith to faith, glory to glory, strength to strength
A Divine recovery, a restoration, a reformation!
(Tim Sheets, Oasis Church, March 16, 2025–Joel 2:20-32; John
7:37-38)

September 29

How will you know if you have made the transition from the old wineskin to the new one? The change will be evident, the attitude will be one of praise and gratefulness to God, and there will be a lack of judgment and criticism. Speech will be positive and encouraging to others. Passion for the Lord's will to be done will be the priority, and more time will be spent in prayer and meditation. His voice will become clearer. "When I act, who can reverse it? Do not remember the olden days, I am doing a new thing, now it shall spring forth, can you not see it? I will make a road in the wilderness and rivers in the desert" (Isaiah 43:13-19). There are people who like the idea of change, of an outpouring of God's Spirit, but then realize it requires giving up comfort, convenience, and electronic entertainment. The great revivals of recent years saw churches full of people every night of the week. There may come an uprising of naysayers who have excuses for why this change is not a good one. They may become angry, saying that it is emotionalism or the devil's devices. It is not a good idea to become an obstacle to God's will (Psalm 55:19). It is time to "Uproot, tear down, and destroy" so we can "build and plant" (Jeremiah 1:9-10). It is demolition time to unlearn what needs to be unlearned to get that new wineskin!

What separates the church from the world is obedience. What distinguishes the remnant from nominal Christianity is obedience. Obedience can turn your years into days. Disobedience can turn your days into years. - Guillermo Maldonado

September 30

"Let us cleanse ourselves from everything that contaminates body and spirit, completing holiness and living a consecrated life set apart for God's purpose in the fear of God" (2 Corinthians 7:1). We are justified before God the moment we confess, repent, and ask Jesus into our hearts. "That Christ may make his home in your hearts through faith..." (Ephesians 3:17). Then we go through the process of sanctification until "Christ is [fully] formed in you" (Galatians 4:19-20). The more we surrender, the more we become like Christ. A motivation for this great work in us is the future day of his coming. "Who can stand when he appears? For he is like a refiner's fire and like launderer's soap" (Malachi 3:2). "Christ loved the church and gave Himself for her, that he might sanctify and cleanse her with the washing of water by the word, that he might present her to himself a glorious church" (Ephesians 5:25-27). "When Christ, your life, appears, then you also will appear with him in glory" (Colossians 3:4).

The remnant church is undergoing deep cleansing, detoxification, purging, and purification. -Guillermo Maldonado.

October 1

We choose to follow Jesus, then his blood, his word, and his Holy Spirit cleanses us. But we also cleanse ourselves, "His bride has made herself ready...for the fine linen is the righteous acts of the saints" (Revelation19:7-8). Righteous acts are important; it is what we wear in Heaven, but what contaminates, giving us spots and wrinkles? Our words do, it is what comes out of the mouth that defiles us (Matthew 15:11). The tongue is a flame of unrighteousness, it stains the whole body, a fire set by hell which has the power to ruin someone's life. It is wrong that from the same mouth come blessing and cursing (James 3:6,10). If anyone does not bridle his tongue, this person's religion is worthless (James 1:26). Our words are to be "apples of gold," full of wisdom, truth, and honesty, "in settings of silver," words used appropriately and at the right time (Proverbs 25:11). True and honest words can also cut, damage, and wound; let your words be led by the Spirit.

Men seek earthly honors, worldly gain, promotions, and high positions. Their quest is to 'make it to the top,' but I am looking for people who will go the other way and sit at My feet as Mary did. I am looking for those who are willing to be lowly that I might be exalted, emptied of self that I might fill them, and foolish in the eyes of the world that I might be their wisdom. I will make the place of My feet glorious. Before I ascended, I first descended. You are to do the same.
(Dick Mills had a vision of Jesus. His feet were dazzling fine brass, then he heard the above words.)

October 2

"If you will listen carefully to God's voice, do what is right, and obey his commands, then I will put none of the diseases on you which I have put on the Egyptians; for I, the Lord, am your Healer" (Exodus 15:26). You might think this verse is impossible, but for forty years in the wilderness he keep the Israelis healthy; they lacked nothing; their clothes did not wear out, and their feet did not swell (Nehemiah 9:21). They were supernaturally cared for, even after failing all ten of their tests. Psalm 103:5 says that the Lord "satisfies your mouth with good things, so that your youth is renewed like the eagle's." Health is important but seems to be eluding us. We must care for our souls by being stress- and anxiety-free and support our immune system by getting enough rest and eating healthy food. Take a literal weekly Sabbath Day rest and daily enter the rest of connecting to the Spirit of God. Pay attention to a warning when you are about to do something. It could be going into a restaurant (God knows where food-poisoning is lurking), taking an Rx (maybe you were given the wrong pill), or accepting a diagnosis (maybe God has a different one, which could be, "you will live and not die!"). Health is important; the Lord will lead you in what to eat, drink, and what medicines to take. We must listen and obey. He cares about the details of our lives and has a cure for everything. God does not love us any less than he loved the Israelis in the wilderness.

Do we put God first one day a week, or first every day? Colossians 2:16; Romans 14:5-6

October 3

Second Corinthians 6:14-18 says we are not to be in partnership with an unbeliever because they are lawless and live in darkness. There are lawless believers, so we would not want to go into business with them either. How do we know whether a person is living for the Lord? We know this by their fruit (character qualities), actions, morals, and convictions. We are not to judge by our standards alone. A person calling themselves a believer may turn out to be corrupt, and a person who has not confessed Christ may be in process and may soon do so. What draws them in? It is the kindness and love of Christ operating through us that will usher them all the way to the cross. We represent Christ on this earth. Pray about your partnerships and your future spouse. God will show you who you should link your life to. "Do not be misled, bad company corrupts good character." (1Corinthians 15:33; Romans 2:4)

None of us lives or dies to himself alone; we belong to the Lord.
Colossians 2:17

The Right One
Don't kiss that toad
He will leave you when winter comes
Wait for the right one
Who will be there in every season

October 4

We are told in Ephesians 4:16, "The whole body is joined together by what every joint supplies, building with unselfish love, every part doing its share, causing growth and edification." Every member in our family and every member in the Lord's family is important. We miss out when we fail to appreciate one another. Everyone has something to offer. The poor are rich in faith; we learn about faith from them. The elderly are rich in wisdom and understanding, offering us pointers on life and sharing amazing stories of their adventures when they trusted the Lord. The young have zeal and creativity, motivating us to get out and do good works. Every joint supplies and love is the glue that sticks us together. We must draw people in and find out their interests and what wonderful things God has done in their lives. Encourage one another so we all may find joy in being a part of kingdom building. "Practice hospitality, even to strangers, and do it without grumbling." (1 Peter 4:9; Hebrews 13:2; Romans 12:13).

Mercy is the heart of Jesus, servant is his hands, he is a leader with authority, a giver with generosity. He exhorts with wisdom, and as a prophet, he shows us the way. He is an orator, teacher, and the administrator of his kingdom.

October 5
A New Day, A New Era

You will dance the dance of Miriam's Victory; the horse and rider are thrown into the sea.
You will shout the shout of Gideon; the sword of the Lord and the Ecclesia revealed.
You will decree the word of Isaiah 61; there is double for your trouble.
The siege of our enemy has ended, no weapon has prospered, their vengeance has failed.
Our God is mighty to save, giving relief from our tormentors and turning sorrow to joy.
Grieving has turned to laughter. You will say with Mordecai, "Haman's work has boomeranged back upon his head."
You will say with Esther, "The King's mandate is within reach, His scepter of power will be stretched toward you."
We reign in the King's authority. We validate with the King's signet ring.
We change the fate of nations with the King's seal of approval.
You will say, "The tables have turned, and the overpowers have been overpowered."
Hell's overrated power is overpowered by an ever-increasing power.
The evil decrees and doctrines of demons in media, culture, education, government, fake news, propaganda, fake power, and stolen authority—all overpowered.
Real overwhelming power will be seen in my Ecclesia
They will overpower the forever loser.
Whirlwinds of reformation will begin.
The time has come for the grand opening of the church that the King has built for supernatural times.

Power from heaven for the table-turning era will begin, and the ruling and reigning of the remnant will begin.

The signs and wonders and the miracle era will begin, the harvest will begin, the era of the overpowering power will begin.

Smoke, ash, and lava, horses at the gate, waiting for the bell to ring, a sign to begin the race

Hearts yearning and burning for revival, it will erupt in God's delivery room, a great passionate reset back to covenant roots

A sound from Heaven will soon launch this moment, like Elijah's deliverance from Baal's prophets, the puppets no longer dancing to the control of evil music

Freedom from the constraints of Jezebel's wickedness, her planned fall is imminent.

Isaiah 61:7

This entry was given to Tim Sheets through vision and prophecy

October 6

You will succeed if you refuse to listen to the advice of evil people. Do not follow their plans, or adopt their attitudes of cynicism, sarcasm, and skepticism. Stay away from them. Do not walk away from your blessing. Refuse the counsel of those who are ungodly, the self-help gurus who deny the Lord, even if their counsel is good. Receive amazing ideas from God, then agree by saying, "I can do that!" Standing idly by and deciding to live your own life will not bring you happiness. Don't sit lazily complaining, being critical bystanders like those who mock and make fun of others. You will be successful if you take pleasure in God's word, think about it often, and let it cause change in you. Be addicted to his word, fill your mind with it at all times, for then your life will be fruitful, you will age well, and enjoy your many accomplishments. All things are possible for those who believe, so run with endurance, never give up! Unfortunately for them, the wicked of the earth will encounter God's presence with fear and trembling and will lie prostrate before him. The ungodly will not be able to join the righteous group in Heaven, those known by the Lord, but they will indeed perish. (Psalm 1 paraphrased).

Pastor Jesus makes sure I have everything I need. He takes care of me and gives me the rest, enjoyment, and restoration I need after going through dark, terrible times. He always arranges my journeys and is with me. I have no fear in those valley-of-death times; in fact, I feel his comforting presence even more during those seasons. He hedges me in and protects me from my enemies. I am joyful as I experience his mercy and kindness, and I look forward to being with him forever.
(Psalm 23 paraphrased).

October 7

Churches, you are diligent and avoid evil people. You even look into those calling themselves apostles and find them to be liars. I commend you and your perseverance, patience, and hard work; you haven't given up. I am sorry to say, though, you have made a grave error. You have departed from me, your first love, so hurry and repent and do those things you did at first. Yes, I know that you hate the deeds of the Nicolaitans who think that I will accept their indulgent lifestyle and immoral deeds, but what I really desire is your love. If you can do this, I will give you fruit from the Tree of Life that is in my Garden of Paradise. (Paraphrase of Revelation 2:1-7). The Church at Ephesus was soon turned to rubble, as was the entire town. "Nicolaitan" means "conquering the laity." Leaders in some churches exercise lordship over the laity or the non-clergy. This exaltation of men was one development that began in the early church. This church did have its candlestick removed, and it is a warning to modern-day churches to have a deep and devout love for the Lord Jesus and for people. We have not seen the Act 2:42-47 type of church since 325 A.D.

I remember the devotion of your youth, how, as a bride, you loved me and followed me through the desert. Jeremiah 2:2

https://www.diggingforthrth.org/digging-deeper/church-of-ephesus
https://www.abarim–publication.com/Meaning. Abarim Publications'
Biblical Name Vault: Nicolaitans

October 8

Churches, I know what you are encountering right now, the persecution and poverty. But you are rich in faith, and that is what pleases me. I know what they are doing, those blasphemous false Jews who worship at Satan's throne. Don't fear what is about to happen to you. Some of you will end up going to prison for your faith, be faithful even to death, for your reward will be a crown of life, and the second death won't affect you. Remember that I am the First and Last, was dead and came back to life. I know what it is like to be persecuted—I am with you, beloved. (Church of Smyrna paraphrased. Revelation 2:8-11). Smyrna means myrrh, which was used for healing and for embalming. This perfume is made by crushing and 'bleeding' this thorny plant; the resin is dried and turns into "tears." The more it is crushed, the more this bitter-tasting plant emits a beautiful fragrance. This persecuted church was crushed. Although Smyrna and the Christians who lived there had a gruesome history, its local Christian church still thrives. It is said that more Christians have lived in Smyrna than in any other Turkish city. This is also every persecuted church in the world today!

Behold, I am coming like a thief. Blessed is the one who stays awake, and remains clothed, so as not to go naked and be shamefully exposed (Revelation 16:15).

https://www.diggingfortruth.org/digging-deeper/church-at-smyrna
Kenneth Cox
https://igneous-products-inc.myshopify.com/blogs//myrrh-origin/
Exploring the Myrrh Plant and its Harvesting Process. August 22, 2023.

October 9

Churches, I know where you live, and I know where Satan has set up his throne. Thank you for holding fast to My name and for not denying Me, even during the time of the murder of My faithful one. However, you need to make a few corrections. Remember Balaam, who taught the heathen King Balak how to trick the Israelis into sinning? It is going on in your church! Some are participating in things that have been dedicated to idolatrous practices and are committing sexual immorality. You are putting your leaders on pedestals and are allowing them to have authority over you when that is my place in your life. Repent quickly, or I will come, and you will experience the edge of the sword of my mouth. Each one who overcomes will be rewarded with hidden manna and a white stone with a new name on it. (Church of Pergamos paraphrased. Revelation 2:12-17). Hidden manna is what the jar of manna was called that was placed in the Ark of the Covenant. Christ himself is the manna or "Bread of Life." These overcoming believers will have a special relationship with the Lord. Pergamos was where Rome had its supreme court, and the double-edged sword was its emblem of the highest official authority, which was given to the proconsuls. Jesus is showing us that his authority is even higher than that, because it is his words that cut and judge. The Temple of Zeus, Satan's throne, was in Pergamum; a replica is in the Museum of Berlin. This is the church of compromise.

https://www.diggingfortruth.org/digging-deeper/church-at-pergamos
https://library.biblicalarchaelology.org/article/satans-throne/ Satan's Throne-The BAS Library

October 10

Churches, your increasing works, love, service, faith, and patience are amazing. Nevertheless, there are a few things on this report card that need your attention. You are allowing a spirit of Jezebel, who operates through a false prophetess, to teach and seduce my servants to commit sexual immorality and to participate in idol worship. I have given her time to repent, but she has not, so she and her followers will be cast into great tribulation. Everyone will be rewarded according to their works. If you haven't participated in this false teaching and haven't known the depths of Satan, then hold fast to what you have until I come. You will rule the nations with an iron rod, and I will give you authority and power over them. (Church of Thyatira paraphrased. Revelation 2:18-29). This town was industrial, poor, and known for its labor union. They manufactured items of brass, bronze, and other metals, and they made and dyed cloth, especially the royal purple. Jesus presents himself to this church as having eyes like a flame of fire, and feet like fine brass. "Hold on to what you have until I come" (Revelation 2:25). This religious church as a whole has not focused on righteousness and holiness.

Positive morality is sweet tasting to the mouth of God—immorality, a dagger in His heart. Morality is a manifestation of a love for God, the way a married couple is faithful to each other. Biblical metaphors are relational. -Don Miller

https://www.diggingfortruth.org/digging-deeper/the-church-of-thyatira

October 11

Churches, I am sorry to have to say this, you think you are alive spiritually, but you are dead. You had better wake up and bolster the things that are barely alive and are ready to die. Your works are not perfect before God. Ponder the past, the day you received Christ, and repent. I am coming as a thief in the night. If you repent, you will know the hour I will come. There are a few of you who have not soiled their garments; they will walk with me dressed in pure white, and their names will not be erased from my Book of Life. I will tell my Father and His angels their names. (Church of Sardis paraphrased. Revelation 3:1-6). The warning to watch came because the church at Sardis was overconfident. It is said that Prime Minister Winston Churchill gave this warning to the British Empire: "But I must drop one word of caution, for next to cowardice and treachery, overconfidence leading to neglect and slothfulness is the worst of martial crimes." Sardis had a good beginning but a bad finish. Sir William Ramsay called it "the city of death." It was attacked in 549 B.C. by the Medes and in 218 B.C. by the Cretans. Sardis represents the splintered church–it has no Jezebel, Balaam, or Nicolaitan teachings, but also no Spirit life, no unity. "A form of godliness but denying its power" (2 Timothy 3:5).

But the cowardly, unbelieving, sexually immoral, sorcerers, those who practice magic arts, idolaters, and all liars shall have their part in the lake which burns with fire and brimstone. Revelation 21:8. *Part of Jezebel's plan is to entrap youth into pornography. 'If you are watching pornography, you are watching a crime scene, or you are funding one.'* Troy Brewer. https://troybrewer.com/

https://www.diggingfortruth.org/digging-deeper/the-church-of-sardis

October 12

Churches, doors are wide open for you, and I will keep them open. You have a bit of strength, have kept my word, and have not denied my name under pressure. You have persevered, and now I will keep you from the hour of trial that is coming upon the whole earth to test them. Those who declare they know me but do not, will fall at your feet and worship because they will finally see that I have loved you. I am coming quickly; hold fast so no one can take your crown. I am going to write on you my new name. (Church of Philadelphia paraphrased. Revelation 3:7-13). This church was in the best condition of all the churches. It was small but dedicated and remained faithful. Love was evident in the Philadelphia church, and, amid suffering, Smyrna was the only other church to receive no rebuke and is the only one that still remains and is active in Turkey today. A third of the city's 15,000 people are true-believers. In the 1700s, the Historian Edward Gibbon wrote this, "In the loss of Ephesus, the Christians deplored...the extinction of the first candlestick of the Revelations. The circus and three stately theatres of Laodicea are now peopled with wolves and foxes; Sardis is reduced to a miserable village; the God of Mahomet, without a rival or a son, is evoked in the mosques of Thyatira and Pergamos...Philadelphia alone has been saved by prophecy or courage. At a distance from the sea, forgotten by the emperors, encompassed on all sides by the Turks, her valiant citizens defended their religion and freedom about fourscore years... Among the Greek colonies and churches of Asia, Philadelphia is still erect–a column in the scene of ruins–a pleasing example that the paths of honor and safety may sometimes be the same." (Gibbon, Volume 2, Chapter 64.) He referred to the lone pillar that stood among the ruins of that ancient city. This represents those churches concerned with others, supports, and sends missionaries around the world. It is engaged in evangelism because it loves people.

I will make you [Philadelphia, city of love] a pillar in the temple of My God.

https://www.diggingfortruth.org/digging-deeper/the-church-of-philadephia

Overcomers

Those who overcome eat from the tree of life in the paradise of God
They will not be hurt at all by the second death
Hidden manna will be given to them, and a white stone with a new name
God will give them authority over nations and the morning star
Dressed in white, they are worthy, their names in the Book of Life
They will be announced before the Father and the host of Heaven
They will carry God's name, New Jerusalem's name, and Jesus' new name
As pillars in His temple, they are secure in the city of God
They will have the right to sit with Jesus on his throne.
He who has an ear, let him hear what the Spirit is saying to the churches

October 13

Churches, Here I am! I know you and your works. You are wishy-washy and apathetic concerning your walk with me, and I am about to spit you out. You think you are rich, high and mighty, that you need nothing. You don't realize that you are poor, blind, and naked. Buy, from spending time with me, the gold of my word that you may be rich in faith and wisdom; buy white robes of my righteousness to cover your shameful deeds; and buy the eye ointment of my Spirit to have spiritual eyes to see. I love you; that is why I am warning you to repent and become zealous for the things I care about. I am standing at your door. Let me in, and so we may fellowship and get to know each other. If you do, I will let you sit on my expansive throne with me. (Church of Laodicea paraphrased. Revelation 3:14-22). Laodicea was famous for its gold. The city produced a beautiful, silky black material that everyone wore. Eye salve was made in the temple of Aesculapius, the Greek god of medicine known as "The Great Physician." Hot and lukewarm springs were also there, and these mineral baths were great for bathing but made sick those who drank it. This church is the last days' apostate one, which won't be rescued, only individuals. (Proverbs 16:16).

Your leaders are rebels, friends of thieves who love bribes, demand payoffs, yet refuse to help orphans or widows. They make alliances that I did not condone and plans contrary to mine. They refuse to heed the Lord's instruction and tell the seers and prophets to shut up. They want lies and pleasantries, saying, 'Get off your narrow path and quit telling us about your God [and your Jesus].' Isaiah 1:23; 30:1,9

https://www.diggingfortruth.org/digging-deeper/the-church-of-thyatira

October 14

"The Lord looked around and was displeased that there was no justice. He was appalled that there was no one to intercede; so he put on righteousness as his breastplate, and the helmet of salvation on his head; he put on the garments of vengeance and wrapped himself in zeal as in a cloak. According to what they have done, he will repay wrath to his enemies. From the west, they will fear the name of the Lord, and from the rising of the sun, they will revere his glory. He will come like a pent-up flood that the breath of the Lord drives along. 'The Redeemer will come to those who repent of their sins,' declares the Lord. 'This is my covenant with them, My Spirit, who is on you, and my words that I have put in your mouth will not depart from your mouth, or from the mouths of your descendants from this time on and forever'" (Isaiah 59:15-21). Jesus adorns himself in the warfare attire similar to ours when he comes for his people.

Jesus also tells us to pray for more workers to enter his field. We can intercede for the world for hours a day, but there comes a time when we must obey the call to do something to make a difference. Prayer with faith is followed by works; we must get involved in some way in society to effect change.

The purpose of God's judgment is to destroy the works of the devil. -Andrew Whalen 12/28/25

HIS ARM

The arm of the Lord is not too short to save, nor his ear too
dull to hear
Don't let iniquities separate you from God, so that he hides
His face from you
Speak no lies or wicked things, nor conceive trouble by
empty arguments
It is like the hatching of viper's eggs, or the spinning of a web
If they eat the eggs, they will die, and cobwebs cannot cover
and protect them
The way of peace they do not know, they do not take the
path of justice
They walk on crooked roads, their feet rush into sin
We look for light, but all is darkness and deep shadows
We growl like bears and moan like doves; deliverance seems
far away
Our offenses are many, and our sins testify against us
We acknowledge our rebellion and treachery against the
Lord
We have turned our backs on God, truth has stumbled in the
streets, and honesty is nowhere to be found
He is displeased and appalled at the lack of justice
For it is the foundation of His throne

"It is time to arise and shine for your light has come and
God's glory now rises on you."

Isaiah 59, 60

October 15

God will open doors for you; will you walk through? Paul had an open door for effective work, and he knew the opposition would be fierce, but he went through. The prophet Agabus bound his feet and hands with Paul's belt, then prophesied that Paul would be bound by the Jewish leaders in Jerusalem and be handed over to the Gentiles. Paul answered the local believers who were begging him not to go, that he was ready to be jailed and die for the sake of the Lord Jesus (Acts 21:10-14). He fearlessly went through that open door and, for two years, taught, preached, and wrote letters from prison. With his letters, now a large part of our New Testament, he is still making headway against the enemy authorities or "gates" of Satan's kingdom. "On this foundation (that Jesus is the Christ, the Son of the living God), I will build my church, and the gates of hell shall not prevail against it. I will give you the keys of the kingdom of Heaven, and whatever you bind on earth will be bound in Heaven, and whatever you loose on earth shall be loosed in Heaven" (Matthew 16:16-19). We can bind the encroachments of hell, so more people are brought to the knowledge of the Lord. Jesus shares his authority with us so we can bind and loose. The antichrist spirit is already at work; we need to push back against the darkness and go through the doors of opportunity God opens for us. (Revelation 3:8; 1 Corinthians 16:9; 1 John 4:3)

Raise a banner on a bare hilltop, shout to them, beckon to them to enter the gates of the nobles. I have commanded my holy ones; I have summoned my warriors to carry out my wrath–those who rejoice in my triumph. Isaiah 13:2

Here is a mystery for you! "We will not all sleep, but we will all be changed–in a flash, in the twinkling of an eye, at the last trumpet. For the trumpet will sound, the dead will be raised, and we who are alive will be changed. That is when Death is swallowed up in victory" (1 Corinthians 15:51-54). "You must understand, though, that in the final days mockers and scoffers will say, 'Where is this coming he promised? Ever since our fathers died, everything has gone on as it has since the beginning of creation.' They forget that the world was created from water and with water and then destroyed by water. These present heavens and earth are reserved for the judgment day of fire and the destruction of ungodly men. The Lord isn't slow in keeping His promises; He is patient, not wanting anyone to perish, but to come to repentance." We are in the scoffing generation. "We should live holy and godly lives as we look forward to His soon return. God's patience means salvation" (1 Peter 3:3-16). "We don't need to write to you about dates and times, you know, He is coming like a thief in the night. While people are saying, 'peace and safety,' sudden destruction will come. But you are not in darkness, that day surprising you like a thief, be watchful, alert, and self-controlled. God did not appoint us to suffer wrath but to receive salvation through Jesus Christ our Lord" (1 Thessalonians 4:13-5:9).

Whoever believes in the Son has eternal life; whoever does not have faith and reliance in the truthfulness of the Son, shall not see life, but the wrath of God remains on him. John 3:36 (Strong's 4100, 4102).

October 17

Charles Finney, a social and cultural reformer during the Second Great Awakening, tells about a group of young people he once taught. One particular girl would not respond to the salvation message, no matter how hard he tried to lead her to the Lord. He finally visited her parents and told them how worried he was about her eternal soul. His concern convicted them, and they confessed their sins, repented, and asked Jesus into their lives. At that exact moment, somewhere else, their daughter did the same thing, giving her heart to Jesus. It was a miracle; God wanted the whole family to serve Him. Was that why the daughter was hardened to the Gospel, so that Finney would minister to the parents, or was there a spiritual influence that needed to be broken between parents and child for the child to receive? There isn't a more frightening Scripture than what Jesus said in Matthew 18:6-7, "Whoever causes one of these little ones who believe in Me to sin, it would be better for him if a millstone were hung around his neck and he were drowned in the depth of the sea." "Understand the present time: the hour has already come for you to wake up from your slumber, because our salvation is nearer now than when we first believed. The night is nearly over; the day is almost here. Let us put aside the deeds of darkness and put on the armor of light" (Romans 13:12-13).

A true awakening will often lead to a reformation of societal morals. -Cindy Jacobs

Glory! Glory! Hallelujah!

Mine eyes have seen the glory of the coming of the Lord;
He is trampling out the vintage where the grapes of wrath
are stored;
He hath loosed the fateful lightning of His terrible swift
sword; His truth is marching on.

I have seen Him in the watch-fires of a hundred circling
camps;
They have builded Him an altar in the evening dews and
damps;
I can read His righteous sentence by the dim and flaring
lamps, His day is marching on.

I have read His fiery gospel writ in rows of burnished steel!
"As ye deal with my condemners, so with you My grace shall
deal!
Let the Hero, born of woman, crush the serpent with his
heel," Since God is marching on.

He has sounded forth the trumpet that shall never call
retreat;
He is sifting out the hearts of men before His judgment seat;
Oh, be swift, my soul, to answer Him; be jubilant, my feet!
Our God is marching on.

In the beauty of the lilies Christ was born across the sea,
With a glory in His bosom that transfigures you and me;
As he died to make men holy, let us die to make men free!
While God is marching on.

(Julia Ward Howe, William Steffe)

October 18

My mother's mother, number 6 of 10 children, road from Iowa to Oklahoma in a covered wagon; I fly. She wrote a lot of letters; I text. She had a large built-in flour bin in her kitchen, and she baked biscuits, cinnamon rolls, and chicken pot pies. I have a small bag of almond flour. Going back 14 generations, her forefathers came over from England right after the Mayflower in1637. They were Puritan preachers, teachers, lawyers, and scholars. One of my English ancestors built the church in Massachusetts where the "One if by Sea, Two if by Land" lantern hung. My great-great-grandfather began college and spoke several languages. Grandma Civilia Viola (Godwin) Reid lived on earth until she was 92. She was on my best friend list. She loved the Lord and loved to talk about the Bible. She especially liked John 15. She walked differently, having been born without hip joints, and it was not clear how much pain it caused her.

Sally Aurora (Silander) Orle, my *farmor*, Swedish for father's mother, was born and raised in Finland, was part Sami from the North country, and was number 14 of 14 children. Her father fell from a ladder, broke his back, and died when she was two. They hosted Smith Wigglesworth during his visit to Finland. She married a Swedish man, moved to Sweden, had four children, then moved to America when my dad was 16. They were among the last immigrants to arrive at Ellis Island. They took a bus to Los Angeles. Three of the children got jobs, and they all worked to improve their English. After two years, they moved to Denver and were able to buy a house and two cars, which they never could have afforded in Sweden. My parents met in church and married when

Mom was 18. When Dad was drafted into the army, my mom found out she was pregnant with me, so he didn't have to go. He became a United States citizen after I was born.

In that time, a present will be brought to the Lord of hosts from a people tall and smooth of skin, and from a people feared far and wide from the time of their beginning, a nation powerful and conquering, whose land the rivers divide–to the place of the name of the Lord of hosts, to Mount Zion. Isaiah 18:7. Could this be America?

Patterns

Wounds cause thought patterns, hard to forgive, can't forgive self
Arrogance to think your standard is higher than God's
He forgives, why can't you?
I forgive, but can't say their name
I forgive, but do not want to see them
Mind is always going to the offense, always replaying the dirty deed, no matter how good they try to be
There is a ditch of trauma in the brain
Thinking on good things is how you will heal
Battle the thoughts, fill in the ditch, pray for them, Forgive.
  Philippians 4:8

Self-Eval

If someone is an irritant
Like a pebble in your shoe
Maybe it is because
You are like that too
Tempted to be angry?
Then ask yourself a question
Is that something I also do?

October 19

Have you ever met someone you wished you could be like? They were probably happy, cheerful, and positive. I loved the Happy Hunters. They had a healing ministry where my friend was healed of a back problem. They were happy. We want people to understand us and understand the pain we are in. We want our depression, dysfunction, and self-pity to be validated. We want people to be sad with us, but what we need is encouragement. Ten spies coming back from spying out the land of Canaan had no reason to be negative. They brought Israel into a depression. God had amazingly delivered them out of the hands of Egypt by sending plagues and opening the Red Sea, then he provided food and water for them in the desert. Neither should we be negative and unhappy, affecting friends and family with our attitudes. God gives us so many wonderful promises, keeps us alive, provides for us, and best of all, he gave his life for us. If you want to be grumpy, then grumpy, negative people will be your friends; happy folks will avoid you. Do you really want to infect others with your complaints and grumblings, making them negative also? Parents, you must be positive toward each other, toward your children, and toward others. You are responsible for the atmosphere of your home. If your children are uncomfortable, they will not want to be there. The home is supposed to be a haven of safety, security, and peace, with family praying together and expectantly believing for God's goodness in every circumstance. God is as concerned with our family as he is with nations. Have fun, be happy, and praise the Lord.

The Lord inhabits the praises of His people. Who inhabits our mummerings? Psalm 22:3

October 20

False teachings or doctrines force people to live under laws that impose weighty systems of creeds, rituals, or taboos, with a prescribed form of worship. People then judge each other for their failures, giving Satan a foothold. They will say that if you do not believe the way they do, you aren't going to Heaven. They say that their rules of when and where to worship, what to eat, and what not to eat make them holy. Some teach that anything the world participates in is sinful, yet these rules do nothing to curb sensual appetites. In fact, it makes them more pronounced (Romans 7:7-9). The law cannot and never will make a person holy and righteous. "In the latter times, some will depart from the faith (faith in Christ alone for salvation), and they will listen to deceiving spirits and doctrine of demons. These hypocritical preachers will lie and have no remorse for their sin. They forbid people to marry and command them to abstain from certain foods which God sanctifies with prayer" (1 Timothy 4:1-6). Baptism in water and taking communion are not rituals. Baptism in water is "considering ourselves dead to sin and alive to God in Christ Jesus" (Romans 6:11). Communion is eating "His body and drinking His blood," partaking in his death and resurrection, and remembering his sacrifice. Baptism in the Holy Spirit is being continually immersed in him, giving us power to be witnesses. Baptism by fire prepares us for service. "He who suffers in the flesh is done with intentional sin" (1 Peter 4:1).

Fear of man keeps some religious people from accepting Jesus publicly. They do not want to be kicked out of their church, ward, temple, mosque, or synagogue. They choose religion instead of the divine.

October 21

"Occupy until I come, take care of my kingdom business by extending my government into the earth. Disciple the nations, cultures, and tribes. The keys of My kingdom are voice-activated by decrees. Hell cannot withstand the church. I have given you the kingdom keys to open and close doors." The Chamberlain Eliakim was the highest-ranking chief executive officer to the king. He managed everything and carried the keys, which were up to a foot long and hung from a hook or ring sewn onto the shoulder of his robe of authority. He was a doorkeeper and had the power to lock and unlock every room. Shebna, who had this position, was rebellious and abused his authority. The prophecy said that his authority would be stripped from him and given to Eliakim. This is a picture of Jesus descending into hell and removing Satan's authority. The government is upon the shoulders of Jesus. "Now begins a merger of Christ's spiritual kingdom on earth with the kingdom of heaven in ways never seen before—a new era of Pentecost. The enemies of God will become disoriented and fight each other, and we will gain freedom by our decrees and with angel assistance. There will be a series of suddenlies. The Lord is cleansing the lips of his prophets; a holy cleansing will arise. Let the breakthrough events begin. With commanding voices, with confidence, cause gateways of promise to open. Supernatural miracles and great victories are coming." -Tim and Dutch Sheets (Isaiah 22:15-24)

To this end I labor, struggling with all His energy, which so powerfully works in me. Colossians 1:29

The Bible Church Online. https://bibleword.or/the-key-of-david. April 17, 2021

October 22

Ask the Lord what he wants you to pray for, then fervently pray until the spiritual darkness is weakened, and prayers are unhindered. The Lord may call you to fast from food, social media, television, sugar, or sleep. People are desperate, ready to give up, time to pray for revival and awakening. When watching a show or movie, pray for the actors, especially the elderly ones. They are on the edge of eternity; anyone can be on that edge! Pray with deep groanings over serious matters in our culture and society. After casting all the burdens on Jesus, expect to see the answers. Take time to celebrate God's victories, realizing that you had a part in God's will coming to earth.

The word 'revival' comes from the Latin root 'revivere,' meaning to live again. The Greek word for revival is 'anazopureo', which means to stir up or rekindle a fire that is slowly dying, to revive. It is used metaphorically when the apostle Paul wrote to Timothy to 'stir up the gift of God which is in you.' 2 Timothy 1:6
https://studyingprayer.com/2013/04/12/five-definitions-of-revival/

That is what happens to those who pluck and eat fruits at the wrong time and in the wrong way. The fruit is good, but they loathe it ever after.... Length of days with an evil heart is only length of misery...all get what they want, they do not always like it...He has made himself unable to hear My voice, Oh Adam's sons, how cleverly you defend yourselves against all that might do you good.
-Aslan about Uncle Andrew in *The Magician's Nephew*, C.S. Lewis, 1955

October 23

There are three important gardens in the Bible. The Garden of Eden, a place of utter perfection and beauty; nothing on earth has ever matched it. We do not know how long Adam and Eve lived there; some think it was a long time, while others say Eve was quickly deceived. The Garden of Gethsemane is where Christ spent a painful hour of communing with his Father before he bore our sins on the cross. Jesus sweated drops of blood in this garden, buying back what the devil stole in Eden. The third garden is a future one referred to in Isaiah 51:3, "The Lord will surely comfort Zion and will look with compassion on all her ruins; her wastelands like the garden of the Lord. Joy and gladness will be found in her, thanksgiving and the sound of singing." God's kingdom is not of this world, but it is in this world. He wants us to be in perfect harmony with him and with one another, where the serpent is kept at bay, and every promise is "yes," because there is nothing to hinder God's perfect will. We can believe this because it is what he wants! The angel still guards the garden; all we need is the password to enter– "Jesus."

A Samaritan Text

There is a Well of living water dug by a Prophet
Whose like has not arisen since Adam
And the water which is in it is from the mouth of God
Let us eat from the fruit that is in this garden
Let us drink from the waters that are in this well
In the depths of an abundant spring is the life of the world
Let us rise with understanding to drink from its waters! We thirst for the waters of life.
Memar Marqah, 6.3, 2.1 (4th century A.D.)

Back to the Garden

Take back dominion in the God-planted earth,
Streams of the Spirit watering the spirit of man
The Tree of Life, at its center, offering fruit to all
His nail-scarred hand beckons to eat of his fruit
"Work the land, take care of it, watch over it,
Subdue and fill the earth, take dominion
Do damage to that serpent's takeover plan
Outrun him, halt the damage he aims to do."
Worship and walk with the Father each evening
The Garden is open, time to enter
Father welcomes us with peace, love, and rest
His purpose now being fulfilled on earth

Half Taken Half Left

A verdict is handed down, and with a mighty shout,
The war trump announces with a booming thunder
Before the court of Heaven, all evidence is laid out
The dead in Christ rise first, graves torn asunder
The remaining saints arise, meeting Jesus in the air
This emergency event is a crisis, the whole world is in wonder
Four billion children, believers, the readied are all there
Four billion left behind, foolish empty vessels, void of Spirit life
Yet many will wake up, pick up the sword, and fight

October 24

Jesus paid our debt with every drop of blood he shed. His blood paid to have our sins washed away. Adam and Eve gladly accepted that payment and were ushered into Heaven. "Christ suffered once for sins, the righteous for the unrighteous, so He might bring you to God. He was put to death in the flesh but made alive by the Spirit. After this, he went and preached to the spirits in prison, to those who were disobedient long ago" (1 Peter 3:18-19). He paid for the curse over sweating and toiling over the thorn and thistle-filled ground when he sweated great drops of blood in the garden. Jesus was struck in the face, the place of his presence, so the devil's authority to stand against us was broken. On his back were placed 39 stripes so that every type of the 39 leading causes of death could be healed. He broke the poverty over us with his crown of thorns. The nails in his hands purchased our success, and the ones in his feet purchased our destiny. Like Eve, who came from Adam's side, the church came from his side when the spear pierced his side, and water and blood flowed out. He also paid for the suffering of betrayal. Jesus did nothing wrong yet was sold for thirty pieces of silver. "Did I not choose you, the twelve, and one of you is a Devil?" (John 6:70). He died naked on the cross to pay for our shame. He paid the price for every sin so we can participate in God's promises. Take communion often to remember his sacrifice. "Everyone who trusts in Him will never be put to shame" (Romans 10:11).

https://hhdw.org NCHS 39 Leading Causes of Death
The Deep End w/Taylor Welch. *The Spirit of Fear (legal system of spirit realm, agreements, & authority)* w/Dr. Michael Cocchini. YouTube 2024 @ 1:10 minute mark.

October 25

"My children, give attention to my words, incline your ear to my sayings. Do not let them depart from your eyes; keep them in the middle of your heart, for they are life to those who find them, and health to all their flesh. Diligently guard and protect your heart, for from it flow the issues of life. Ponder the path of your feet, and all your ways will be sure. Don't swerve to the right or the left, turn your foot away from evil" (Proverbs 4:20-27). The demonic hooks in the thought life need to be detached, and the fortress of captivity torn down piece by piece. Be determined to disassemble, brick by brick, those strongholds and lies that have built destruction to your soul. These thoughts have dug trenches in the brain that, unless desire is there to pursue change, you will be stuck. This false evidence, which has pre-determined the course of your life, is a stronghold. Ask, what do I believe that opposes the truth of God? What is the root of that lie? Who and what do I listen to? What do I think about? Compare this to God's word, and take one lie at a time, removing it. Repeat the truth until you believe it. Fight for a breakthrough by letting go of false beliefs and distorted views about yourself, others, and God! Journal the progress. "Make haste with diligence, earnestness, and zeal to study to show yourself to be approved by rightly, and correctly analyzing, accurately dividing, rightly handling, and skillfully teaching the word of truth" (2 Timothy 2:15).

If truth isn't true for all people, in all places, and for all times, it is not truth.

October 26

King David loved the law–Why? Because "Blessed are those who keep his testimonies, who seek him with their whole heart. They do no iniquity; they walk in his ways. Your testimonies are my delight and my counselors. I will walk in liberty, for I seek your precepts. This is my comfort in affliction, for your word has given me life. Before I was afflicted, I went astray, but now I keep your word. The law of your mouth is better to me than thousands of coins of gold and silver. Unless your law had been my delight, I would have perished in my affliction. You, through Your commandments, make me wiser than my enemies. I have more understanding than all my teachers, for your testimonies are my meditation. I understand more than the ancients, because I keep your precepts. My flesh trembles for fear of you, and I am afraid of your judgments. It is time for you to act, O Lord, for they have regarded your law as void. The entrance of your words gives light; it gives understanding to the simple. Your word is very pure; therefore, your servant loves it. Your law is truth. Great peace have those who love your law, and nothing causes them to stumble" (Psalm 119). Without the law, there are no restraints, and people perish. The law holds the mysteries of God, revealing his character. It points to Jesus, the Word of God.

I will not be ashamed when I look into all Your commandments. Your word I have hidden in my heart that I might not sin against You.

October 27

God's will is not automatic or Jesus would not have had us pray that God's will would be done on earth. His will, that none should perish, is accomplished by us speaking words of life to others, and Holy Spirit making sure those words are not forgotten. Being guided by Holy Spirit leads to encounters with those seeking truth. "I would that none should perish" (2 Peter 3:9). Don't miss the opportunities to bring in the harvest of God. "How can they call on the one they have not believed in? And how can they believe in the one of whom they have not heard? And how can they hear without someone preaching to them? And how can anyone preach unless they are sent? How beautiful are the feet of those who bring good news" (Romans 10:13-15). Apostle Paul evangelized in synagogues; our church buildings should also be places to lead people to Jesus. (Acts 19). The Lord allowed other people groups to join Israel as long as they served him and followed the law. The Jews accepted them. We must accept people into our circles and help them know the Lord and his goodness. (Joshua 6:25; 8:33; Exodus 12:38; Leviticus 19:33-34; Isaiah 19:16-25).

Cousin Annette, who lives in Seattle, dreamed:
A group of Christians was praying for young people. The teens had problems, but the girls were worse and had emotional issues. The boys were aggressive, mean, and angry. The group said, 'Amen,' then there was a knock on the door. A Samoan prophet came in; he was big and gentle; peace came in with him. He was serious and had a job to do, he said to us, 'I feel something, fishermen in the past are now fishers of men.' The ground shook beneath us; he said it was the thunder of feet rushing to God, and that it was an earthquake to come.

October 28

God gave us thousands of promises, and not all of them are conditional. He promised never again to destroy the earth with a flood. Here are some conditional promises. You will receive what you pray for if you believe you have received it (Mark 11:24). Those who remain in Christ will have a fruitful life (John 15:4). Those who repent will be worthy and will not have their names blotted out of the Book of Life (Revelation 3:5). If we ask for wisdom, he will give it generously (James 1:5-7). If we seek first God's kingdom and righteousness, then everything we need will be provided (Matthew 6:32-33). You will have eternal life if you believe in Jesus as God's only Son (John 3:16). If we stand firm in the Lord, he will give us a new glorious body that will never perish (Philippians 3:21). We can do all things if Christ strengthens us (Philippians 4:13). Those who love his appearing and are faithful to preach God's word will receive a crown of righteousness (2 Timothy 4:7-8). We will receive a crown of life if we love the Lord and endure trials and tests (James 1:12), and the victor's crown if we are faithful to the point of death (Revelation 2:10). Leaders, who are a good example, will receive a crown of glory that will not fade if they feed the flock willingly, not for money (1 Peter 5:2-4). You will keep your crown if you hold on to it (Revelation 3:11). "Resting on your laurels" is a saying from the time when the Caesars wore a laurel crown on their heads. We aren't to sit on our crowns, but to live as if we already deserve them, not being so self-satisfied with our already won achievements, but going after every new challenge God is handing to us.

Look to yourselves, that we do not lose those things we worked for, but that we may receive a full reward. 2 John 1:7-8

October 29

Faith sees things others cannot see. Many have had undeniable and supernatural encounters, and others have had near-death experiences. Jesus said, "Blessed are those who have never seen and yet believe." (John 20:29). Believe these testimonies and don't be jealous of their experiences, pursue a close relationship with the Lord because he loves our faith when we do not see and yet believe. "Without faith it is impossible to please him, for he who comes to God must believe that he is, and that he is a rewarder of those who diligently seek him" (Hebrews 11:6). We will hear from God like Abraham did, giving us a choice to obey. He had to leave family and friends and move to an undetermined location. If you have desired to have a child, as Sarah did, do not limit God. If you tell the Lord that it is too late, then you cut off the blessing that comes from faith. Sarah laughed at the Angel of the Lord when he told her at age 90 that she would have a child. In our shorter-lived days, she would have been in her 60s! Faith is knowing we have a heavenly homeland before we arrive, and we choose to live accordingly. No matter what our life is like here on earth, we know that this is not our home.

Faith is trust, confidence, assurance, courage, and action. -Dick Mills

Dead faith has no action, no works. 'I will show you my faith by what I do.' James 2:16-18

October 30

It takes faith to subdue kingdoms, work righteousness, obtain promises, stop the mouths of lions, quench the violence of fire, escape the edge of the sword, be strong and valiant, and turn and fight enemy armies. By faith, women received their dead raised back to life; others faced trials of torture, mockings, scourgings, chains, and prison. They wandered in deserts, mountains, in dens and caves of the earth. These people never received their Promised Land while on earth, but that did not deter them. They were looking forward to the Kingdom of Christ, to the multitudes who would be added to their numbers (Hebrews 11:40). More of God's people are being persecuted in this present time than ever before, but also more resurrections, deliverances, blessings, and miracles than ever before. "We are surrounded by a cloud of witnesses who have gone before us, let us lay aside every burden and the sin which entangles and defeats us, let us run with endurance the race that the Lord set before us. Let us focus on Jesus, who for the joy of having us in his family, endured the suffering of the cross, and is now at the right hand of the throne of God" (Hebrews 12:1-13). When you are discouraged, read Hebrews 11.

Many are the afflictions of the righteous, but the Lord delivers them out of all of them. Psalm 34:19.
In all their suffering, he also suffered, and he rescued them. Isaiah 63:9

Joseph, Egypt's number two ruler, was not satisfied. He had riches and influence but had not received the desire of his heart–to be reunited with his father and brothers. He had received a promise in a dream twenty-two years earlier, but he did not know whether his father was still alive or how his brothers were treating his full-brother Benjamin. No matter how successful we are, it matters little if we have no family or friends. Joseph was the only light of God in a pagan, idol-worshipping culture. He married the daughter of a heathen priest and made the best of it, but his life became fulfilled when he was able to hug his brothers and his father. Church is important because it is the family of God. Like Joseph's brothers, church leaders may treat people without love and care. Believe that Jesus will adjust and fix those wrongs like he did for Joseph. A great church rejoices with those who rejoice, weeps with those who weep, and rejoices when other churches succeed (Romans 12:15). Hospitality has fallen by the wayside and needs to be resurrected (1 Peter 4:9). Getting to know and understand people one on one, praying for them, and listening to the testimonies of what God has done, are wonderful body-of-Christ encounters.

God sets the lonely in families...Psalm 68:6

Do we have the same mandates given to Adam and Eve to multiply, fill the earth, subdue it, and take dominion? Satan took dominion away from Adam through lies, and mankind has submitted to those lies. But God never rescinded those first commands he gave Adam and Eve. The enemy became prince of the air, god of this world, but we have a mandate to take it back. The fall of mankind brought us into a world war that has continued for 6,000 years. *Nelson's New King James Version Study Bible* gives this insight, "God placed humankind as living symbols of Himself on earth to represent His reign. We are made to reflect His majesty on the earth, have dominion: Rule as God's regent" (Genesis 1:26). As far as multiplying and filling the earth, Western developed countries' birth rates have dropped, leaders are concerned. Jesus didn't start a religion; he was inviting us to join him in taking back what the enemy had stolen. "The Spirit of the Lord is upon Me, because He has anointed Me to preach the gospel to the poor. He has sent Me to heal the brokenhearted, to proclaim liberty to the captives and recovery of sight to the blind, to set at liberty those who are oppressed; to proclaim the acceptable year of the Lord...Today this Scripture is fulfilled in your hearing" (Luke 4:18-19, 21). His government subdues the works of the devil by us exercising our authority. (John 8:44)

Go, for you are my chosen instrument to take my message to the Gentiles and to kings, as well as to the people of Israel (Acts 9:15). *My name will be honored by the Gentiles from morning till night. All around the world, they will offer sweet incense and pure offerings in honor of my name.* Malachi 1:11

https://ourworldindata.org/grapher/children-born-per-woman

November 2

We are God's ambassadors, carrying upon us the name of Jesus Christ. We are not looking to overthrow worldly powers but to replace injustice with God's justice, and to usher the world into his kingdom. This happens by reformation, *Coram Deo*, "all life lived before the face of God." There should not be a separation between the sacred and the secular, living for the devil all week, then feeling holy by repenting on Sunday. Every day is church, living for Jesus, and being a light to the world. Holy is his name in my family, my neighborhood, my city, my nation. Jesus tells us to go and disciple nations, not social justice, which does not lead people to God, but biblical justice–inserting God's wisdom and righteousness into our laws, government, education, business, and technology. We have accepted the devil's plan to separate church and state, which has resulted in an increase in crime and unjust laws exerting control over people. Looking to man's wisdom instead of God's has reaped for us a harvest of godlessness and enmity. "You are a chosen people, a royal priesthood, a holy nation, God's special possession, that you may declare the praises of him who called you out of darkness into his wonderful light. Once you were not a people, but now you are the people of God...Dear friends, I urge you, as foreigners and exiles...live such good lives among the pagans that, though they accuse you of doing wrong, they may see your good deeds and glorify God on the day he visits us" (1 Peter 2:9-12).

Maintain justice and do what is right, for my salvation is close at hand, and soon my righteousness will be revealed. Isaiah 56:1

November 3

"Now therefore, if you will indeed obey my voice and keep My covenant...you shall be to me a special kingdom of priests and a holy nation" (Exodus 19:5-6). This was written to a group who had been enslaved for 400 years; their worldview was one of scarcity, and there was never enough. They were certain of their dim future of having to measure up to Pharaoh's harsh demands and needing to focus on self-preservation. After forty years, they were transformed from having a slave identity to the identity of God's holy people. They went through periods of falling away from God because they feared God was not enough. We are children of Abraham and have the full benefits given to him, as long as we know that God is enough and that we do not lack anything, because God is a good father who calls us to be holy. Holiness is when what you do and what you believe aren't in conflict. Do what you say you believe. Judge your thoughts; those thoughts that encourage you are from God, the devil's thoughts are insulting, predict future calamity, bring you down, and make you fearful. Fix your mind and imagination on God and fight life's battles from a place of rest. "We can't," the words Israel grumbled that kept them out of God's promise for forty years. Obedience means hearing and responding with no "what ifs" (Numbers 13:33; 14).
(Lessons from *Living Fearless* by Jamie Winship)

In the last days, the mountain of the Lord's temple will be established as chief among the mountains; it will be raised above the hills, and people will stream to it. Micah 4:1

November 4

When God's laws are broken, creation crumbles. A person's secret sins have serious ramifications. You are important, and your soul is important. Imagine a culture where everyone secretly sins. In Israel's law, adultery was illegal. Protecting marriage protects society. The Lord calls sexual perversion defilements (Leviticus 18). God does not change his mind about these things. When the land is polluted by sin it "vomits" out its inhabitants (Leviticus 18:25). The Sahara Desert at one time was green and lush. The land cried out over Abel's blood that was spilled on it (Genesis 4:10). "Hear the word of the Lord...for the Lord brings a charge against the inhabitants of the land: 'There is no truth, mercy, or knowledge of God in the land. By swearing, lying, killing, stealing, and committing adultery, they break all restraint, with bloodshed upon bloodshed. Therefore, the land will mourn; and everyone who dwells there will waste away with the beasts of the field and the birds of the air; even the fish of the sea will be taken away" (Hosea 4:1-3). Does this not read like the news of today, dead fish covering beaches, sick chickens, and sick cows? God removes his blessing from an evil nation, and also from creation itself. Repentance, turning from evil ways, and breaking evil covenants with secret sin will cleanse and bless the land. "Your Father sees what you do in secret" (Matthew 6:18).

We acquire knowledge through study, experiential knowledge through participation, and revelatory knowledge through supernatural encounters with the Holy Spirit.

November 5

What can we possibly do about the world's condition? The answer is in 2 Chronicles 7:13-14, "When I shut up heaven and there is no rain, or command the locusts to devour the land, or send pestilence among my people, if my people who are called by my name will humble themselves, pray, seek my face, and turn from their wicked ways, then I will hear from heaven and will forgive their sin and heal their land." The word "heal" here is *Rapha* and it is the word used to refer to healing someone's body. We are given the privilege of redeeming the land by repenting for the sins of our forefathers. Cindy Jacobs tells a story in her book, *Reformers Arise,* about a team that prayed over the cursed Hinnom Valley where Israel had sacrificed their children to Molech. Later, a tour guide told them that no birds had been there for some time, but that they had returned. Intercessory prayer includes praying over the land, "So I sought a man who would build a wall and stand before me in the gap on behalf of the land, so I would not have to destroy it; but I found no one. Therefore, I have poured out my wrath on them...and I have brought upon their heads all they have done, declares the Lord God" (Ezekiel 22:30-31).

Listen to me, all you who remain of the house of Israel, you whom I have upheld since you were conceived, and have carried since your birth. Isaiah 46:3

November 6

Revivals do two things: they bring spiritual awakening and spiritual opposition. Most are short-lived; even the famous Welsh Revival lasted only two years, yet 100,000 were born again. This revival brought about societal transformation: curses stopped, bars closed, and prayer meetings became more popular than sports events. Evan Roberts, the catalyst of the Welsh revival, was 26 years old. What was needed during that time were Bible teachers who would build a firm foundation in the face of secularism and Darwinism. A nation's worldview will affect how children are educated, how laws are enacted, and how courts mete out justice. We need reformation at the heart of society. We have become polluted by humanism, rationalism, naturalism, and secularism. People in the Western world three hundred years ago were largely theistic–they were God-centered and had a biblical foundation. They knew there was a connection between the physical world and the spiritual one and that God was over all. They knew God as creator, believed the Bible to be true, that his laws were just, and that disobedience led to consequences. They knew that hell was real.

All over the world, this gospel is producing fruit and growing.
Colossians 1:5

The finished work of the cross was more powerful than we can imagine. We need to imagine it because in it lies our healing and deliverance. Many of the sick and infirm whom Jesus healed had a demon cast out of them; we should consider using this ministry method. Jesus healed all who were oppressed by the devil. Acts 10:38

November 7

The Age of Enlightenment began when intellectuals came to believe that God created the world, then left it and us to our own devices. This is called deism. Rationalism became the philosophy and the foundation for truth. If they couldn't understand a Bible passage, they would toss it. Sin began to be rationalized, and criminals were seen as victims of circumstances. In the last two hundred years, we have seen philosophies transform the Western world. Now they say God does not exist, reality is fluid, morality is relative, and absolutes are nonexistent. Teachers are playing the "what if" games of situational ethics, leading children to think that wrong choices can be right. Values clarification is when all absolutes are removed, so that there is no higher power, no rescuing angel, and no guiding love. Rebellion surged, selfishness blossomed, but the hippy type of love did not satisfy, and drugs were needed as a supplement. The self-centered hippies were not happy. The revival of the 70s exploded on the scene, and with it came the much longed-for love and joy. The only way to stifle the sin nature is to accept the boundary line of God's love, which keeps us on the right path. Psalm16:6 says, "Boundary lines have fallen for me in pleasant places." Outside those boundary lines can become quite unpleasant. (*Jesus Revolution* 2023 movie)

Reductionism is the evolutionary idea that the whole equals the sum of the parts. This idea believes that from molecules we can reconstruct everything, even our bodies. This removes meaning. It cannot explain everything. You cannot take DNA and put it in a petri dish and expect a body to grow, even in a million years. -Don Miller

November 8

Do we know right from wrong? What about the acceptable language in movies that was unacceptable and frowned upon fifty years ago? Clothes that were embarrassing are now acceptable in public; are we dressing for the throne room or for dark city streets? We no longer feel the need to limit alcohol use and are justified as long as we get a ride home. Taking illegal drugs is called self-medicating, and legal drugs can also be dangerous, with many side effects. We have become ungrateful, wild, loud, and abusive as a culture. Our opinion is always right, and no one else should have a voice. Communism, the alternative to Christianity, has become popular, and classes on how to overthrow the government are taught in our universities. Revival is not enough to change this; we need reformer universities, teachers, and churches that will teach us how. Jesus told us to make disciples of nations, not just individuals. This discipleship happens in colleges, Christian schools, homeschools, Sunday schools, books, media venues, conferences, and in homes. Christians a hundred years ago wrote the curriculum, built the schools, and taught children how to live. If you are in your 60s, you remember praying at the beginning of the school day. We have chosen to focus all of our attention on saving the spirit of man so he may enter eternity, when in fact, redeeming all of the material world by teaching God's health, morals, ethics, character, principles, and doctrines of the Bible is what Jesus mandated. This brings all mankind closer to the truth of Christ. We, as Christ followers, have become an irrelevant part of society to be ignored and controlled.

There is confusion in our understanding of our physical bodies and the meaning of 'the flesh,' the part of us that tends toward sin, the lower nature we were born with. "It is the Spirit who gives life, the flesh profits nothing" (John 6:63). This confusion has affected how we teach, leaving out how our bodies are the temple of God, and if we destroy our bodies, God's temple, He will destroy us. 1 Corinthians 3:17

Math

Jesus is the Lord of Math
He multiplies bread and fish
He adds to the church daily
He subtracts from the Book of Life
He divides the sheep from the goats
He came to bring division
(Revelation 3:5; Matthew 25:31-46; Luke 12:51-53)

November 9

Dennis Peacock reveals to us how dualism has affected the area of business and finance: "The marketplace was 'carnal' because it dealt with 'earthly things' like business and money... the worldly realm of economics was viewed, like politics, as some kind of 'neutral zone' where Christianity had no real place in trying to affect the system of economics, production, management, or distribution. Hence, no Christian ministry was possible in that realm." Darrow Miller calls this thinking "evangelical Gnosticism," placing a wide gap between the spiritual and natural, believing that faith, theology, and missions are for Sundays, and feeding the poor, science, government, and the laws of society are not spiritual but secular. The Old Testament reveals God's opinion about dualism. First, God created the physical world, including our bodies, and said it was good. Since God, who is spiritual, created everything, whatever job we have in life is spiritual. There is no neutral ground; he holds everything together and gives man the wisdom and understanding to build and create. God loves beautiful expressions of art: painting, poetry, drama, and music. God brought order from chaos at creation, and now we must be the caretakers and administrators of society, bringing it into order. "Whether you eat or drink or whatever you do, do all to the glory of God" (1 Corinthians 10:31).

We don't start with theology; we start with Father.

Peacock, Dennis. *On the Destiny of Nations.* January 1, 2012
Miller, Darrow L. *Discipling Nations.* July 30, 2018

Racism has its evil roots in the belief that only certain races were more evolved, and others were mere animals. Darwin's *On the Origin of Species* was subtitled *Preservation of the Favoured Races*. Eugenics, the perfecting of the human race by ridding it of its undesirables, was not just popular in Nazi Germany, but presidents and others supported it in America. Germany was euthanizing its people who were disabled, had syndromes, or were born "imperfect" two years before Hitler came into power. The scientists and psychiatrists of the time paved the way for his atrocities. Cindy Jacobs tells the story of Erasmus Darwin, Charles's rich and influential grandfather, who belonged to a group of fourteen industrialists, philosophers, and intellectuals who called themselves the Lunar Society. They said the Bible was the obstacle to achieving its social goals. They wanted to remove the power of the church in Great Britain, so they concocted a story of how the earth came into being without a creator, discrediting God. James Hutton, another Lunar member, then called the great flood a farce, saying that the earth was much older than the Bible's six thousand years. This is called naturalism, where the supernatural is not deemed a viable source of information. Social Darwinism is now humanism—a rationalization based on what society needs and not on God's absolutes. He [Jesus] is the image of the invisible God...For by him all things were created...He is before all things, and in him all things hold together (Colossians 1:15-17). He is the glue that holds atoms and society together.

Martin Niemöller, a Lutheran pastor prior to World War II, wrote this. It is posted in the Holocaust Museum's Halls of Remembrance: "First they came for the Socialists, and I did not speak out–because I was not a Socialist. Then they came for the Trade Unionists, and I did not speak out–because I was not a Trade Unionist. Then they came for the Jews, and I did not speak out–because I was not a Jew. Then they came for me–and there was no one left to speak for me." Why do we think we are immune to what happened in Germany?

https://encyclopedia.ushmm.org Martin Niemöller Quote

John Dewey and his philosophy are at the root of every public school in America and in other countries as well. Here is one of his quotes from "My pedagogic creed," "I believe, therefore, that the true center of correlation on the school subjects is not science, nor literature, nor history, nor geography, but the child's own social activities." He saw school primarily as a social institution. "Examinations are of use only so far as they test the child's fitness for social life." In 1973, Catherine Barrett addressed the largest teachers' union, "We will need to recognize that so-called basic skills, which currently represent nearly the total effort in elementary school, will be taught in one quarter of the present school day. The remaining time will be devoted to what is truly fundamental and basic: time for academic inquiry, time for students to develop their own interests, time for a dialogue between students and teachers; more than a dispenser of information, the teacher will be a conveyer of values, a philosopher." She stated that the timeframe for this goal was the year 2000. Harvard psychiatrist Chester M. Pierce addressing the Association of Childhood Education, said this, "Every child in America entering school at the age of five is mentally ill... because he comes to school with certain allegiances to our Founding Fathers, towards our elected officials, towards his parents, toward a belief in a supernatural being, and toward the sovereignty of this nation as a separate entity. It is up to you, teachers, to make all these sick children well by creating the international child of the future." William Holmer McGuffey (1800-1873) wrote the McGuffey readers for children. They taught morals and good character qualities, and between 1836 and 1960, 120 million were sold. They continue to be sold at a rate of thirty thousand a year. A godly voice in a world growing dim. We can make a difference by praying and being informed. We can no longer drop off our children at a school and expect them to be properly educated or kept safe. When we see corruption in the classroom, we can make formal complaints to the heads of the school or university, to those funding the school, and to our government officials. We can make a difference!

A broken hedge weakens the moral stamina of the family and allows the serpent to gain entrance. -Dick Mills

Pierce, Chester M. Keynote Speaker. http://eric.ed.gov *Becoming Planetary Citizens: A Quest for Meaning.* Denver, Colorado. April 1972
Dewey, John. *My pedagogic creed. The School Journal*, Volume LIV, Number 3. January 16, 1897, pages 77-80.
Dewey.pragmaism.org/creed.htm. John Dewey: *My Pedagogic Creed.*
Barret, Catherine. (1973, February 10). [Title of article unknown]. *Saturday Review of Education.* Cited in 2018, April 18. https://tdn.com.opinion/letters-to-the-editor-april-18/article Letters to the editor. TDN.com.
Jacobs, Cindy. Reformers Arise. 2021

November 12

It is clear why science is no longer emphasized in schools. The foundation of the modern scientist's belief is evolution (though that belief is falling by the wayside), the Big Bang theory, and, more recently, the belief, advanced by the cosmologist and theoretical physicist Stephen Hawking (1942-2018), that our planet was seeded by aliens. True science must follow the scientific method and must be repeatable. None of the ideas of how we came to exist can be scientifically proven. Creation depends on faith in the God of the Bible and that what Hehe says about himselfHimself is true. Evolution is a philosophy and a theory, a humanistic religion that also requires faith. Many conclusions touted as facts from experiments have been proven to be rigged*. Schools have downplayed the importance of math because God is a God of math; it is concrete and indestructible, which does not look good for the theory that the world accidentally exploded into being. Stephen Hawking was the closest to getting it right. God, who is alien to us, did seed this planet through Adam and Eve after creating it with survivable conditions. Where did your aliens come from, Stephen? "From one man he made all the nations, that they should inhabit the whole earth..." (Acts 17:26).

See to it that no one takes you captive through hollow and deceptive philosophies. Colossians 2:8

*Lindsay, Dennis, *The Origins Controversy: Creation By Design or Chance*. January 2007

November 13

"When we act biblically, the righteous judge of the universe fights on our behalf. Where there is corruption, it is not possible to receive true justice. We cannot expect our nation to act any better than we do ourselves. We cannot be reformers when we have no higher standards than those around us, no matter how small we think the issues may be...Only a godly judge can step out of his or her own selfish perspective enough to judge fairly every time." (Cindy Jacobs, pages 126-127, *Reformers Arise*). Adding to this, we cannot expect our children to be better than we are. We are the light in the world, a city on a hill, an example of love and godliness and joy. There are leaders claiming to know the God of the Bible yet demanding of their employees a departure from the holiness of God for the purpose of success: actors sinning on camera, media icons who mock, curse, and cuss, politicians who rage in anger at their opposers, and parents who abuse their children. When we care about what he cares about, he will care about what we care about: our children and our grandchildren. Too many of our sons and daughters have been drawn away from God, from loving his word, and from the church by poor "Christian" examples.

Since the Lord knows what we need before we ask him, we can ask him for what we need, but he wants to hear our requests. That way He gets the glory when we realize the answer was from him. Thank him with the same passion, and as often as you spent pleading with him for the answer.

November 14

Many do not feel bad when breaking the law, yet they want justice when they have been wronged. What does God say? "For the person who keeps all of the laws except one is as guilty as a person who has broken all of God's laws" (James 2:10). "Defend the poor and fatherless; do justice to the afflicted and needy" (Psalm 82:3). Doing justice is making things right when injustice has been done. Joseph Fletcher, an Episcopal priest turned atheist, published his thesis, *Situation Ethics: The New Morality, in 1966.* He touted that right and wrong are defined by the situation itself. But "Law and situation ethics are complete opposites, there can be no law based on situation ethics. Law without an ultimate judge and lawgiver can only deteriorate into anarchy or tyranny. Law without the fear of the Lord turns our cities into police states." (Cindy Jacobs). Without knowing what the Lord thinks and fearing his eternal judgment, people will always look for loopholes, seeking sneaky ways to steal and cheat. The only society that works is one whose God is the Lord; people suffer. God's grace isn't a license to sin, and knowing the law doesn't make us repentant. "We know that the law is not made for the righteous, but for lawbreakers and rebels, the ungodly, sinful, unholy, irreligious, murderers, adulterers, perverts, slave traders, liars and perjurers—and anything else that contradicts sound teaching" (1 Timothy 1:9-10).

Righteousness and justice are the foundation of His throne. Can we legislate morality? We already do! Psalm 89:14, Psalm 97:2, Matthew 6:10

https://learn.ligonier.org/devotions/situational-ethics-and-the-word-of-God/ *Situational Ethics and the Word of God*. September 2, 2020.

November 15

William Blackstone (1723-1780), an English barrister (lawyer), was very interested in the common law and was the first to give lectures on the subject. He was an excellent orator from his years of studying the classics, was zealous for order and improvement, and wrote the *Commentaries on the Laws of England*. He wrote, "It is proposed to lay down a general and comprehensive Plan of the Laws of England; to deduce their History; to enforce and illustrate their leading Rules and fundamental Principles; and to compare them with the Laws of Nature and of other Nations." His amazing lectures served as the basis for his four-volume *Commentaries*. He wrote this, "Blasphemy against the Almighty is denying His being or Providence or uttering contumelious [insulting] reproaches on our Savior Christ. It is punished at common law by fine and imprisonment, for Christianity is part of the laws of the land." In Daniel Boorstin's book, *The Mysterious Science of the Law*, he wrote that Blackstone's Commentaries were the second most influential book after the Bible in creating America's judicial system. Here is a ruling from a recent 1980 court case: "It is unconstitutional for students to see the Ten Commandments since they might read, meditate upon, respect, or obey them." (Stone v. Graham; Ring V. Grand Forks Public School District, and Lanner v. Wimmer, 1981).

It shall be, when the king sits on the throne of his kingdom, that he shall write for himself a copy of this law in a book...and it shall be with him, and he shall read it all the days of his life, that he may learn to fear the Lord His God and be careful to observe all the words of this law and these statutes, that his heart may not be lifted above his brethren...and that he may prolong his days in his kingdom, he and his children...Deuteronomy 17:18-20.

https://www.britannica.com/ Sir William Blackstone summary
https://americanminute.com/blogs/american-quotations-by-william-j-blackstone Sir Willian Blackstone (July 10,1723-February 14,1780) January 4, 2025
Boorstin, Daniel J. *The Mysterious Science of the Law: An Essay on Blackstone's Commentaries.* June 1, 1996.

Satan's Bait

Theism, naturalism, deism, and evolution
Fail the test if your answer is "Creation."
The Discovery Channel, Animal Planet
Cartoons, movies, entertainment
Evil doctrines entrapping children
Every day in schools and universities
Few even notice, few even care

November 16

William Wilberforce (1759-1833) was a reformer who fought and persevered in ridding England of slavery. It took him forty years, but he never gave up, thanks to his friends who encouraged him to continue when he wanted to quit. Wilberforce was twenty-six when he began his calling and was the youngest member of parliament. His education and his natural ability to orate eloquently, slowly swayed the government to abolish the selling of slaves in 1807, and finally slavery itself in1833, three days before Wilberforce passed away. John Wesley, the revivalist, wrote this to Wilberforce:

February 24. 1791

Dear Sir:
Unless God has raised you up to be *Athanasius contra mundum [Athanasius against the world], I see not how you can go through your glorious enterprise in opposing that execrable [unpleasant] villainy which is the scandal of religion, of England, and of human nature. Unless God has raised you up for this very thing, you will be worn out by the opposition of men and devils. But if God be fore [sic] you, who can be against you? Are all of them together stronger than God? O be not weary of well doing! Go on, in the name of God and in the power of his might, till even American slavery, (the vilest that ever saw the sun) shall vanish away before it... [abolished in 1865]. That he who has guided you from your youth up, may continue to strengthen you in this and all things, is the prayer of, dear Sir,
Your affectionate servant,
John Wesley

Wilberforce was born for a purpose, and he accomplished it. We are born for a purpose. He had friends who partnered with him and encouraged him. God will put a person, a group, or a church in your life to encourage you. Always, the Spirit is with you and will never leave!

This Bible is for the government of the people, by the people, and for the people. - John Wycliffe, 1384, of his translation of the Bible into English.

*Athanasius defended orthodoxy in the 4th-century battle against the heresy that the Son of God was not of the same substance as the Father God.
https://www.britannica.com Saint Athanasius.
Evangelical Advocacy: *A Response to Global Poverty, Last Writing of John Wesley (a letter to William Wilberforce) (2012). Papers, PDF Files, and Presentations.*
http://place.asburyseminary.edu/engaginggovernmentpapers/10/
https://www.focusonthefamily.ca/content/a-few-good-men-friendships-that-put-an-end-to-the-slave-trade-in-britain

True Riches

Whoever can be trusted with very little can be trusted with much

Whoever is dishonest with very little will be dishonest with much

If you have not been trustworthy in handling worldly wealth

Who will trust you with true riches?

If you have not been trustworthy with someone else's property

Who will give you property of your own?

What is highly valued among men is detestable in God's sight

Everyone who has will be given more, and he will have an abundance

Whoever does not have, even what he has will be taken from him -Jesus (Luke 16:10; Matthew 25:29)

November 17

Assumptions cause conflict. Assuming is mind-reading, and mind-reading is guessing about what people are thinking. Instead of assuming the worst, ask if the things you think are true, then ask them what things they assume about you. We easily create our own false mental world. It is laziness at its core and takes others for granted. The solution is to ask questions, be honest, and step out of the comfort zone of isolation. We need each other, not as a means to an end, but to inspire and encourage. It may be a fearful thing to speak up and reveal your soul to someone; it is worth the risk. This comfort zone of safe, surface relationships leads to acquaintances rather than deep friendships. There will be conflicts because we have expectations of each other. We assume the other person thinks the same as we do. We must express our desires without being offended by what they say in return. Be curious about them. Try to understand them by asking about their past and their upbringing. Mercy wants to understand, give grace for faults and foibles, and loves them no matter what. Differences are beautiful; we are unique creations, and that is how God wanted it. So, honor one another, comply with their wishes, agree on expectations, listen, and be sensitive. Take one another seriously and give them the benefit of the doubt. "I shouldn't have to ask for help" assumes a lot about someone. Don't have unrealistic, unspoken, and unagreed-upon expectations. Challenge your assumptions, ask yourself questions, and be your own counselor.

Past trauma can create triggers; strong reactions linked to an experience. Discuss and expose them. Maybe it is time to grow out of them?

November 18

Since the dawn of television, passive parenting has been the way to raise children. Now, we have all types of electronics to keep them busy. Sunday school, vacation Bible school, and even Christian school are not enough to build a strong foundation for children and their future. We need a plan that will help our children and grandchildren thrive. Leading them into the presence of God so they can learn to love him more than anything needs to be an intentional daily objective. Have them memorize the books of the Bible so when the Lord gives them a scripture verse, they know where to look. Lead them into salvation, water baptism, and Spirit baptism. Encourage godly friendships and reach out to those who need to hear about Jesus. Guard them, be discerning of adults with hidden evil intent, even relatives and professionals. Teach children that God is our protection and have them memorize Psalm 91. Show them how to rebuke the enemy, those visible and invisible, and how to scream if cornered by criminals. Both parents must be involved. Keep the home's atmosphere one of peace, joy, and love. They must be obedient at age 3, or they won't be at age 14 when it counts. Freedom is earned, and trust is given when teens are trustworthy.

There cannot be two ruling authorities over one geographical region. There will either be ruling powers of God or ruling power of Satan. Each generation needs to watch and pray over their own generation. -Cindy Jacobs

"Christ has redeemed us from the curse of the law, having become a curse for us, that the blessing of Abraham might come upon the Gentiles in Christ Jesus, that we might receive the promise of the Spirit through faith" (Galatians 3:13-14). Because Gentiles can be grafted into the vine, we can receive the same blessings given to Abraham. We work out our salvation with fear and trembling lest we be pruned from the vine. Adam and Eve were told to be keepers of the garden, and somehow the serpent slithered in. We have the authority as keepers of the land to block those asps and the "little foxes from destroying the vines" (Song of Solomon 2:15). The second law of thermodynamics is partially about entropy; systems left to themselves move toward disorder. God's decree is that we must manage our earth, reversing the chaos of entropy, which is poverty, corruption, disease, and all other resulting misery. God will show you what he wants you to correct. Be faithful in the small things, and he will make you stewards of his house. "When the children of God are revealed, the frustration of creation will end. It will be liberated from the bondage of decay from which it has been groaning since the fall of man."
(Romans 8:19-23; Philippians 2:12; John 15:2)

But my God shall liberally supply your every need according to His riches in glory. Philippians 4:19

November 20

A book published in the late 60s by Paul Ehrlich, *The Population Bomb*, insists that the earth could not sustain its population (3.5 billion at the time), and that it was our patriotic duty to reduce and control the numbers. Now that we are around 8 billion, each person could receive a half-acre of land in North America, leaving millions of square miles over. It was a hoax nullifying God's first command. The belief that a lower population would boost employment rates is not true. The free-market capitalist economic system is based on a flat tax rate, no income tax, and the belief that people will be innovative in growing the economy, as it will be in their own best interest to do so. It is how our country began, and it works. This economic idea thrived until socialism infiltrated our educational system, media, and government. God's economics are not like ours. The economy of the Gadarene region was disrupted when the demon-filled pigs rushed into the lake and died. The people begged Jesus to leave—they were not keen on their income being disrupted. When God cleans out our region, will we be angry and send him away? (Matthew 8:28-34)

You shall keep the commandments of the Lord your God, to walk in His ways, and to fear Him. For the Lord your God is bringing you into a good land...in which you will eat bread without scarcity, in which you will lack nothing. Deuteronomy 8:6-9.

Ehrlich, Paul R. *The Population Bomb.* 1968

November 21

If you are stuck between lack and debt, repent of anything you have done that is against God's principles or is illegal: cheating on taxes, lying, or stealing, which means never doing those things again. Then break the curse of poverty over your life and lineage. Study what God says about money, greed, prosperity, generosity, faith, and make a covenant with God on these issues. Pray to receive the blessing of Abraham as one of his grafted-on heirs, then do what he tells you to do, no matter how small or large. Prosperity, according to Webster, is the condition of being successfully thriving. In Greek, it means having a successful journey, full of well-being and flourishing. This non-greedy attitude cares about people. We are told not to charge interest to our own people or to the poor (Exodus 22:25). In the New Testament, it was the job of the church to take care of the widows, not the government's. Jesus said that we would always have the poor with us, but that does not give us the right to ignore them. (Deuteronomy 8,15, 28; John 12:8)

Sin always leads to lying. -Dr. R.T. Kendall

November 22

We love the Lord with our mind by renewing it so we can prove what is the good, acceptable and perfect will of God (Romans 12:2). "Everything is permissible for me—but not everything is beneficial, and I will not be mastered by anything" (1 Corinthians 6:12). The mind is the battlefield where the strongholds of arguments and opinions get in the way of God's will. Wash the mind with Scriptures; a corrupted mind needs much time reading or listening to the word. "The weapons we fight with are not the weapons of the world. On the contrary, they have divine power to demolish strongholds" (2 Corinthians 10:4-5). We are far from defeating strongholds in American thought. "For we do not wrestle with flesh and blood, but against the despotisms, powers and world rulers of this present darkness, against the spirit forces of wickedness in the heavenly sphere" (Ephesians 6:12). Corruption and evil are our enemies, and we must stand in prayer for victory. It is active-duty time, we are deployed! Worship is a weapon, and we must war like never before. The walls of Jericho will come down, shout, obey, and have faith. We are entering a short period of supernatural outpouring and harvest. Pray daily from Psalm 91 and 1 Chronicles 4:10, and make sure you are wearing your full armor. There are societies held captive by evil forces, and it is our responsibility, through prayer, to combat them, our faith in action, God's perfect will. (Matthew 22:37). "Lord, keep us in your will."

He put all things under His feet and gave Him to be head over all things to the church, which is His body, the fullness of Him who fills all in all. Ephesians 1:20-23

November 23

We are saved by grace, but it is a costly grace. It cost Jesus Christ his life in the most despicable way. What should this grace cost us? It could cost us our lives if we are confronted with the choice of "deny Christ or die." It also costs us our life if we choose to be a "living sacrifice." We could lose our reputation if we speak up for our faith in Jesus; it could cost us our money if he requests we sell everything and give to the poor. It could cost us sleep if he wakes us up in the middle of the night to pray for something or someone. During the American Revolution, pastors led their men into battle to secure freedom from the crown's bondage. One pastor, Peter Muhlenberg, preached a moving sermon and then announced, "There is a time to preach and a time to fight, and now is the time to fight!" He then removed the black robe of the clergy, and underneath was the uniform of an officer of the Continental militia. Three hundred men joined him. King Solomon said that there would be a time for war. David dealt with the giant Goliath, who was intent on destroying Israel; he was the only one brave enough to face him head-on to take his head off. Corruption and evil are our enemies, and we must stand in prayer for victory.

Everyone who calls on the name of the Lord will be saved.
Romans 10:13

https://www.nps.gov/york/learn/history/culture/muhlenberbio.htm
Brigadier General John Peter Gabriel Muhlenberg-Yorktown

Rebellion is at the core of everything anti-truth, anti-Christian, anti-church, and anti-family. People want attention by touting their brazen, polluted views and the sin that they decline to repent of. "They glory in their shame" (Philippians 3:19). They change God's word to meet their desires. One such man who had a negative impact on the church was Julius Wellhausen. People believed scripture was the absolute truth until he introduced a movement called higher criticism through a book he published in 1883. It taught that the Pentateuch, the first five books of the Bible, was a conglomerate of several authors and not from Moses hearing from God on Mount Sinai for 80 days. It brought doubt and unbelief over the story of creation and over God's eternal qualities; it affected the faith of spiritually weak believers. The Bible began to be seen as moral and historical rather than as the inspired word of God. This doctrine, plus Darwin's theory and Marxism, was the devil's seemingly perfect plan to destroy Truth. Thinking became, "If the Bible could not be trusted as God's word...then perhaps Darwin was right. If Darwin was right, then maybe there isn't a God after all, and Marx was right that religion was merely 'the opiate of the people.'" Universities that began with the glory of God are now liberal in their thinking and hold to the religion of secular humanism. They may have wanted Jesus's moral teachings but not his salvation. Christianity, hiding behind the walls of their churches, fled to the suburbs, and many ignored the fight for civil rights. It is time for the church to return to the cities and fight to save our nation. (Lessons from Chapter 10, *Reformers Arise*).

'How can the tribes in the darkest jungles be sent to hell when they have no knowledge of God?' The question should be, 'How can the Western culture, with its knowledge of Christ's sacrifice and love which paid for their salvation, turn from God and reject him and his eternal Heaven?' The people who have never heard are judged for their deeds. Those who have heard are judged for their rebellion.

https://www.blueletterbible.org/Comm/torrey_ra/fundamentals/01.cfm.
R. A. Torrey: The History of the Higher Criticism. Canon Dyson Hague, M.A. 2025.
Nicholson, Ernst. *The Pentateuch in the Twentieth Century. The Legacy of Julius Wellhausen.* 2003.

Spirit of the Age
Ignorant, indolent, dull, and unfeeling
Hasty, lazy, poor, and presumptive
Fierce, conceited, and complacent
Know-it-alls with no illumination
Stuck in the past, judging the new
Hearing suspended, opinionated
Afraid of the future, denying the past
Suspiciously questioning everything
Not wanting to know the Truth

November 25

Take God out of the box and realize that he is supernatural and when he is allowed to be supernatural, people come to him. "And these signs will follow those who believe: In my name they will cast out demons..." (Mark 16:15-18). There are many people right now who are dealing with demonic attacks, night terrors, night paralysis, demon nightmares, and many, even children, are seeing evil spirits. Who can they talk to? Would you listen and believe them? Do you have the boldness, power, and sensitivity to Holy Spirit's leading to be able to confront the unseen world? When was the last time you laid hands on the sick? You won't have power or see the recovery until you act on the directive. We will also raise the dead, multiply food, and see miraculous provision. Why? Because Jesus said that we would do his works and also do greater works. This will bring the intellectuals, those in cults, the religious, and the atheists to the Lord. Are you ready for the Book of Acts evangelism? "Make it your habit to heal the sick" (Matthew 10:8 TPT). "The Lord added daily those who were being saved" (Acts 2:47).

With God helping you, here is what I want you to do: Take your everyday, ordinary life-your sleeping, eating, going-to-work, and walking-around-life and place it before God as an offering. Embracing what God does for you is the best thing you can do for him. Don't become so well-adjusted to your culture that you fit into it without even thinking. Instead, fix your attention on God. You'll be changed from the inside out. Readily recognize what he wants from you and respond quickly. Unlike the culture around you, always dragging you down to its level of immaturity, God brings the best out of you, developing a well-formed maturity in you. Romans 12:1-2, The Message

Forty-two percent of Americans believe Jesus could return in their lifetime, 14% of agnostics, and 9% of atheists. https://www.pewresearch.org/short-reads/2022/12/08/about-four-in-ten-u-s-adults-believe-humanity-is-living-in-the-end-times/

No Boxes for God

We cannot manage, predict, control, or trick
God can't be in a box; He will not fit
We want instant answers and self-sufficiency
He wants our surrender to His majesty
I do not understand, but I will trust
With faith in His hidden mystery
He is the author and finisher of the story
Convinced of His unending history
His qualities were revealed throughout the galaxy
His vast creation was given to humanity
His divine nature and eternal power
Seen clearly in this, the final hour
Romans 1:18-20

TEST

Are you a Christian in name only?
A religious compromiser or a true believer?
A purchased shepherd or a wakeful watchman?
God's heir and joint heir with Christ?
A follower of the Way, a living stone?
Part of a spiritual house, warriors in the Lord's army?
Jesus' holy temple in which dwells Holy Spirit?
(1 Peter 2:4-8; Romans 8:17; Acts 9:2; Ephesians 2:19-22)

November 26

Let's take the power of God, Holy Spirt within us, to the streets and begin to see the transformation the world is crying out for. That is what happened during the Jesus Movement of the 60s and 70s. It was a glorious time where the atmosphere felt alive. As an eighth-grader, our youth group from a church in Denver, Colorado, went to Pirate's Cove Beach in California, where thousands were, and are again being, baptized. We visited Sunset Strip, where Arthur Blessitt (1940-2025) chained himself to a pole for 28 days to protest being kicked out of his building. He went on to carry a 110-pound wooden cross 43,340 miles through every country of the world. "Jesus Freaks" was what this revolution produced; they were willing to do anything for the Lord and were not ashamed to be called Christians at a time when the Summer of Love event was being held in San Francisco. This hippie movement drew in 100,000 people with their loose lifestyle and hallucinogenic drugs. Many of these hippies were set free from addictions and turned to Jesus. Cindy Jacobs tells of a friend of hers who was raised by hippie parents. They gave him drugs from the time he was a small child. When he was saved, God restored his mind, and he is an influential Bible teacher today. "Jesus is the Way," with the index finger pointing upward, was the sign of this revival. The young people will again be leaders of a new wave of God's movement, "Do not let anyone despise your youth, but set an example in speech, conduct, love, faith and purity" (1 Timothy 4:12).

Will You not revive us again, that your people may rejoice in you?
Psalm 85:6

If we join the next move of God by reforming the seven mountains of society, we will effect change. We will see postmodernism fall by the wayside. It cannot be a reformation of the church alone, but of society as well. The revivalist Charles Finney understood this when he called Freemasons to the altar to repent of the idolatry presented in the oaths of their rites. Finney had been a Mason. He exposed the secrets of their society and how they would curse themselves with unmentionable torture if they ever exposed these oaths. These curses affect their children to the fourth generation and must be repented of and renounced. He was never afraid to expose evil and stood strong against slavery. He was the president of Oberlin College, a stop on the Underground Railroad. He would not allow slave owners to take communion. Francis Schaffer, in *A Christian Manifesto,* argues that our culture's downfall stems from the church's failure to fulfill its duty to be the salt of the earth. We look back at our history and are appalled at how our government allowed slavery, the mistreatment of Native Americans, and wouldn't allow women to vote. It seems like it was the dark ages. But aren't we allowing things that are even worse? "It is necessary to obey God rather than men" (Acts 5:29 TMB). We need to speak out and sometimes disobey men to obey God. Passivity means a failure to confront; evil needs to be confronted!

Mercy to the guilty is cruelty to the innocent. -Adam Smith

Weighing the counsel of Finney and Moody re: Freemasonrywww.ephesians5-11.org/finmood.htm.1996

Alice Paul led a march in Washington, D.C. on March 3, 1913, to fight for the right of women to vote. She had been jailed and went on hunger strikes, and finally, on June 4, 1919, Congress passed the 19th Amendment to grant women the right to vote. A 42-year-old black woman, Rosa Parks, refused to sit in the back of the bus and was jailed for it. This led to marches in protest against racism and segregation. Our country knew that "We hold these truths to be self-evident that all men are created equal," and yet it took disobedience for people to finally realize it. Martin Luther King Jr. gave a speech on August 28, 1963, in it he said, "...When we allow freedom to ring, when we let it ring from every village and every hamlet, from every state and every city, we will be able to speed up that day when all of God's children, black men and white men, Jews and Gentiles, Protestants and Catholics, will be able to join hands and sing in the words of an old spiritual song, 'Free at last! Free at last! Thank God Almighty, we are free at last!'" Screen every thought through the lens of God's word, and we will begin to see the sins of our own generation.

In the United States, Canada, and England, we at least have a memory of what a Christian society should look like, but the memory is fading fast. However, God's light is a bright light. It is stronger and more intense than any darkness Satan can gather. It is time to release that light into our culture again and chase out the darkness! -Cindy Jacobs, *Reformers Arise*, page 219

https://www.britannica.com/biography/Alice-Paul
https://www.britannica.com/biography/Rosa-Parks
https://www.marshall.edu/onemarshallu/i-have-a-dream/ "I have a Dream" Speech by Dr. Martin Luther King, Jr.

November 29

On February 17, 1739, George Whitefield began preaching to the coal miners in Britain; the meeting grew to 20,000. George Whitefield preached 18,000 sermons during his lifetime, and John Wesley preached 42,000 sermons. They were dedicated to the saving of souls in their generation. Prayer is the spark that ignites revival fires. Hearts were hardened toward the plight of the slaves until people began praying in earnest. Three and a half years before the Civil War, Jeremiah Lanphier, a businessman in New York, was burdened for lost souls, but no one seemed interested. He handed out 20,000 invitations to a meeting, seemingly to no avail. He was praying alone in the room he had obtained for this purpose, when another man walked in and knelt beside him, then there were ten. In a month, he had to get a larger room, then on October 10th, the banks folded, and panic ensued. Soon, thousands were praying during their lunch hour. It is too bad that it often takes a crisis to get people on their knees. This prayer movement was labeled the Third Great Awakening and influenced all of Europe. One puts a thousand to flight since it is the Lord your God who fights for you, just as he has promised (Joshua 23:10).

Whenever God is ready to do something new with His people, He always sets them praying.
-J. Edwin Orr.

https://seedbed.com/when-george-whitefield-and-john-wesley-met-radical-things-happenedHoward Snyder, June 27, 2017
https://christianhistoryinstitute.org/dailystory/permalink/jeremy-lanphier Dan Graves. Christian History Institute. 2025

"Awakenings begin in periods of cultural distortion and great personal stress, when we lose faith in the legitimacy of our norms, the viability of our institutions, and the authority of our leaders in church and state" (Keith Hardman). When it seems darkest, and hearts begin to cry out in desperation, God shows up. Want to be an awakener? How much are you willing to give to God? A verse read from the Bible and a minute of prayer, fifteen minutes while you drive to work, a prayer meeting at church once a week, does that seem like enough? How desperate are you? A tithe of time in 24 hours is over 2 hours. This will depend on the level of desire; give it your all, and God will give his, and it will be done! Edith Moules was sent by God to the lepers in Belgian Congo in 1927. She was afraid, but she did it, and many came to Christ. The Puritans who first came to Massachusetts Bay came with a burden for the Native Americans. Rev. John Eliot spent 12 years translating the Bible into Algonquin; it was the first Bible printed on American soil. Paula Akerson, my college friend, spent forty-five years in Papua New Guinea, ministering to a language group and helping translate the New Testament.

For this people's ear has become calloused; they hardly hear with their ears, and they have closed their eyes. Otherwise, they might see with their eyes, hear with their ears, understand with their hearts, and turn, and I would heal them. Matthew 13:14

https://dacb.org/stories/guinea-bissau/moules-edith/ Dictionary of African Christian Biography, Edith Moules.
Hardman, Keith. *Seasons of Refreshing: Evangelism and Revivals in America.* 1994
https://www.britannica.com/John-Eliot-British-missionary. John Eliot

December 1

"Christ is the power and wisdom of God" (1 Corinthians 1:24). Power is seen, and wisdom is heard. "Many believed in His name when they saw the miracles He was performing" (John 2:23). The Jewish people wanted signs and miracles to confirm to them that Jesus was their coming Messiah. The Greeks, on the other hand, were interested in wisdom and intellectual proof by means of logic and philosophy (1 Corinthians 1:22). Our Western cultured Christians are good with the Greek method but think that it is a sin to want to see a sign or wonder. Some even doubt that God still does them. "The Pharisees and Sadducees came to Jesus and tested him by asking him to show them a sign from heaven. He replied, '...a wicked and adulterous generation looks for a sign.'" (Matthew 16 1-4). This was after they had seen the healing of a deaf and dumb man. They doubted his deity, even after seeing a miracle. Desiring to want miserable people healed is merciful and brings God glory. Many religious leaders today deny signs, wonders, and miracles while wondering why no one is coming to Jesus. We need to win people over with power and with wisdom. "When he taught in the synagogue, everyone was amazed and said, 'Where does he get this wisdom and the power to do miracles?'" (Matthew 13:54).

I tell you the truth, anyone who believes in me will do the same works I have done, and even greater works, because I am going to the Father. You can ask for anything in my name, and I will do it, so the Son can bring glory to the Father. John 14:12-14

December 2

"You will seek me and find me when you seek me with your whole heart" (Jeremiah 29:13). What is it that you are seeking? What do you desire deep down in your soul? Expand your horizons, break out of the norm into God's creative adventure. We were created in his image, and we are called to be creative in whatever we do. The first time the Bible says that God filled someone with his Spirit is in Exodus 31, when Bezalel was chosen to do the artistry for the tent of meeting. No matter what career or calling we have, God will fill us to do amazing things for his glory. We were created to create, an act of worship!

The greatest days of church history is now. -Tim Sheets

Be a Builder, Not a Blocker

Ask more questions, give out less judgment
Be open, not rigid, see the person, not his opinion
Is God doing a new thing? "We've never done this before!"
If it is true, biblical, joyful, community-building, then go for it!
Don't be the only voice in the room; embrace the voices of others
No competition, put people first, not tasks
No: "Yes, buts"; only "Yes, ands!"
Lessons from *The Magic of Curiosity* by Drew Worsham

December 3

In 1922, Henry B. Garlock (1897-1985) and his wife, Ruth, served as missionaries to Liberia. This area in West Africa was nicknamed "The White Man's Grave." The book of his life, *Before We Kill and Eat You,* tells how they faced cannibals, witch doctors, disease, and superstition. They were among the last missionaries to enter the mission field and survive solely by the power of the Holy Spirit. Soon after arriving, his wife became sick with malaria, and the medicine supply was depleted. The quickest way to get medicine was to walk through the cannibalistic Pahn tribe. A group of Christian tribesmen agreed to make the journey but couldn't get past the tribe. One fellow was captured. Mr. Garlock took a few warriors and went to rescue him. He arrived at the village, walked into the prison hut, cut off the man's bonds, and walked out, only to find that he was surrounded by the tribe, its chief, and its witchdoctor. The missionary prayed, then the verse came to mind, "When you are arrested, take no thought what you are to speak, whatever is given to you in that hour, speak it, for it is not you who speaks but the Holy Spirit" (Mark 13:11). He opened his mouth and for twenty minutes spoke in a language he did not understand. They let them go. After that, many accepted Christ, ended their sacrifices, began educating their children, brought in modern medicine, gave up cannibalism, and accepted deliverance from demons. The Lord is looking for those he can trust, who will give their lives to the work of advancing God's kingdom on earth.

It has always been my goal to preach the gospel where Christ was not known...rather it is written: 'Those who were not told about him will see and those who have not heard will understand.' Romans 15:20-21

https://www.godreports.com/2022/11/god-gave-missionary-the-language What language did God supply to keep the missionary from being eaten by cannibals? John Sherill. Nov. 9, 2022
https://www.jstor.org/stable/175101 *The White Man's Grave*. Image and Reality, 1780-1850

December 4

Murphy's law, which says, "Anything that can go wrong, will go wrong," is a curse. If you have quoted this in a moment of frustration, renounce it. This is related to coincidence: the occurrence of events that happen at the same time by accident but seem to have some connection (Webster). Coincidence is not a part of the Christian viewpoint any more than Murphy's law. We must believe that our sovereign God sees every event and arranges them for a purpose. Things we see as accidental or coincidental may be a part of God's bigger plan. There are billions of movable parts on earth, and he is the only one who can see all of them at once. Our trust must be that "He works all things together for our good" (Romans 8:28). That is why we praise him in every circumstance. He does, however, mention the phrase, "by chance" in the story of the Good Samaritan, where someone passes a person in need "by chance," but this refers to an unexpected moment within a larger divine purpose. "Providence," a word used by our forefathers, refers to God's active involvement in the world. "He works all things after the counsel of His will" (Ephesians 1:11). We know nothing of our future, and that is why we trust God always, in every situation, and during every crisis.

This is what the past is for! Every experience God gives us, every person he puts in our lives is the perfect preparation for the future that only he can see. -Corrie ten Boom

December 5

Sean Feucht holds massive "Let Us Worship" rallies in cities where Jesus is badly needed. He takes worship to the streets, to the inside of our Capitol building, and in places that seem impossible to rescue. The Lord had him purchase a piece of property on Capitol Hill where worshipers gather to pray and intercede. He calls this place Camp Elah, after the brook where David picked up five smooth stones to slay the giant. Our praise and worship are weapons. When Paul and Silas were praising in the jail cell, an earthquake shook their chains off, the jailor and his family believed in Jesus, and a door opened in Europe for the gospel (Acts 16:25). "Let the saints be joyful in glory; let them sing aloud on their beds. Let the high praises of God be in their mouth, and a two-edged sword in their hand, to execute vengeance on the nations, and punishment on the peoples; to bind their kings with chains, and their nobles with fetters of iron; to execute on them the written judgments–this honor have all His saints. Praise the Lord" (Psalm 149:5-9). Part of our devotion to God begins with heaven opening through worship, drawing his full attention toward us. "Give to the Lord the glory due His name; worship the Lord in the beauty of holiness!" (Psalm 96).

Religion points to the future for relief–leaving earth instead of affecting it. It uses future hope to justify its ineffectiveness. If you do not believe the kingdom of God is now, you will not expect to experience it. -Miles Monroe

December 6

We do not need to be anxious or worried about the future. Dread comes from the spirit of fear and "God has not given us the spirit of fear, but of power, love and a sound mind" (2 Timothy 1:7). If you dread a project, being with people, a vacation, or even leaving your house, you have this spirit, and it needs to be repented of and renounced. Pause and do this now. We cannot fear the future; he says the life he has for us is abundant. If you receive a blessing, have a particularly great day, or hear good news, automatically think that something bad must surely be coming next, you need to renounce that way of thinking. God does not work that way–it is a joy robber; those thoughts become a stronghold. God has protected you in the past, he is here in the present, and he will be with you in the future. He brought you this far, and he will not drop you, no matter what you think of yourself or what you think you deserve. What God sees when he looks at you is his beautiful child, cleansed by the blood of his dear Son. Pray about this until you receive the faith, peace, and joy to venture out with boldness. "The steps of the righteous are ordered by the Lord" (Psalm 37:23), and "you are the righteousness of God through Christ Jesus your Lord!" (2 Corinthians 5:21).

If you look at the world, you'll be distressed. If you look within, you'll be depressed. But if you look at Christ, you'll be at rest. - Corrie ten Boom

December 7

Do you feel like your will is not engaged with God's will? This is apathy and complacency. Don't worry, there is a solution. Ask the Lord to give you the will and desire to do his will. "It is God who works in you both to will and to do His good pleasure" (Philippians 2:13). He can rekindle in you that flame of fire, or maybe you've never had it. In earnestness, tell him how you are feeling, tell him that you struggle to want to pray and read his word. Tell him the areas of sin that draw you away from him and away from his perfect will. He already knows but wants to hear it from you. He will give you the strength to do what is right and the courage to say no. We are in a process, and even though we may think we have missed our opportunities, or failed so badly that there is no hope, it is not true. If you are reading this book, then you want progress. He is growing your faith, increasing your understanding, and maturing you. He loves you so much that he will never leave or forsake you. Allow his Spirit to be the fire-starter in your heart!

Teaching others comes from knowledge gained, and in teaching others comes greater knowledge.

Knowledge of the Holy One is understanding (Proverbs 9:10).

December 8

We have dynamite in us! "I can do all things through Christ who strengthens me" (Philippians 4:13). The word "strengthen" is made up of the Greek word meaning "power within." We are positioned as instruments of action and power, and the same Holy Spirit who dwells within us raised Christ from the dead. The Spirit of Jesus Christ dwells inside our mortal bodies! Isaiah 11:2 lists the seven-fold, or seven manifestations, of the Holy Spirit. In us is the Spirit of the Lord, of wisdom, understanding, knowledge, counsel, power, and the Spirit of the fear of the Lord, which is the beginning of wisdom. If we do not fear the Lord, we won't want to obey Him. Holy Spirit is our counselor, "You will hear a voice behind you saying, 'This is the way you should go,' telling you when to turn right or turn left" (Isaiah 30:21). Whatever strength and endurance is needed for us to accomplish great exploits for God resides in us and is active and ready to cause demons to flee, fear to vanish, weakness to become strength, poverty to become success, infirmities to be healed, obstacles to be removed, and impossibilities to become possible. God is on our side; what can man do to us? God is rooting for us, cheering us on, and making us a powerful tool that overcomes the world (Psalm 118:6-7; Romans 8:11).

Why should we limit either the goodness or the power of God by our own knowledge of what we call the laws of nature? -George Müller.

When being baptized into the name of the "Lord Jesus Christ," the fullness of the godhead is declared over us. Father God is Lord, as revealed in the Old Testament, the Son's name is Jesus or Yeshua, and "Christ" or Messiah means Anointed One, representing Holy Spirit's anointing on Jesus. Before Jesus had defeated death and the grave, he told His disciples to baptize in water using the name of the Father, Son, and Holy Spirit (Matthew 28:19). They had to wait for him to die, be buried, and rise before they could be baptized into his full name. He had not yet been revealed as Lord Jesus Christ; this wasn't until after his resurrection. The first time is in Acts 2:36, "God has made Jesus both Lord and Christ," also this title is used in 1 Corinthians 8:6, "And there is one Lord, Jesus Christ." In the book of Acts, they always used parts of the name Lord Jesus Christ when baptizing people. "For in Him dwells the fullness of the godhead bodily" (Colossians 2:9). It wasn't God's plan for baptism to be a formula, but a public demonstration and identification with the death, burial, and resurrection of Jesus Christ. He rose from the grave having conquered sin and death; that is what happens to us as we come out of the waters of baptism to a newness of life (Romans 6:3-4). Every knee will bow, and every tongue confess that Jesus Christ is Lord to the glory of God the Father. Philippians 2:10-11

If anyone is thirsty, let him come to me and drink. Whoever believes in me, as the Scripture has said, streams of living water will flow from within him-Jesus (John 7:38).

Baptize in the name of the Father, the Son, and the Holy Spirit, the Lord Jesus Christ.

December 10

He is the potter; we are the clay. He is the Creator; we are his creation. Jesus, the creator, spat in the dirt, made clay, and healed a man's blindness; eyes formed from the dust of the earth, the same way Adam was created. We are his workmanship; in Greek, this means poem (Ephesians 2:10). We are God's poetry; he calls us a work of art. We are on the potter's wheel and may be there until we are taken to glory, but through the process of sanctification, there will be fewer and fewer imperfections to remove. Because we are this beautiful work of art, we have purpose and meaning. He takes a life of chaos and discord and turns it into sweet music; he begins the second we submit to him. He is working on us because that is what he loves to do. What great things God can do with a lump (Isaiah 64:8).

Jesus healed all who came to him. But in Nazareth, he did few miracles; they knew Jesus personally, yet were unbelievers, and they did not come to him. There are unbelieving believers who think they know Jesus yet do not believe he heals. There are believing believers who know Jesus, believe it is his will to heal, so why are there so many ailing Christians? 'Those who eat and drink without discerning the body of Christ eat and drink judgment on themselves. That is why many are weak, sick, and die.' Jesus' body is the church, and a lack of insight into how we are to honor God's people causes sickness and death. Having the elders pray and lay hands on the sick leads to recovery, so do gifts of healing, miracles, faith, and walking in forgiveness. The gifts of the word of knowledge, wisdom, and discernment are for showing people what is making them ill. It is body ministry, and if you block that blessing, you block health. We not only make sure we haven't offended Christ when we take communion but also take care of our relationships within His Body, the Church.
Matthew 4:23-25; Mark 6:4-13; 1Corinthians 11; James 5:14-16

We pray for a need until the peace of God confirms that our prayer is answered. We tend to pray then worry; instead, pray then believe. In the parable of the woman who needed justice and persistently knocked on the door of a grumpy, godless judge, who cared nothing for people, Jesus teaches us that God will bring about justice for those who cry out to him. Justice will be quick, unlike the wicked judge who was slow to help. Then he said right after that, "However, when the Son of Man comes, will he find faith on the earth?" Treating God unjustly by banging on the door instead of asking, believing, and being patient demonstrates a lack of faith (Luke 18:1-8). But then in Luke 11:5-13, Jesus tells a story of a man who goes to a friend's house in the middle of the night and asks to borrow three loaves of bread because a visitor has arrived. The friend tells him to go away; he does not want to be bothered, but because of the relentless knocking, he finally gets up and gives him as many loaves as he needs. Then Jesus tells us to ask, keep on asking; knock, keep on knocking; seek, keep on seeking. "For everyone who asks receives, and he who seeks finds, and to him who knocks it will be opened." In the first story, the woman begged a judge for justice for herself, teaching us to view God as a kind and just judge. In the second parable, a man begs a friend for someone else, we must keep praying for others until the answer comes. "The fervent prayer of a righteous man accomplishes much." We plead with our friend Jesus for the unsaved ones who have no bread of life.

Don't pray when you feel like it. Have an appointment with the Lord and keep it. A man is powerful on his knees. -Corrie ten Boom

December 12

"Praise waits for you, O God" (Psalm 65:1). The word in Hebrew for "wait" in this context means "silent" with a sense of awe and expectancy. The opposite is a frenzy of anxiety and worry. We should be silent and have our hearts at peace, knowing the answer is on its way. Don't doubt God's care and love, wondering if he is listening. If we say, "Que Sera, Sera, whatever will be, will be," or say, "it is what it is," that is fatalism, believing in chance and not in Father God. The Bible never gives us that idea. Instead, we wait, pressure- and stress-free, entering into God's perfect rest with excitement, knowing the answer is on its way. "But I have stilled and quieted my soul; like a weaned child with its mother, like a weaned child is my soul within me" (Psalm 131:2). A weaned child takes nothing from its mother yet wants to be close to her. The relationship we have with the Lord shifts from what he can give us to waiting peacefully near him, believing that he is acting behind the scenes on our behalf. "Wait for the Lord and keep his way; he will exalt you to possess the land; when the wicked are cut off, you will see it, so wait for the Lord and keep his way." (Psalm 37:34).

Whoever does the will of my Father in heaven is my brother and sister and mother. Matthew 12:50

Que sera, sera, Whatever Will Be, Will Be. Song by Doris Day. Jay Livingston and Ray Evans. 1955.

December 13

One reason we encounter trials is so we can, in turn, comfort others who are going through the same troubles. "Blessed be the God of all comfort, who comforts us in all our misery, so we can comfort others in their misery with the same comfort with which we have been comforted" (2 Corinthians 1:3-4). Instead of our past being an open door to minister to others, we hide, feeling shame and guilt. Dick Mills had this problem when he was twenty-four years old. A godly man had a vision of him being bound to past memories; he prayed that Dick would be freed from the chains of his past. That night, as Dick was praying, he had a vivid picture of himself chained to twenty signposts with dates on them. His back was to the future, and he was facing the past. In desperation, he cried out to God, "Lord, I will never be able to adequately minister to the needs of people until these chains are removed. Dear Jesus, free me from this bondage!" He thought of the verse, "Forgetting those things which are behind and reaching forward to those things which are ahead" (Philippians 3:13). Other verses came to mind and immediately the chains fell off. He became a tremendous blessing and comfort to many people. If your past sins and the identity of failure are keeping you from freedom and ministry, confess this to God, and let him give you a new identity. Listen, and God will answer; your past will never bother you again, and you will become a comfort to others.

Do you think these...were worse sinners because they suffered this way? I tell you no! -Jesus Luke 13:1-3

December 14

"We know that everyone who has been born of God does not keep on sinning, but the One who was born of God protects him, and the evil one does not touch him" (1 John 5:18). Keeping in relationship with Christ will keep us from habitual sin, the kind of sin that gives ground to the roaming enemy seeking whom he may devour. He has already devoured the unbeliever; he is not targeting them; he targets threats; we are the threat. Satan attacks with words of fear, failure, and other lies about who we are, who others are, and who God is. This verse can be translated, "The one born of God keeps himself." We keep ourselves in Christ, so we are protected by Christ. Jesus said in John 14:30-31, "The prince of this world is coming, and he has no claim on me. [He has nothing in common with me; there is nothing in me that belongs to him, and he has no power over me.]." "Be angry, and do not sin, do not let the sun go down on your wrath, nor give place to the devil" (Ephesians 4:26-27). The word "place" here is the Greek *topos,* which gives us the word "topography." Do not let the enemy take ground or get a foothold in the soul or the body by playing around in his domain. He can only take what we offer to him and be on guard against his lies. "If you fear failure, you will expect failure. Perfect love casts out fear" 1 John 4:18.

Satan has asked to sift all of you as wheat. But I pray for you, that your faith should not fail; and when you have returned to Me, strengthen your brothers. Luke 22:31-32

December 15

God is patient. He says that the cup of iniquity has to be filled before he will pass judgment. He was patient with the Amorites for 400 years, then, because of their corruption and perversion, they were destroyed. The cup of iniquity of this world is not yet full. There are the vials of judgment seen in the book of Revelation. "For in the hand of the Lord there is a cup and the wine is red; it is fully mixed, and He pours it out; and all the wicked of the earth will drink it down" (Psalm 75:8). "If anyone worships the beast and his images and receives his mark on the forehead or on the hand, he, too, will drink the wine of God's fury, which has been poured full strength into the cup of His wrath" (Revelation 14:9-10). In chapter 16, verse 1, seven angels are commanded to pour out the vials of God's wrath on the earth. Just before he was crucified, Jesus took a cup of wine and passed it around to his disciples, "Drink from it, all of you; for this is my blood of the covenant, which is poured out for many for the forgiveness of sins" (Matthew 26:27-28). Jesus' cup of suffering represents his life being poured out for our salvation. Those who refuse to accept his free gift of salvation will be given a cup of suffering to drink during the time of judgment. "But the rest of mankind, who were not killed by these plagues, did not repent of their worship of demons and idols, and they did not repent of their murders, sorceries, sexual immorality, or their thefts" (Revelation 9:20-21).

Behind idols lie demon spirits. Be careful what you bring into your home.

December 16

A hundred years ago prophesies from the Old Testament about Israel seemed impossible. Israel was not a country; they had been scattered, and the land was desolate. This is what Mark Twain said about the land, "The hills are barren; they are dull of color... The valleys are unsightly, deserts fringed with a feeble vegetation...It is a hopeless, dreary, heartbroken land. Over it broods the spell of a curse that has withered its fields and fettered its energies...Nazareth is forlorn;...Jordan, where the hosts of Israel entered the Promised Land with songs of rejoicing, one finds only a squalid camp of fantastic Bedouins of the desert; Bethlehem and Bethany, in their poverty and their humiliation, have nothing about them now to remind one that they once knew the high honor of the Savior's presence; the hallowed spot where the shepherd watched their flocks by night, and where the angels sang Peace on earth, good will to men...Jerusalem itself, the stateliest name in history, has lost all its ancient grandeur, and is become a pauper village, the riches of Solomon are no longer there..." Mark Twain would be surprised that the Jews have returned to their land and that it is a beautiful, flourishing country today. Now the prophecies make sense. They will again have a temple. Antisemitism among believers is because they have never read the Old Testament!

But you, mountains of Israel, will produce branches and fruit for my people Israel, for they will soon come home. Ezekiel 36:8

https://www.wayoflife.org/reports/the_land_of_israel_in_1867.html The Land of Israel in 1867. David Cloud. Way of Life Literature. March 29, 2016.

Kingdom Come

Israel, small, unloved, persecuted, unaccepted
At odds with all nations
When will you receive Yeshua, your Messiah?

144,000 come forth, lead your people
Carry them through Jacob's trouble
Usher in the Holy One

New Jerusalem, come down
Refuge for all men, a resting place
For eternity, In saecula saeculorum

Right above me, a crystal city, twelve floors, pearl
doors
Golden glassy streets, twenty-four elders on
Throne-like seats

The angels singing "Glory, Holy, Holy, Holy,"
The saints tell their story, incense prayers arising
The sound of waters roaring

The fields are ripe and golden, servants now
emboldened
The Spirit and the bride say, "Come!"
Let one who hears say, "Come!"

"Pray for the peace of Jerusalem" (Psalm 122:6)

December 17

Conditional love is painful. Acceptance depends on how well you match up, fit in, and succeed. If you lose, rejection fills the hole that unconditional love was meant to fill. But God loves us unconditionally, not because of what we do, who we are, or how righteous we try to become. We cannot add or subtract from his love; it is eternal. We can hinder his blessings and promises, but he never stops trying to get us to accept his love. "I have loved you with an everlasting love; therefore, with lovingkindness I have drawn you" (Jeremiah 31:3). God loves us so much that he does not leave us to ourselves; as a good father, he disciplines us. Discipline is painful, but don't give up and quit, keep going and growing (Hebrews 12:5-13). We sometimes think of him as a judge standing over us with a great gavel ready to declare us guilty when we mess up, but his judgment is reserved for the end of the age for those who reject him. Discipline from Father is crafted by him for our own personality. He is tender with those who are compliant, harder with his rebellious sons and daughters, but eternity with us is always his goal. Sometimes he lets us get by with no consequences at all because "It is the Lord's kindness that brings us to repentance" (Romans 2:4). "His love endures forever" (Psalm 136).

They did not know that I healed them. I led them gently with kindness, with ties of love, and I lifted the yoke from their neck. I stooped down and fed them. Hosea 11:3-4

December 18

Jesus told a parable about a man (Jesus), who sowed good seed (sons of the kingdom) in his field (the world). In the middle of the night, the enemy (devil) came and sowed weeds (sons of the evil one) among the field. When both sprouted, the servant went to the master and asked if they should go pull the weeds. The master said no, that in pulling the weeds, some of the wheat might also be pulled up. "Let both grow together until the harvest (end of the age). At that time, I will tell the harvesters (angels): First collect the weeds (all who do evil) and tie them in bundles to be burned, then gather the wheat and bring it into my barn." Perhaps a few of those weeds will turn into wheat, and that is why they shouldn't be pulled up. The harvest is at the end of the age, before the millennial reign of Christ, when the beast and the false prophet are cast into the lake of fire, and Satan is bound for a thousand years (Revelation 19:20). Then God's scattered people and those in Heaven will be gathered into his barn, his glorious reign on earth. (Matthew 13:36-42; Revelation 14:14-20)

Loving our enemies is one of the good works we do. Jesus said we would be perfect if we did this. See them as your neighbors, not as enemies. Matthew 5:43-48

God's Planting
A seed planted in the ground, covered in dirt, is dead
Drowned with water, now growing
We are that seed, dead to selfishness
Covered with His glory, watered by the Word
Growing into holiness, beautiful to behold

December 19

Have you heard the term "self-fulfilling prophecy"? It is a belief that becomes a reality simply because it is believed. One with deep rejection emits rejection, so people reject him. You feel like a failure, so you struggle with studying and memorizing, and you end up failing. This is taught in secular psychology and is also in the Bible. "As a man thinks, so is he" (Proverbs 23:7 KJV). The heart is revealed through the mouth: "What comes from the mouth proceeds from the heart, and that is what defiles a person" (Matthew 15:17-19). "If anyone does not stumble in what he says, he is a perfect man, able to control his whole body" (James 3:2). Even salvation is based on believing and then confessing (Romans 10:9). It all begins with the heart. "May He grant you the desires of your heart and make all your plans succeed" (Psalm 20:4). If good things from the Lord begin in the heart, bad things from the devil begin there also. Believe the worst about people, and you will see the worst in them. This is the time to confess to assigning false identities to others. Ask the Lord to show you those things that are false, embrace the truth, then resist negative thoughts that fly through your brain by saying out loud, "I do not believe that lie, I resist it in Jesus' name."

Our soul is like a book; one page is in heaven when we accept Christ. Do not give a page to the devil. Sever evil attachments in the soul and call back all that has been stolen by unholy relationships, witchcraft, sin coming in through the eyes and ears, and words and thoughts that you repeat. Get those pages back and invite the Holy Spirit to help build a beautiful book of your life.

December 20

The Lord knows when I sit and when I rise, when I come and when I go. Even though he is far away, he can read my mind and knows beforehand what is about to come out of my mouth. He surrounds me, hems me in, and has his hand on me, this is hard to believe! There is nowhere I can go to get away from him, not to outer space, to the ends of the earth, or even to the place of the dead. Even if I go to the remote far side of the sea, you will guide me and take care of me. Darkness is not dark to you, and night is like day. You were involved in my creation; you knit me together and did a wonderful job. You saw me being formed, and my life was recorded in one of your books. Your thoughts about me are vast; there is no way I could count them all. There are as many as the grains of sand on the seashore. I wake up, and you are there! During the times of dealing with wicked enemies, take over, they are fighting against you, not me. Test me to see if I have missed the mark and have offended you. Set a guard over my mouth and do not let my heart be drawn to an evil path. My eyes are focused on you, keep me from hidden traps and lead me on the path of everlasting life. (Psalm 139, 141 paraphrased).

I know that you can do all things; no plan of yours can be thwarted. Job 21:1

December 21

Picture the cross, a symbol of our Lord's sacrifice, with a draped scarlet cloth over its cross-piece and a crown of thorns slightly skewed on top. The cross sits atop a huge mountain of different-sized scarlet packages. These are the burdens, sins, diseases, failures, and the shame of billions of people who have given their lives to King Jesus. The mountain reaches to the heavens, and the mountain increases daily. Then the cross turns into an evergreen tree, a magnificent sight. It is covered with gold and silver, and on top lies a golden crown. Filling the skies are the glorious host of heaven and a great cloud of witnesses singing:

On a hill far away stood an old rugged cross,
The emblem of suffering and shame;
And I love that old cross where the Dearest and Best
For a world of lost sinners was slain.

> *So I'll cherish the old rugged cross,*
> *Till my trophies at last I lay down;*
> *I will cling to the old rugged cross,*
> *And exchange it someday for a crown.*

Oh, that old rugged cross, so despised by the world,
Has a wondrous attraction for me;
For the dear Lamb of God left His glory above
To bear it to dark Calvary.

> *In that old rugged cross, stained with blood so divine,*
> *A wondrous beauty I see.*
> *For 'twas on that old cross Jesus suffered and died,*
> *To pardon and sanctify me.*

To the old rugged cross I will ever be true;
Its shame and reproach gladly bear;
Then He'll call me someday to my home far away,
Where His glory forever I'll share.
(songwriter George Bennard, 1912)

December 22

He is born; there is a reason now to carry on
Toot your horns, write another song
Love is here, seated at your table now
Not living in a stable now

So let us sing, Love is king
Angels sing, let us sing
Let it ring, Love is king
Love is king, Love is king

The song "El Niño" by Willie Nelson, from the album "Hill Country Christmas, released in 1997

I love this song because it tells the meaning of Christmas in a few short sentences. It presents the message of hope, Jesus at our table; he loves us. We do not need to fear the coming year. It will be a great year of the Lord working in and through us. We do not have to wait to be better people; he makes us better by binding up our wounds and pouring the oil of joy upon our heads. He is Lord of our past, present, and future, and is willing and able to make all things work together for our good. No matter what you are facing at this moment, give it to the Lord and add it to the pile of gifts underneath his Christmas tree. Toot your horns, as Willie says, worship him in Spirit and truth with all of your heart. He is sitting at your table. He died to give you an abundant life. Receive it and have a Blessed New Year!

Long lay the world in sin and error pining, till he appeared, and the soul felt its worth.
Words from the song "O Holy Night." -Adolphe Adam, 1847

December 23

Jesus blessed the food several times in the Scriptures. Never before have we needed to bless our food as much as we do now. With so many of us facing health problems coming from many directions, we should begin our days and meals with prayer. When a health problem arises, "let him call for the elders of the church, and let them pray over him, anointing him with oil in the name of the Lord. And the prayer offered in faith will make the sick person well; the Lord will raise them up. If they have sinned, they will be forgiven" (James 5:14). Pray before calling a doctor. Taking care of your body when you're young will help prevent problems later. Get enough sleep, drink pure water, give up sugary and diet sodas, fried and fast food, and desserts after every meal. "Feed me with the food that is needful for me" (Proverbs 30:8 ESV). God can prescribe what you need for your health. Let him guide you. Read labels and avoid these products, Red 40, Yellow 5, aspartame, sucralose, high fructose corn syrup (HFCS), trans fats BHA, BHT, sodium benzoate, MSG, sodium nitrate and nitrite, sulfites, carrageenan, high maltose (IMO), and the oils: canola, corn, soybean, vegetable, palm, and the gums: xanthan and guar. These additives and chemicals are also dangerous: titanium dioxide, brominated vegetable oil, propylparaben and potassium bromate. Dextrose is a simple sugar that is processed quickly and is known to cause health problems, including obesity. There is a reason 88.6% of Americans ages 65 and older take prescription drugs. One-third of those between 60 and 79 take five or more of the 23,000 prescription drugs on the market. We have a problem! "Eat and drink to God's glory" (1 Corinthians 10:31).

Beloved, I pray that you may prosper in all things and be in health, just as your soul prospers. 3 John 1:2. One can diminish health because the soul is not whole. Our soul needs to prosper!

https://realfoodbar.com
https://www.hackensackmeridianhealth.org
https://www.cdc.gov. *Therapeutic Drug Use*. March 2020. National Center for Health Statistics.

Immanuel

Here is my servant whom I have chosen
The one I love, in whom I delight
I will put my Spirit on him
And he will proclaim justice to the nations
He will not quarrel or cry out
No one will hear his voice in the streets
A bruised reed he will not break
A smoldering wick he will not snuff out
Till he leads justice to victory
In his name, the nations will put their hope
Isaiah 42:1-4; Matthew 12:18-21

December 24

The shield of faith extinguishes the fiery darts of the enemy. Listen to the illusions to fire in these statements, flaming anger, fiery jealousy, burning passions, afire with lust, consumed by hatred, devoured by the flames of prejudice– all coming from the darts of the devil. *Diaballo* is from the Greek word for devil, *dia* meaning "through" and *ballo* meaning "to throw." He throws fiery darts through the believer, causing trouble in an area of life that is not protected by the shield. We must leave our comfort zone for the combat zone, the nursery for the trenches. "We are to get off the charismatic love boat where life has been all fun and games and onto the spiritual battleship from which we can shell the enemy's fortresses and demolish his strongholds" (Dick Mills). By faith, we are safe during warfare while taking ground from our enemy. We must be careful to enter this battle with faith on our lips, not defeat. It is a daily walk of watching our hearts and our words. Going into battle already defeated by negative self-talk is not going to lead to victory. Using words like divorce, bankruptcy, hate, doctors, disease, sickness, is a pre-planned failure. Don't plan on losing, plan on winning!

Make no provision for the flesh, Romans 13:14 KJV. The Greek word for provision means thinking about something ahead of time. Don't think about giving in to temptation or predetermining your failure.

December 25

Do you want to make God happy? Give him a gift! He deserves our best. God is merciful and full of lovingkindness. He created us and has great plans for us: "All good and perfect gifts come from the Father of lights who does not change like shifting shadows" (James 1:17). What can we give him that pleases him and brings him joy? Faith, obedience, loving his word, praise, worship, our journey in life, our joy and happiness, our children and their progress, helping the poor, widows, and orphans, caring for animals, giving a cup of water to one in need, blessing our brethren, resting and trusting in him completely, meditating on his word, prayer, fighting for the future of our country and the world, defeating the enemy with our words, resisting temptation, and having a heart full of compassion and merciful love. He takes pleasure when we are having fun, enjoying life, and nature. Our relationship with him isn't about being legalistic in tithing money or time; it is about wanting as much of him as we can possibly contain. The Sabbath of "doing all for the glory of God" is about our relationship with Jesus: "There remains a Sabbath-rest for the people of God, let us make every effort to enter that rest." (Hebrews 4:9-11). As Jonah said, we do not want to forfeit a single blessing from the throne of God (Jonah 2:8). "I no longer call you servants, but friends" (John 15:15).

His name is Immanuel. God is with us. Matthew 1:23

December 26

"One who puts on his armor should not boast like the one who takes it off" (1 Kings 20:11). In our country, we have little respect for the aged or the "ones taking off their armor." They are veterans of life, having survived many trials and tests. They have earned bragging rights as they leave this world. They have learned to understand the enemy, his strategy and cunning trickery, and that it is possible to defeat him. This soldier of his time has many stories of victories, has earned the respect of his peers, and quickly gives credit to the soldiers who assisted him along the way. He is humble and grateful for all God has done in helping with rescue missions, providing needs, and giving him times of rest. The rookie thinks he knows it all, even though he has seen few battlefields. His conceit keeps him from seeking advice from the one who is fading away. He does not want to waste his time, but with zeal feels ready to go out and win. He will, with time, become more mature and somber, having a more humble attitude and wishing he had spent more time with the veteran. "Let not the wise boast about his wisdom, or the strong about his strength, or the rich about his riches, but let him boast that he understands and knows me, that I am the Lord, who is kind, just, and righteous, for in these I delight" (Jeremiah 9:24).

Give everyone what you owe him: If you owe taxes, pay taxes; if fees, then fees; if respect, then respect; if honor, then honor.
Romans 13:7

December 27

"To make ready a people prepared for the Lord" (Luke 1:17). The Greek words for "ready" and "prepared" have two different meanings, "to make ready" is used to describe preparation internally, covering the range of qualifications necessary to meet the Lord at his return; integrity, humility, holiness, submission, the Christ-like attitudes and motives of the heart. This is the readiness of overcoming unforgiveness, bitterness, resentment, and unbelief. "Prepared" is the external work of bringing the body of Christ into unity. It is corporate worship and praise, standing together against the enemy's plans and working together to help in times of crisis; all that we do is visible to the world around us. The Lord is readying his corporate bride for his arrival. They will be "without spot or wrinkle." In Greek, spot can also mean fault, stain, or blemish, and is used to describe internal moral or spiritual blemishes. Wrinkle is used in the context of skin or fabric—a visible imperfection, defect, or flaw, the fleshly sin "that so easily entangles" (Hebrews 12:1). "We have this treasure in fragile, earthen vessels, to show that the power is from God and not from ourselves" (2 Corinthians 4:7). He chose frail humans to display the power of his glory and might. The treasure in us is the Holy Spirit, much finer than pure gold! -Dick Mills.

Submission to the government protects us from anarchy, leading to great slaughter and violence.
Submission to teachers protects us from rebellion, leading to spiritual death and blindness.
Submission to parents protects us from the spirit of antichrist, leading to eternal death.
Submission to one another protects us from division, broken relationships, and judgment.

December 28

"You will receive power when the Holy Spirit comes on you; you will be my witnesses to the ends of the earth" (Acts 1:8). The word "witness" in Greek is *martus*, where we get the word "martyr." It also means "to testify." We need Holy Spirit's power to be willing to die for him and to live for him. To testify means "to give evidence or produce facts, to exhibit truth, to confirm claims." We can be great defenders of the Truth, using logic and proofs, as Josh McDowell does through his books (1 Peter 3:15). We also have the power from the Holy Spirit to operate in supernatural signs, wonders, and miracles. "And these signs will follow them who believe...they will take up serpents; and if they drink anything deadly, it will not hurt them...The disciples went everywhere and preached, and the Lord worked through them, confirming what they said by many miraculous signs." (Mark 16:15-20). Paul was bitten by an asp while in Malta, and the whole tribe came to Jesus because he did not die. He laid his hands on the chief official's father, who had a fever, and he was healed (Acts 28:1-9). These gifts did not die with Paul. Arthur Blessitt, when carrying a cross through every country, drank from unclean streams and lakes and never became sick. Have you received the power to die and to live for Christ? Has the Holy Spirit come upon you? Do you testify for Christ? Do you lay hands on the sick? We still need those gifts (1Corinthians 14).

No more delays! None of my words will be delayed any longer; whatever I say will be fulfilled. I the Lord have spoken. Ezekiel 12:28

December 29

In Isaiah 58, the Lord rebukes Israel for fasting while complaining that he was not listening. He points out their sin of living for pleasure, exploiting their workers, their angry abuse, and wanting God to intervene in their heated debates. God then paints a beautiful picture of what he desires from fasting: "To break the bonds of wickedness, to undo heavy burdens, to let the oppressed go free, to break every yoke, to share bread with the hungry, and to welcome into your home the poor who are cast out. When you see the naked, to clothe them, and never ignore your own flesh and blood." He wants repentance, a change in attitudes and actions; fasting is a pride-deflator, a cure for unbelief. "Then your light shall break forth like the morning, your healing shall spring forth speedily, and your righteousness shall go before you; The glory of the Lord shall be your rear guard. Then you will call, and the Lord will answer; you will cry, and he will say, 'Here I am.' If you take away the pointing of the finger and speaking wickedness, extending your soul to the hungry and satisfying the afflicted soul, then your light shall shine in the darkness. The Lord will guide you continually and satisfy your soul in drought and strengthen your bones. You will be like a well-watered garden." We should fast and pray for the coming new year. (James 1:6-7; Psalm 102:16-17; Romans 12:11-12; Hebrews 11:6)

When you fast, you will be tempted just like Jesus was. You will be tempted to eat, to accept praise, to focus on yourself and not on what God wants.

December 30

"It is more blessed to give than to receive" (Acts 20:35). It is important to give, but also to receive. A giver is not blessed unless the person graciously accepts the gift. Be a giver, but also have a heart that is ready to receive. Jesus offers forgiveness; receive it. Receive kindness from others. Thinking that being a self-made person is something great, it is pride. Humbly receive help when you are needy with the faith to believe that someday you will be able to help those who are in need. If you find yourself being a bit like Scrooge, make yourself be generous. "It is possible to give away and become richer. It is also possible to hold on too tightly and lose everything" (Proverbs 11:24). Opening clutched fists, letting go, and beginning to tune in to where God wants our generosity to land is freeing. He may ask us to spend our time and energy on a community endeavor. He may want us to support an orphan in another country. Solomon, in Ecclesiastes 11:1, wrote that we are to cast our bread upon the waters, and after many days it will come back to us. The waters represent people, bread is money, food, and God's word. It means to be generous, and someday you will be rewarded. Giving takes faith, and faith takes patience. Putting money in God's savings account pays off. "Store up treasures in Heaven" -Jesus.

Tithing is a law from the Old Testament covenant; now our giving comes from a heart of gracious generosity to those in need, not from a legalistic, mandated, obligatory directive. Any type of coercion to tithe puts people under the law. Obligation does not foster cheerful giving or sacrifice. Feeling like the financial duty of paying tithe absolves me from considering the needs of others is a law, not the Spirit. Threats of curses and disasters for not giving the church ten percent come from leaders and not from God. Giving is to be based on love, need, and God's leading (Proverbs 28:27). Be led by the Holy Spirit in your giving with the attitude of cheerfulness and generosity. The early church had no needy among them. 2 Corinthians 8:3-5

Teaching by Jonathan Cahn–YouTube, Cahn Words. March 26, 2025

It Is War!

There is no time to oscillate, fluctuate, or vacillate
Into the trenches! It is time for war! Prepare for impact!
This is not a religious playground or a sports arena
Not an Olympic tournament but a grim, bloody conflict
Light against darkness, truth against error, good against evil
The forces of God against the devil's minions, a collision
It looks impossible, yet triumph is assured, nock the arrow
Hemmed in, front and back, no escape, yet no surrender

Standing still, waiting for "All Clear."
The Captain has not abandoned us
He did not bring us out to desert us
It is darkest before the dawn
Not a hair of our head shall be lost
The door of victory is now visible
March on through, you will see evil no more
(Zephaniah 3:15; Luke 21:18)

December 31

Romans 16:1-16 is the last chapter of Paul's letter to the church in Rome; it contains personal greetings to individuals, some of whose names look familiar: Junia, Narcissus, Persis, Hermes, Olympas, all believers named after Roman gods. Their parents were idol worshipers. "Greet one another with a holy kiss," then he tells the Romans that all the churches send greetings. It is a picture of the first church and its unity, care, and love for one another. Then Paul warns them to watch out for those who cause divisions by teachings that are contrary to what they had already been taught. Be warned, he continues, of smooth-talking scammers who use trickery and flattery to deceive naïve people. "Be wise about what is good, and innocent about what is evil" (verse 19). Then, right in the middle of his personal greetings, he says, "The God of peace will soon crush Satan underneath your feet." The Greek word for crush is *suntribo*, meaning "to shatter, annihilate, torpedo, disintegrate, totally demolish." It is an encouragement, a banner to plaster on the wall, something we must remember and have faith in. But, if this happens under our feet, we must be out there marching, our feet shod with the gospel of peace for treading on snakes and scorpions, fighting the good fight of faith, engaging in our culture and society, warring for peace, for justice, for the goodness of heaven to come to earth. "I will give you every place where you set your foot" (Joshua 1:3). Let us stomp on fear, insecurity, poverty, sickness, trouble, discouragement, and over all the works of the enemy, in Jesus' name!

He who began a good work in you will carry it on to completion until the day of Christ Jesus. Philippians 1:6.

When we are young, we talk about our fun, our future, our dreams

When we have families, we talk about our children, their hopes, their dreams, their future

When we are old, we talk about our pain, our past successes, and our exploits

When our days are nearly over, we share what matters most

I don't mean to say that I have already achieved these things or have reached perfection. But I press on to possess that perfection for which Christ Jesus first possessed me. No, dear brothers and sisters, I have not achieved it, but I focus on this one thing: Forgetting the past and looking forward to what lies ahead, to the end of the race and the heavenly prize. We must hold on to the progress we have already made. Philippians 2:12-16

Live Faithfully Ever After!

BIBLIOGRAPHY and Suggested Reading

Barton, David. *Original Intent: The Courts, the Constitution, & Religion.* Wall Builder Press; 5th edition, August 30, 2008.

Blessitt, Arthur. *The Cross: 38,102 Miles, 38 Years, One Mission.* Authentic Media, 2009.

Calder-Ritchie, Lord. *The Lunar Society of Birmingham.* Scientificamerican.com, June 1, 1982.

Chesterton, Gilbert K. *What's Wrong With The World.* Dodd, Mead And Company, 1910.

Diaz, Ben. *Supernatural Healing of the Soul.* Harrison House Publishers, July 1, 2025.

Darwin, Charles. *On the Origin of Species the Preservation of Favoured Races in the Struggle for Life.* John Murray III, 1859.

Gibbon, Edward, *The Decline and Fall Of The Roman Empire, volume 2, 1781-1789, The* Folio Society, January 1, 1999.

Ham, Ken. Ware, A. Charles. *Darwin's Plantation: Evolution's Racist Roots.* Master Books, 2007.

Harber, Frank, PhD. *Sherlock's Faith: The Investigation of Christianity.* Heartstring Media, 2004.

Jacobs, Cindy. *Reformers Arise.* Destiny Image Publishers, Inc., 2021.

Johnson, Phillip E. *Defeating Darwinism by Opening Minds*. InterVarsity Press, 1997.

Kendall, R.T. *God Meant It For Good*. Destiny Image Publishers, Inc., 2024.

Klavin, Andrew. *The Great Good Thing*. Zondervan, 2016.

Kralik, John. *365 Thank Yous*. Balance, December 28, 2010.

Lindsay, Dennis Gordon. *The Dismantling of Evolutionism's Sacred Cow: Radiometric Dating*. Christ for the Nations, Inc., 1994.

Maldonado, Guillermo. *The Latter Glory of God Revealed*. Destiny Image Publishers, Inc., 2024.

Milligan, Ira. *The Ultimate Guide to Understanding the Dreams You Dream*. Destiny Image Publishers, Inc., 2012.

Miller, Darrow L., Guthrie, Stan. *Discipling Nations: The Power of Truth to Transform Cultures*. Emerald Books, 2001.

Miller, Don. *Searching for God Knows What*. Nelson Books, January 2004.

Mills, Dick. *The Spirit-Filled Believer's Daily Devotional*. 1995.

Nance, James B. Wilson, Douglas. *Introductory Logic: The Fundamentals of Thinking Well*. Canon Press, 2014.

Peck, Josh. *The Lost Prophesies of the Qumran*. Defender, Sept 15, 2021.

Sandford, John Loren. *Healing the Nations: A call to Global Intercession*. Chosen, 2000

Sarfati, Jonathan PH.D., F.M. *The Greatest Hoax on Earth? Refuting Dawkins on Evolution*, 2010.

Scazzero, Peter. Emotionally Healthy Spirituality. Zondervan, 2017.

Shaeffer, Francis A. *How Should We Then Live?: The Rise and Decline of Western Thought and Culture*. Crossway Publishing, 2022.

Smalley, Gary. *The Key to Your Child's Heart*. 2000

Strong, James. *Strong's Exhaustive Concordance of the Bible*. Abingdon Press, 1890.

Taylor, Ian T. *In the Minds of Men: Darwin and the New World Order*. TFE Publishing/Creation Moments; 6th edition, 2008.

Winship, Jamie. *Living Fearless*. Revel Books, 2022.

Worsham, Drew. *The magic of curiosity.* Blue Hat Publishing. 2025.